The Afghan Amulet

The
Afghan
Amulet

*Travels from the Hindu Kush
to Razgrad*

Sheila Paine

MICHAEL JOSEPH
LONDON

MICHAEL JOSEPH LTD

Published by the Penguin Group
Penguin Books Ltd, 27 Wrights Lane, London W8 5TZ
Viking Penguin Inc., 375 Hudson Street, New York, New York 10014, USA
Penguin Books Australia Ltd, Ringwood, Victoria, Australia
Penguin Books Canada Ltd, 10 Alcorn Avenue, Toronto, Ontario, Canada M4V 3B2
Penguin Books (NZ) Ltd, 182–190 Wairau Road, Auckland 10, New Zealand

Penguin Books Ltd, Registered Offices: Harmondsworth, Middlesex, England

First published in Great Britain 1994

Copyright © Sheila Paine 1994
Line drawings by Imogen Paine
Maps by Martin Collins
Photographs by Sheila Paine, except where indicated

Photoset by Datix International Limited, Bungay, Suffolk
Printed in England by Clays Ltd, St Ives plc
Typeset in 11/12½ pt Janson

A CIP catalogue record for this book is available from the British Library.

ISBN 0 7181 3729 9

The moral right of the author has been asserted.

Author's Note: The names of one or two people have been changed for their protection.

For my grandchildren
Daisy and Tamsin
David and Alexander
with apologies for the world we hand on

And for the BBC World Service

Contents

The Quest

The Kohistani dress was like no other tribal dress. It hung on the wall of the London textile dealer's shop with brooding presence. Of black cotton, its immense wide sleeves and bodice were heavily embroidered in red with solar patterns outlined in tiny white beads. Old coins, talismanic coral and hundreds of shiny buttons were set around the embroidery; broken zips and lead shot edged openings; a separate triangular amulet made of beads, with eleven dangling loops of shells, hung over the stomach. All these devices protected the wearer from the djinn, those evil spirits that in Islamic mythology lurk among men and angels, ready to attack but known to be frightened by dazzle, by colour, by curving lines and by the tinkling of a woman's clothing as she moves.

The skirt of this bizarre dress flounced in an incredible frill of six hundred and forty-seven small triangles of black fabric painstakingly stitched together by hand. This extraordinary skirt, unlike almost any other in the world, nevertheless showed a curious link with Europe: though the skirts of the royal guards at

Athens are pleated rather than made of godets, the flared effect is precisely the same. Could such a costume possibly be a hangover from Alexander's campaigns in Asia and the Hellenistic settlement of those mountainous regions west of the Indus, known indiscriminately as 'Kohistan', from where the dress was reputed to come? Questioned on its more precise origin, 'Kohistan' was all the London dealer could say. Then 'Swat Kohistan, I think.'

'Yes, Kohistan but the bit known as Nuristan' other dealers said.

'Kalash. Chitral' said others.

As for the shawl worn with the dress, this too was black, embroidered with solar patterns and with a triangular motif dangling with tassels. Three, five or seven. This motif was the same as the beaded amuletic triangle that hung on the front of the dress, only it was stitched as a pattern. Embroidered in the same style were the cuffs of the trousers and also the helmets that were all part of the costume. Peaked at the head and falling in a triangular flap over the nape, some of the helmets had appliquéd above the forehead a silver horn amulet. 'Worn when the woman is regarded in her village as a soothsayer' said the ethnographer in Basel. 'From somewhere in Kohistan we believe.'

Other eminent ethnographers gave their opinion. One at the National Museum of Sofia, shown a photograph of a detail of the Kohistani shawl, was sure it was an embroidery from Bulgaria, from Razgrad to be precise, a town that was the site of one of those earliest burial grounds of mankind that neighbour the Black Sea. He produced a marriage cushion from Razgrad, which did indeed have the same embroidery patterns on it. But his was the only dissenting voice and mostly it was agreed that my photograph was of the costume of Kohistan. No, no one knew exactly where in Kohistan this costume came from, nor indeed *which* Kohistan. No one had ever seen a woman wearing it. No one had ever even seen any photographs of a woman wearing it. Its origin remained a mystery.

It was a mystery that intrigued me. In all the years I had spent travelling the world researching embroidery traditions I had never come across a costume whose origin was unknown. It was always possible to pinpoint it to a precise village or tribe, often even to know from the pattern and colour whether the woman who wore it was single or married, young or old. But this time no one knew. The occasional examples of this flamboyant costume that found their way to market were traded by dealers in Europe and Pakistan nonchalantly writing out little price tags labelling them 'Kohistan', 'Kalash', 'Nuristan', or even just 'tribal', 'ethnic'.

Then there was the nagging suggestion that the patterns on the costume, and in particular the pattern of a triangle with pendants, were also found in Bulgaria. Already fascinated by the links between the embroidery of Central Asia and Eastern Europe, I engaged in prolonged correspondence with the ethnographers. Some were world authorities who knew the Kohistani regions of Afghanistan and northern Pakistan well. One sent comments that were encouraging:

> The task you have set yourself is quite extraordinarily interesting ... Now to your problem. I have seen similar material with dealers in Kabul. They say they get the pieces from Swat – they're made either by Pashtuns or by Kohistanis under strong Pashtun influence, as those people love the combination of black and red. As for the helmet-shaped cap, I've never come across anything like it. In Kohistan the men wear caps with a flap over the nape that extends to the shoulders and back. It could have derived from that.

Another, too modestly, was reluctant to commit himself:

> Your hopes are too high if you have been led to believe I know exactly where the type of dress in your picture comes from. I worked in the valley of Sazin in particular (5 months), but also visited Tangir, Darel, Yasin, Harban, Thor, Hodar & Gor and Chilas fairly extensively in 1987. I am fairly certain that the type of costume does not come from any of those valleys: the impression I had (though it is very dangerous to look at any woman too closely) was that throughout the Shin area the costume is fairly similar, and certainly of less finesse than your example. The embroidery in Sazin, of which I was able to obtain some examples in the shape of caps, was very crude. The only piece approaching the sophistication of yours was a gun-case I bought from its owner in Thor. The people in Palus, just south of Dassu on the left bank of the Indus, may have a different tradition, but they were mostly in the mountains

when I visited the valley in July: glimpses of costume were promising. I suspect the main source may be the valley northwards from Dassu, Kandia.

P.S. Sazin: the dresses there were very full-skirted, like yours, but embroidery (or appliqué?) limited to stripes over the shoulders and round the waist, front & rear. In one case a rosette on the back.

Things looked encouraging and I continued writing and sending photographs of the Kohistani costume, which I had by now bought, not only to international ethnographers, but also to local experts. One, living in Karachi, attacked my credentials:

Are you at all conversant with the basic ancient ethnological structure of B.C. Eurasia – the Scythians, Sarmatians and Gettae for example? And do you know the tribal structure of Pakistan in relation to those basics? Those basics apply to both Asia as well as Europe of course. And do you know anything about Cosmic symbology in designs?

I hung my head. In the next letter he continued the theme and confused me further:

The most important ethnological group of people in the North out here are the onetime Siahposhe Kaffirs of Nooristan who once ruled the entire Northern Areas, when it was Kashgaria – The Bashgal, Lambgal and Weigal. The Kalash of Chitral represent a Siahposhe slave tribe largely of Ladak origin. I presume you refer to the embroideries of the Siahposhe obtained in Swat and Peshawar? Yes, they are indeed comparable with those of the Mengal Brahuis of Baluchistan – one can also compare them with the embroideries of the Meg (Megwar) of Rajastan, the Kasakh of Central Asia and even the Maya of Guatemala! The Siahposhe influenced the embroideries of Northern Afghanistan, the whole of Pakistan's Kohistan and even the Punjab! There are basic ethnic reasons for this of course.

Though languages are my training and background the same fellow pointed out that these would be of no help, but that it was rather linguistics that I would need 'coupled with hordes of text books and wide field experience'. He added helpfully:

An excellant general book is Gordon T. Bowles 'Peoples of Asia' which covers most of these aspects, going reasonably far back in time. The University of Berkeley Indo-European Studies Department produces somewhat more academic reports, but this is the most important up-to-date research. Most of their work is based on up-to-date modern archaeological findings in the Steppel and Corridor Kurgan Culture of burrials.

By now totally confused – though somewhat cheered by his spelling – I wrote again to the ethnographers who had worked in the area, still determined to find the source of this costume for myself, and asked for practical advice. I received ominous warnings in reply:

It must be said that work throughout this area is extremely hazardous because of the belligerent and extremely parochial attitude of the inhabitants: jealousy over women reaches paranoid dimensions, but at the same time the position of women in society must be one of the lowest in the Islamic world, as they have virtually no rights whatever. It would be *very* difficult for a woman to travel there: impossible alone, and hard to contrive with anyone else, for any woman travelling with an interpreter or a police escort would compromise them automatically.

Lest you suspect I may be exaggerating, I should point out that an Englishman was found dead under suspicious circumstances near Babusar while I was there: he had been travelling alone. The Commissioner told me that the high rate for murders for Indus-Kohistan as a whole was 7–8 a week, but I found out from the police at Juglot (Tangir) that there had been a murder a day in that one tiny town for the last two months: three, sure enough, occurred in the two nights I was there, and a man was killed in my back garden at Shatial. The entire region is still beyond the law.

I remained undeterred, indeed encouraged further by jolly anecdotes:

I was able to get hold of modern costume in Tangir but it was made clear to me that to sell a woman's clothes was equivalent to selling the woman. So I had to pay a lot of money and

immediately put my purchase into a locked iron chest. Then I
rode off into the high meadows and on my return found the
whole household in uproar. Hordes of vermin had escaped
from the chest and were tormenting the inhabitants of the
house – fleas, but lice too. So I had to dispose of my chest in a
lonely spot.

In 1955 I was able to buy in Tangir/Darel items of women's
clothing that are now no longer obtainable. They were made
out of the local wool and were shirt-shaped with a flap over
the breast for feeding babies. Presumably such dresses were
worn without trousers. In fact in Baltistan women's trousers
were in no way part of summer costume and while I was there
the mullahs were just launching a campaign for decent dress,
on the curious grounds that the old costume had all too great
a tendency to encourage the women to use fleeting encounters
on the high meadows for purposes of sexual pleasure.

I would be going. Still, not only was the source of the costume
elusive – that was the first thing I needed to find – but also the
significance of the triangle with pendants, worked in beads and
shells on the front of the dress and embroidered on the shawl.
Where might I find it between Kohistan and Bulgaria and what
did it mean? 'Mean?' repeated the dealers. 'Symbol of fertility.
Talismanic. Can be an embroidered pattern or can be an actual
amulet to hang on children's bonnets or round the necks of
donkeys and women to protect them from the djinn and the evil
eye. Usually made of fabrics, threads, tassels and beads. Or it can
also be a piece of jewellery, silver, still a triangle but with bits of
chain hanging down. Even worn as earrings.' You could find
them for sale here and there in all these versions. 'When they're
actual amulets made of fabric or silver, they're Afghan definitely'
the dealers said. No one seemed to have any doubts.

Anthropologists had once held a theory that by establishing the
geographical incidence of ancient embroidery motifs the probable
migrations of early peoples could be charted. The idea had been
discredited but it taunted me none the less that this triangle with
pendants was known to occur embroidered on costume from
somewhere or other in Kohistan – whichever Kohistan that
might be – then as an actual amulet in Afghanistan and again as

an embroidery pattern in Bulgaria. The three versions looked
like this:

THE KOHISTANI COSTUME, where the triangle, precisely the
shape of the Afghan amulet, was embroidered on the shawl and made of
beadwork on the dress.

THE AFGHAN AMULET itself, which was after all only a triangle
of embroidered fabric hung with three twisted tassels, worn to ward off
evil spirits.

THE RAZGRAD CUSHION, where the pattern was still the same
but had overtones of a stylized earth goddess, a deity at the heart of the
mythology of Ancient Europe.

Where else, either in its form as a separate amulet or as an embroidered pattern, might this ancient symbol be found on the routes that linked Eastern Europe and Central Asia? Nomads, traders, emperors – over millennia each had chosen a different path: the steppelands, the Silk Road, the territories of the Golden Horde, the campaign routes of the Persian and Hellenistic empires.

These last crossed a southerly swathe of land between the mountains of Indus Kohistan and the eastern Mediterranean and Black Sea. Most of this region was traversed by the early trade routes of Mesopotamia; it was conquered by Darius, and by Alexander the Great, who turned back at the high inaccessible valleys beyond Taxila, returning down the valley of the Indus river and then through the mountains and deserts that skirt the Indian Ocean and that he called the land of the fisheaters; it was swept over by Islamic conquerors; it was the Ilkhanate of the Mongols; and the British strung across it their telegraph line linking India with Whitehall.

Over time, conquests, political decrees, tribal movements and religious wars have fractured the region into Pakistan, Afghanistan, Baluchistan, Iran, Iraq, Kurdistan and Turkey. Here the Trapezus of Alexander became Trebizond and then Trabzon, the Black Sea port from where boats still go to Istanbul. They once went, and may again go, on to Varna – not far from Razgrad – a harbour and another ancient burial site of Bulgaria, which predates the civilization of Mesopotamia by a thousand years and that of the Indus valley by two thousand.

The journey from Kohistan to Razgrad could logically have been accomplished in one attempt, but immobilizing winter snow and summer heat, riots in Kashgar, the backlash in Pakistan from the Gulf War, the seemingly impenetrable frontiers of Afghanistan and of Iran and Iraq, the military presence in eastern Turkey and escalating war with the Kurds split it into four separate journeys. There was first the search for Kohistan through the valleys of the Hindu Kush mountains, the Swat and Indus rivers, in 1990 and '91. Secondly a return to Pakistan in 1991 – to the closed territory of Makran in the south – and from there, continuing through Iran, to Turkish Kurdistan during early '92. Then a third journey in mid '92, seizing the chance to get into Afghanistan. Finally a return to the Kurds of both Northern Iraq and Turkey, and from there round the Black Sea to the end of the trail at Razgrad in eastern Bulgaria. Perhaps fortunately, it wasn't possible to know at the beginning that the journey would be so splintered.

And so it was that, in the late spring of 1990, wearing the Afghan amulet itself, armed with photographs of the embroidered versions from Kohistan and Razgrad, and carrying five kilos of baggage and a litre of vodka, I began my travels in the high valleys of the Hindu Kush.

Kohistan

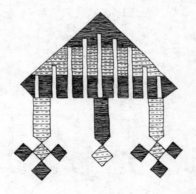

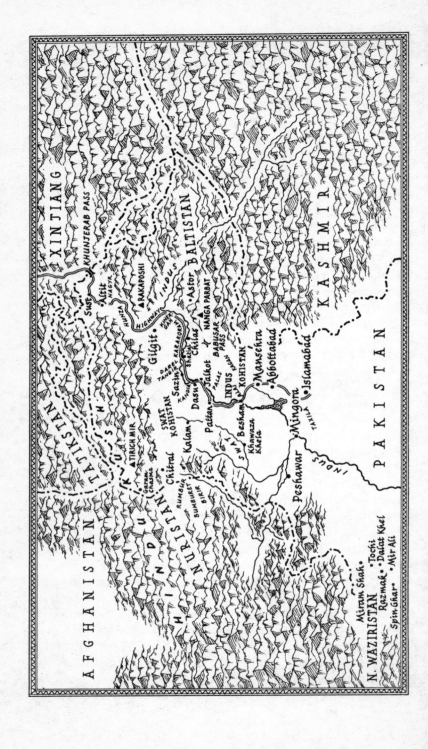

Chitral

The Major had 'stayed on' as the Indian Army left, overseeing partition and then reverting to his old job of teaching, being offered headmastership of a school he described as the 'Winchester plus Eton' of Pakistan. Now nearing unprepared retirement, he found himself beached in an isolated valley of the Hindu Kush as headmaster of a small English-medium primary school.

A lonely man, he pounced on each newcomer to recount the tale of the ten years he had spent in a walled tribal encampment, where men have no truck with the laws of the land, where he never met nor spoke to a woman, where he set himself the task of bringing to the boys the benefit of an English education, and from where he was ultimately kidnapped before being released a year or so ago and making his way north to Chitral. The story had lost none of its fascination for him in the oft-repeated telling. That he had succeeded in instilling his moral values in the sons of the wildest tribesmen, Pathan and Waziri, whom the British, the Russians and the puppet Islamic rulers had failed to quell, had indeed been an achievement, and the Major felt justly proud. Having exhausted a new listener, of whom he knew and learnt nothing, and had merely come across sitting alone in the garden of the Mountain Inn, he turned and walked away, his gait rigid, his head bent and his hands clasped behind his back, affecting the little bounce in his step that he had cultivated when approaching his troops or pupils with unpopular instructions.

Northern Waziristan he had disclosed was the setting for this life among the tribes, a disclosure that eliminated him from my interest as rapidly as he had eliminated me from his. 'Land of the Wazirs' he had explained. It was like a child's game: knock off the 'istan' meaning 'land of' and you could find the people you were looking for. Afghan, Baluch, Uzbek, Turkmen, Kafir, even 'Pak', 'the clean ones', as opposed to the dirty Hindus. But I was looking for Kohistan, 'land of the mountains', and in this most mountainous part of the whole planet there were a considerable number of Kohistans: Indus Kohistan, Swat Kohistan, the

3

Kohistan of Afghanistan. The latter had also been called Kafiristan until the pagan inhabitants were forcibly converted to Islam in the late nineteenth century, when it was renamed 'Nuristan', 'land of those who have seen the light', with those who had not taking refuge across the frontier in Pakistan. These are the last pagan people of the Hindu Kush and are known as Siah Posh or Kalash Kafir, meaning Black Kafir, distinguishing them from the Red Kafir of Afghanistan, who used to wear red robes. They live in three interconnecting fertile strips, Bumburet, Rumbur and Birir – buried high in the mountains and until recently inaccessible to vehicles – that are part of the complex of valleys of Chitral where seemingly haphazard events, shirked decisions and his widowed brother's letters from home had settled the Major at the tag end of his life.

His gradual withdrawal from headmastership of one of the highest places of learning in the country to the job of tutor in an untamed tribal encampment in frontier territory and then to the task of setting up a small primary school in these remote northern valleys seemed only to have been achieved with some unease. He employed a series of young girls from England to help him, even, it has to be said, to do the work for him. They gave the little school considerable status and also enabled him to leave the valleys from time to time and renew his ever more tenuous contact with the outside world.

The outside world impinges little, less even than it did in the nineteenth century when Chitral was at the wildest edge of the North-West Frontier Province and the British were skirmishing with Afghanistan. The one way in and out of the main valley entails an arduous climb with porters over the pass that cuts it off from the south, the snows melting enough to allow travellers through only in the short summer months. Or by air, though should there be a wisp of cloud or a puff of wind the small propeller plane does not fly and the valley is left isolated. This for the whole of a long winter.

When it is possible to fly the geography becomes clearer. These are no pretty picture-postcard mountains, they are upheavals of the earth's gut, pushed skyward where the tectonic plates of Asia and India clash. They are wrinkled-skinned as elephant and rhinoceros, primeval and scabby; capped with icy crags. The little Fokker flies straight into them, skirting every crest and slipping between each peak so that the snow and steep scree at its wingtips are almost within reach. Below, the pocked, grey wastes of rock and boulder are sliced by green valleys, as acidly discordant as a field of rape in the English countryside. Their apricot, mulberry and walnut trees, their millet and wheat, though cultivated for centuries, stand as an alien challenge still.

Some valleys are wide and fertile, quilted with green and yellow fields and spiked with poplars. Others are only a flash or flick of green, like a casual Miró brush stroke. These on the ground would turn out to be just spots where the rushing river skirting the mountain was spanned by a precarious plank bridge, wide enough to take a horse from the narrow road on one side across to a small orchard of walnut trees and a garden of rose bushes and irises on the other. On the road side of the valley a locked wooden gate would prevent outsiders from crossing while on the orchard side there would be a small shack of wood roofed in slates. In its dusty yard women would squat patiently winnowing grain, their veils cast aside in the security of their own home. There would always be dirty small children, bejewelled and barefooted, and dogs of the sandy jackal type that in poor and dusty parts of the world skulk around roadside food stalls or lope purposefully down highways, head and tail down, teats swinging.

It would be in such valleys that I might find women wearing dresses embroidered with the amulet, or the amulet itself. When the Major reappeared in the garden of the Mountain Inn to regale me with further instalments of his life story, I tried interrupting the flow with diffident questions about amulets, women and valleys, but to no avail. Until, that is, he was joined by a young Frenchman of Médecins sans Frontières, Thierry. Yes, yes, he knew two young English girls who were going the next day to one such valley, along with one of the local rulers, a Mehtar. One of the girls, Fiona, was spending a few days away from the hospital where she worked tirelessly fitting false wooden limbs on Afghan refugees who had stepped on landmines. The other, her sister Michaela, was out from England on holiday. When asked to take me along they were too polite to refuse, though I was a total stranger to them.

Because we were females we were squashed into the back of the tiny jeep while the Mehtar and a friend sat in the front. A

peacock of a man, whose princely title came to him as son-in-law
of the previous ruler who had personally owned all the valleys of
Chitral, the Mehtar was taking a day trip to call on relatives
living up this remote valley. Though he listed for us his wife's
property as his own there was of course no sign or mention of her.

We followed the road alongside the river, passing several little
gated bridges that crossed it to the strips of orchard on the
opposite bank. Until at one the Mehtar stopped. The dogs barked
when he stood at the locked gate and yoohooed across the river,
holding the fish he had just scooped out of the water with his
hands. The men greeted us, the women sat silently watching.
The fish was taken and cooked on a fire of sticks. Cut into small
pieces, it was handed to us by servants as we sat waiting for
hospitality on the narrow grassy strip that fringed one bank of
the river, walnut trees behind, a flower garden ahead, the mountains close on both sides. The family idiot stood watching our
every movement. His face was small and brown with a strangely
squashed look; his eyes were square and uncomprehending but
expectant below shaggy eyebrows. The Mehtar hugged and
kissed him. 'I love these children of nature' he said. 'I retain three
in my household.'

The intimate touch excited the fool, who got up and began to
dance. He held his hands in the air, in the twisted swanlike pose
of a Balinese temple dancer and, humming to himself, swayed his
body from side to side. Then he moved forward towards me and
said something.

'He wants to marry you.'

'Tell him I'm betrothed.'

He began a strangled chanting, his voice rising and falling with
irregular pauses of rhythm in a plaint ill-learned and half-forgotten.
Suddenly he spun round and round, slobbering with excitement
and trampling the wild irises around the edge of his self-ascribed
stage. Regaining his balance with some difficulty – he was very
short and wore unfastened rubber sandals several sizes too big for
him – he grinned at his audience, his face shining with happiness
and spittle. He rushed to kiss the hands of the three women,
grabbed an iris and thrust it on to Michaela's lap. His joy was
unbearable.

'I thought he wanted to marry *me*.'

'He changed his mind when he realized how old you were.'

In our laughter the fool saw only the reflection of his own happiness.

It was late when we reached the old family home at the head of the valley, a square white fortress of rooms around a high-walled courtyard. The Mehtar rustled up his retainers – the estate manager, Faisal, who was responsible for the lands, the man in charge of buildings and stores and the one paid to have food, wine and musicians ready for any surprise visit. After finding wood to light the fires, music seemed to be the first priority. A small disparate group of musicians was summoned to bang old drums and wail plaintive nasal songs that sounded as if they might be love songs. The other men, far from scurrying about their tasks, sat on the floor gazing intensely at the musicians through wrinkled eyes in a row of filthy bare feet, knees cupped by blackened hands, sharp tribal faces and flat woollen hats. Wooden chairs were brought for us and in the firelight we drank sour, soupy wine and ate walnuts in the sort of quantities that in England we usually only see at Christmas. There was no question of returning to Chitral that night.

Beyond the house the valley split. One path led into the pass through to Nuristan where no one went, now that the Afghan border was closed and the mujahedin's arms cache had blown up. The other path we walked along to the tiny settlement of Garam Chashma where the valley ended, a desolate row of stone shacks dripping with the slush of early spring. A few men with rifles slouched against rickety posts that held up the overhanging roofs, and stared menacingly. The path ended where old hot springs, now disused, rusted stains into the icy ground.

Back at the house, loud gunfire reverberated. On the verandah the Mehtar sat with Faisal, a man with the face of a Persian aristocrat in an old book of miniature paintings – a long aquiline nose, large ears and a thin head topped by the squashed woollen cap all Chitralis wear. The two were blasting away with a Kalashnikov at anything that moved, the shots resounding off every rocky surface. A barefoot retainer soon ran in grinning; in his hand was a beautiful exotic bird, pale lilac, blue and green, a roller. Stiff. Covered with blood. The Mehtar smiled.

*

On the drive back home the Mehtar suddenly braked, his way barred by a sheep lying in the middle of the road. He strode off with his Kalashnikov to chase it away, but it staggered to its feet giving birth. He gently picked up the sticky lamb, kissed it and placed it by the roadside, the mother lurching after it. He carefully placed them together and kissed the lamb again. A woman stood immobile, watching, a basket of firewood balanced on her head. She was dressed in the shalwar kameez outfit of the plains of Pakistan, trousers, shift and shawl.

Nowhere had I seen women in the embroidered clothes of Kohistan. The women who crouched in the Mehtar's pitch black smoky kitchen, one kindling a twig fire to make tea, the other spinning at a wheel of sticks and string, had been wearing long dresses of floral polyester, not the short, flounced-skirt ones of Kohistan. They wore no peaked helmets; their shawls were plain and tatty, devoid of bits of coral, blue beads and the motif of the Afghan amulet.

'This isn't the right Kohistan' said the Mehtar. 'Try the Kalash valleys.'

Kalash

The Granada TV cameraman filming the Black Kafirs of the Kalash valleys for the television series *Disappearing World* had come into town to send off mail, collect the stores and grab a shower. He could be found somewhere down the main street they said, 'and you have to register with the police before you can go to Kalash'.

The main street of Chitral was a gullied stone track that toppled down the hillside, sluiced with melting snows and over-hung with telegraph wires. The open-fronted bazaar stalls that flanked it were flimsy constructions of rubble, tea-chests, stones and cardboard with ladders leading up to an occasional precarious second storey. Their access was cluttered with hessian sacks and brooms, with clusters of rubbish and plastic buckets and with men sitting on stools at low wooden tables drinking glasses of mint tea. Neat displays offered Chinese torches, yellowing note-books, lurid earrings, rubber shoes and Western ephemera. The place thronged with wild-eyed bearded men, some Afghan refu-gees, some Uzbek and Turkmen in embroidered pillbox hats, some Pathan in huge turbans and some Chitrali in their usual flat caps. Guns and jeeps were everywhere and there was not a woman to be seen. Over it all, away in the distance, brooded the sacred mountain of Tirich Mir, one of the highest in the world, and beyond it Afghanistan and the Central Asian states of the disintegrating Soviet Union.

Perhaps the post office. This was a small mud shack, the only indication of its purpose a very British red postbox standing sentinel outside. Inside sacks and sacks of mail were piled on the floor and heaped up against the high barricaded wooden counter. Here they were left for a week or a month or more till the plane flew and one or two could be loaded on and taken to Peshawar. Only by pushing around the sacks was it possible to get behind the counter to find the postmaster. 'I am not knowing this cameraman. I am seeing no one here.'

Perhaps the telegraph office, a rather larger version of the post

office, where an old-fashioned upright typewriter tapped away
on its own into a radio set while the operators lay dozing on
their string and wood charpoys.

I found him eventually at the top of the bazaar in his loaded
jeep, ready to go.

'Sorry. We're working in Rumbur. I'd have to drop you off at
the police station where the valleys fork. That's a couple of
hours' walk in the dark before you'd find somewhere to stay. Too
risky. Sorry.'

Following more suggestions I located a rather seedy man who
offered to take me there. He haggled with ferocious intensity,
revolving his cap between his fingers and glancing down at it
each time he raised the price still further, but in the end it wasn't
his jeep that turned up the next morning. He had farmed the job
out to a meek little Chitrali, already taking two Americans to the
Kalash valleys, and had gone himself on the more lucrative run
to the airstrip where a group of tourists was said to be arriving.
The Americans turned out to be two friendly young men, old ski
bums from Aspen, Colorado. Slung with shoulder straps advertising brands of expensive Japanese cameras, with leather cases,
canvas bags and tripods, they were on their annual photographic
spree, one having left his mother and the other a new wife back
home. They sold their pictures to magazines, they said, and gave
shows to local clubs. They commented on my generally small
size, my lack of any significant luggage, my status as a lone
female traveller and courteously helped me up into the back of
the jeep. They were not terribly interested in embroidery.

We could hear the shouting before we reached the isolated
police station where the track forked, but at the sight of us the
small fat man in a rather dirty shirt, who held all the power
needed in these valleys, stopped mid-flow and smiled obsequiously. He noted passport details for the three of us and then,
without pausing for breath, began shouting again at the lackeys
who formed his staff, directing most of his invective at an Afghan
who, with a pot of glue and a brush, was trying to paste back the
cover of the file recording details of newly arrived tourists. The
torn cover seemed to be the cause of the entire problem. And
recording tourists a new power base. Twenty years ago there was
no route into these valleys, as in most of this region, bar a path

offering a slithery foothold with a raging torrent far below. Then the few outsiders who struggled for days to get here were greeted by painted women in exotic costumes proffering food and dancing in celebration. Now the food was sold at inflated prices and the dancing had been tidied up into advertised tourist events staged on the roofed dance platform that had been newly built on a spur dominating the valley of Bumburet.

It was generally agreed that we should give a lift to the two backpackers lying on the grass. As they climbed into the jeep the Americans moved protectively to either side of me. Six hours the backpackers said they'd been waiting. Nothing ever came past. 'Thank Christ you turned up.' Australian, two years wandering round the world, taking in the beaches of Thailand, doing a bit of trekking in Nepal, now here. 'Rip-off' they said, as we drove past sylvan glades, meadows with lilting brooks where tattooed women wearing ankle-length black dresses, strings and strings of red beads round their necks and hoods on their heads laden with cowrie shells and pompoms, scrubbed their clothes on stones. The young girls with them were not wearing hoods but wide headbands with a strip of fabric hanging down their backs to the waist, all covered with cowries, red beads and shiny buttons. They took off this headgear, shook their long black hair and then proceeded to wash it in the streams.

'Had to pay two bucks a night for a room in the last valley' said the backpackers. Small children in beautiful embroidered costume stared and then ran to hide. 'And two bucks for dinner on top of that.' Cattle grazed gently among the women and children and this time it was men who were nowhere to be seen. 'Plus when we get out of here we can't get anywhere else. Afghanistan closed, Iran closed, Khunjerab to China closed. Complete and utter waste of time.' Small watermills and streams, channelled into stone pipes that tipped the flow gently downwards along the valley, gurgled beside us. 'Have to pay the fare back to Nepal.' A woman sat on the ground unpicking all the cowries from an old headdress and sewing them on to a new one. 'Might as well have scrubbed this place – would have been cheaper to go straight on to India.' We reached the small village at the heart of the Bumburet valley. Stone houses piled on each other up the mountainside, the roof of each serving as the verandah of the next. Rough wooden looms warped with red wool leant against them. 'Thanks, mate, see you around.'

We crashed in, the ski bums and I, they with their zooms and wide-angles, filters and flashes, I with my dangling amulet, bits of stitchery and incomprehensible photos of patterns – the raw beginnings of tourism, grossly intrusive, rich barbarians, like so many hobnail boots tramping over wild flowers. The women now fled or covered their unveiled faces, the girls giggled, the children still stared or held out a hand for money.

I crept away to the local school where hordes of small boys in grey uniforms were playing football – girls are not educated beyond primary level, they said – knowing that here I might find an interpreter. The headmaster listened attentively, shuffled his papers and told me to come back in half an hour when he would have found the right young man to guide me.

The teacher he chose shinnied up steep grass slopes, across the flat roofs of the piled-up houses, up the notched planks of solid wood that served as ladders to reach upper storeys, along narrow passages between windowless stone walls, presuming I was following but never glancing back, taking his cue from what he had seen of the world outside his valley where a man never acknowledges the quiet shawled woman trailing in his wake. The Black Kafirs were different, a small pocket of a few thousand pagans who still resisted Islam and whose women were not veiled. As they had been left undisturbed until now in their three remote high valleys, this was just where amuletic patterns might be found.

An occasional doorway was flanked with carved wooden effigies of horses' heads and stiff human figures like African fetishes. Twigs and branches swagged the lintels where horseshoes were nailed dead centre. These, I later learned, were the Black Kafirs' pagan temples. Outside some houses tall wooden posts were topped with the women's ceremonial hoods. They were in heavy wool with a flap that covered the woman's nape, like hoods the coalmen used to wear, and were crowned with a huge red pompom and stitched with all-powerful amulets against the evil eye: cowrie shells, Coca-Cola bottle tops, military buttons, red gewgaws and blue beads that itinerant traders brought from the markets of Peshawar and Nuristan. They were like the hoods of Ladakh women further east, revealing interesting links across the mountains in the direction of Tibet. The only difference was that cowrie shells replaced the turquoises. They were not at all the Kohistani helmet I was looking for, but nevertheless I hurried breathlessly after the teacher.

We darted like house martins in one door after another. Girls at sewing machines embroidering zigzag patterns on long black robes – again not the Kohistani dress – answered questions and giggled shyly. A graceful tattooed woman holding an even more deeply tattooed baby, blue markings covering its entire face, showed off the winter dress of her tribe, a dense brown woollen shroud to protect them in the glacial season that lasts most of the year and leaves these valleys impenetrable to outsiders. A season that is to the Kalash Black Kafir as the desert is to the Bedouin and the Arctic to the Inuit – the bedrock which nurtures their values and beliefs and set them on the sidelines of the mainstream of humanity. But the woollen shroud wasn't the Kohistani dress either.

As we stepped into a dark windowless hut, lit only by a smoking fire on the ground that dimly defined beds and cooking pots around the walls, I was grabbed by a small boy and pulled forward to look at some bundles hanging on the back wall that he wanted me to buy. They were hard and dark brown like dried Chinese mushrooms and I wondered whether they were cannabis or some other drug. Whatever they were, the price demanded – 200 rupees for an unspecified quantity – was the equivalent of several nights in a low hostelry or food for almost a week. I politely declined, but curiosity compelled me to step forward and take a closer look. All hell broke loose. Women wailed, men appeared from nowhere shouting and pushing me back as I quivered with fright. It transpired simply that the threshold behind the hearth was sacred and out of bounds to women. Exactly the same situation, in fact, as in the RAC Club of Pall Mall in London where women who step off the circular carpet upstairs find agitated uniformed staff rushing up to warn them they are violating male territory.

'Did you use f8 for that one of the girl washing her hair, or what?' The ski bums compared notes as our jeep took the sole track out of the valley, a narrow path along the flank of the mountain, and was blocked for an hour while a small truck ahead of us loaded logs: trees felled from the higher slopes and rolled down to the path for transportation, precipitating eroded soil into the river below. As we finally set off for the narrow pass out of the valley a little family of would-be settlers trudged in past us, the man bearing all their possessions wrapped in a cloth, a seven-year-old humping a small sibling on her back and the pregnant mother dragging along behind, head bowed, totally shrouded in Muslim black, as menacing as crows alighting on a lay-by of a rural English road.

Peshawar

Peshawar was the springboard to the next Kohistan, the mountains crowding the valley of the Swat river. The hotel on the edge of the old city offered 'Modern emenities, a commercial Enviorment, Get newspapers early in the Morning, a car to the Khyber Pass and viracious atmosphers'. Though I required none of these things it seemed in other respects perfectly adequate for my needs. The room, painted entirely in cabbage green and fluorescently lit, was equipped with a prayer mat but no bedding. Cockroaches were not immediately in evidence. I later felt doubly gratified by my choice when I observed that the nearest hotel down the road proudly advertised that all its toilets came with 'flesh attached'.

Outside the air sagged with heat and humidity – a warm damp towel over an inhalation of Friar's Balsam. The fumes of auto rickshaws and claptrap buses, the dust kicked up from the road by donkeys, horses, goats and sandalled feet smudged the evening lamps along the stall fronts. By morning light the colour, the discord, the cacophony, the shock of images that assaulted the eye at every blink were as if every bazaar, every fairground, every farmyard, every market, every medieval wooden town had been smashed to pieces and then swirled together into one pulsating mass. Buildings constructed of bits of loose sticks and small rough dusty bricks, their carved shutters hanging off corroded hinges, teetered above the crowds. Faces were like an ethnographic museum's chart of all the tribes of Central Asia – every shade of brown and every shape, topped by exotic headgear. And all male. The few women abroad slunk by enveloped from head to foot in burqas. 'Walking tents you British used to call them' the shoeman said. A man stealing jewellery looked me straight in the eye; most tried to push me over as they passed. Some cohesion came from the traders: a street of jewellers, another of bed and catapult makers, a small alleyway where floral garlands hung, another of spice stalls, a square where money changers squatted, a road of grinning false teeth advertising

15

the dentists. But such cohesion was only the background and, like bearings, was rapidly lost in the throng of people.

Among all the textile dealers in the bazaar of Peshawar there was one from the Swat valley who, it was said, was likely to know where the Kohistani embroideries came from. I finally found him, a plump man in khaki, crouched, like all the dealers, on the floor of his little stall which was crammed to the hilt with carpets, embroideries, carved wooden chairs and heavy dull silver jewellery. He beckoned to me to squat on the rugs beside him and offered tea. An old man looked on apprehensively while the contents of the bag of embroideries he had brought to sell the dealer were tipped out on to the floor. Negotiations, which included the dealer trying to sell me the old man's stuff before buying it himself, were long and skilled. Embroideries were passed to and fro among the seller, the dealer and me until the old man left and the inevitable question 'Where's your husband?' was asked. I told the dealer I was a widow. His soft spaniel's eyes drooped. 'How?'

'My husband was killed in an aeroplane crash nearly twenty years ago.'

He grasped my hand warmly as if it had happened only yesterday. 'You have a friend. If ever you need I am here.'

I thanked him politely, but said I thought I could manage. His eyes suddenly brightened, as if a thought had just hit him. 'You are alone!' he exclaimed, squeezing my hand even tighter. 'Come with me to Waziristan! We go to the bus stand and get bus to Miram Shah, then we change to small jeep for Tochi.' He warmed to his subject. 'Then we can go to Razmak, Dalat Khel. It is Pashtun territory, very troubled but hospitable.' He looked very excited. 'Mir Ali and Spin Ghar, we go.' A slight frown troubled his brow. 'I can take only three or four days free. Give to you. Then I must back to my house.'

I concentrated then on the Afghan dealers, who squatted among even more exotic and esoteric merchandise but who always, when a transaction was sniffed, turned out to have smart calculators and credit card facilities. Each offered me green tea and varied explanations of the Afghan amulet. 'Turkmen Lakai.'

'Aren't the Lakai Uzbek people?'

'Name of work. Against sickness and bad spirits. Mullah writes prayer or saying from Koran and stuffs inside. Round Mazar-i

Sharif, Balkh and Samangan. Lot of Turkmen there. Women wear on shoulder or front of neck. Hang on doors and windows. Also in silver. Also on cows and horses.'

Awash with green tea I wandered through the bazaar looking at horses. The first, with a wispy beard, tried to bite me. A traffic jam of carts heavily laden with sacks of grain snarled up a crossroads while a beautiful young man – wide pantaloons astride a wooden box raised above the jute bags, cartons and sacks that his horse refused to pull – twirled his whip in vain. While old turbaned beggars, squint-eyed delivery boys and orphaned kids selling plastic bags pushed between the horses and carts, the jam-up provided me with a grand number of horses to survey. Some hours later I could confirm that none of the horses in Peshawar wore that amulet. Nor, indeed, did any of the women.

All the dealers, once they saw a Westerner, claimed to be not Pakistani but Afghan, selling their heirlooms from Kabul. It seemed to say much for our reputation for being sentimental rather than businesslike. In the end, of the true Afghan dealers, it was Sayell whose information on the amulet was the most trustworthy. A slight man with peaked nose, pale eyes and exuberant whiskers, he sat amid piles of carpets and stacks of cheap pink glass rings and lapis earrings. As soon as I entered his stall he set about preparing yet more green tea, boiling a small metal pot of water on the floor and taking out a small red wooden pestle and mortar in which he ground the cardamom. 'Sugar?'

'Just a little.'

He fetched an open biro and stirred the tea, leaving circles of blue ink in the bottom of the cup.

That formality dealt with he embarked on the story of how he had left his job as an accountant at the Afghan Ministry of Planning to join the mujahedin. His eyes glistened, his beard of thick black hair frothed with grey trembled, he shook his finger at me exclaiming 'You understand?' at every phrase, when it was impossible to understand, so rapidly and incoherently did he talk. He unfurled a nonstop saga relating to Bedford vans and how good, clean and cheap they had been, how wonderful Canadian aid to Afghanistan and British help to the refugees was, how he found himself in a 'cellar' – 'you know, the thing that goes up from the first floor to the top of the building' – when between the first and the second floors a KGB fellow asked him where Kalid's office was. '"On the sixth" I told him – it was my own, I am Kalid, you understand?' He then hastily got out at the second floor, he explained, rushed off and so joined the mujahedin, hiding all his papers in the wooden ceiling of his house. The KGB searched, he said, but didn't find them. He fought together with those he had once been against and then when things got too tough he walked for four days through the mountains with only shoes, a blanket and a hat. He fetched out an album of blue-toned, dimly focused photos of himself and his brothers in the mujahedin in fatigues and Afghan turbans, guns aslant.

'Will you go back, now there's the agreement between America and Russia to stop arms shipments?'

'It's good, it's hopeful. Maybe one year, maybe two.'

On the Road

From Peshawar north-eastward to Swat Kohistan and then on to Indus Kohistan the pattern of travel was almost always the same. Every bus stand was simply a waste lot on the edge of town, waste that is of buildings but not of anything else. It was always cramjammed with people and, of course, with every kind of vehicle that could serve as a bus. These ranged from small Suzuki jeeps to massive coaches with holes in place of windows. All were decrepit, their shabby unroadworthiness disguised under layers of tinsel, rainbow sign painting and pink plastic trinkets. 'SUPERCO ACHPESH' they would proclaim in psychedelic hues, lurid film stars painted in the middle of the word 'coach'.

Old women poured out the lament of their life story to travellers, the lame and the infirm stretched out their hands, small boys tried to sell chewing gum, peanuts and sticky sweets in ones and twos. Goats and stray dogs sniffed around the piles of litter and mooched through the swirling dust, which after each sharp shower turned into a churned quagmire. Men sat on charpoys under a hessian canopy, writing out tickets on bits of flimsy paper.

The scenario that ensued on my arrival at one of these bus stands was always the same. I had only to say the name of my destination – to anyone or even to the open air – and I would immediately be escorted to the right little group of ticket men. Journeys to places an hour or more distant were usually in minibuses that left when full. The men would eye me carefully. 'Woman!' they would say. When no disclaimer came they would continue, 'Two ticket. Front seat'. As no good Muslim man will sit next to an unrelated female the idea was that I should buy the two front seats by the driver, leaving the one between him and me free so that no physical contact could occur. There would inevitably already be two fellows lolling in the two front seats of the first buses waiting in line so that I would be taken back to about the third minibus in the queue, which was empty and would still be waiting an hour or so later. This I always refused.

19

'One person, one seat.' Index finger in the air, I would stand firm, as a crowd of onlookers gathered. In almost all the minibuses there was a single seat by the door, occupied by the man who at each stop took the money, opened and shut the sliding door, shouted the destination, leapt in and out and yanked the passengers on and off. Behind this was another seat separated from the rest of the row by a small gap enabling passengers to clamber into the back. This I indicated: 'This seat good'. Animated discussion would break out and a solution was always found. If there was a family on the bus they were shifted into the rest of the row. The woman, children hanging on to her skirts, would wrap her shawls around her as she settled at the window – where women always sat so as to be as far away from the men as possible – while the father was placed across the gap from my seat. He always looked straight ahead and was careful never to glance my way. If there were no suitable family a young boy or a few grizzled old men would be lined up alongside me. I would pay for one ticket and we would be off.

I was always courteously looked after, always put on and off the right buses in the right places, always charged the right fare. Should I need to change buses *en route*, say from the main road minibus to a large local pantechnicon serving a string of villages, I would be set down at a fork in the road. Here there was always a rickety wooden teahouse astride a murky stream where I would take tea, a dirty little cup of an intensely sweet milky brew poured from a Chinese thermos. I was almost always the only woman and always the only foreigner and, as such, within seconds attracted an enormous crowd of men and boys who would simply stand and stare. When the local bus came along it would be a monster with heads leaning out of every window, the driver submerged under passengers, the roof rack piled with people, chickens and sacks and the steps on to the bus clung to by about twenty youths. None the less I was always thrown on and a young rake with flashing teeth would grab my bag and try to pay my one rupee fare. Minutes later he would be leering 'Where's your husband?' I would tell him he was in Peshawar or Mingora, or whatever other town we had just left, and was about to join me. At my destination he – or if he were unfortunate enough to be getting off the bus before me, the 'brother' to whom he delegated the task – would try to lead me to some louche establishment like the Bright Star Lodgings instead of the local hotel.

That I was alone elicited an entirely different response in the women. Working in the fields or in the courtyard of their homes, they would question me as I walked past, by pointing to me and raising one finger in the air. When I nodded in reply they would invite me in, offering tea. Communication was usually by signs and drawings and, as I began with the advantage of knowing exactly what they were going to ask me ('Where's your husband? How many sons? How old are you'?), even Urdu was possible. Best of all, if there were a schoolboy around he would interpret in basic English.

In one home – one large wooden room with an earth floor and a flat earth roof, built next to a frothing mountain stream for a fresh water supply – an old woman sat with all her daughters-in-law and a clutch of fly-eyed small children, several still breastfeeding. A young boy, who unlike the women had been to school and spoke a little English, followed me in. His hands would be smooth for sure, but I knew not to offer him mine and shook instead the scraped and calloused claws proffered by the women and girls.

The newest daughter-in-law, who had been married only three days before, traditionally had the task of cooking for everyone and was stirring a metal pot on a fire of small twigs on the ground. She appeared still to be dressed in her bridal gear: a vivid pink satin dress and trousers, scarlet chiffon shawls and masses of thin gold jewellery. The shawls trailed dangerously close to the flames. It was common knowledge that many new daughters-in-law died mysteriously from burning, especially when their death opened the way to another dowry for the groom's family.

The walls of the room, as in all the houses, were lined with shelves full of cooking pots and questionable patent medicines. A ghetto-blaster stood prominently on a shelf, covered with an embroidered cloth, and was immediately switched on for my benefit. A few charpoys were the only furniture, apart from the low beautifully carved wooden chairs on which the women sat around the central hearth, idly watching the young bride work.

'Are you Muslim?' the old woman asked, after having established the whereabouts of my husband and the number of my sons.

'Christian' I hesitantly suggested.

She leapt to her feet and started shouting 'You must go, you must go'. I got up from the bed where they had seated me, but they insisted I have tea before leaving. They blew at the fire to hurry it on. When it was ready the old woman tasted it first and then handed it to me. It looked like a delicious cappuccino from the best Venetian café, except for the cracked cup ingrained with dirt. Unfortunately the white froth, enclosing globules of fat, continued all the way down to the bottom of the cup. I held my breath, took a few sips and then started to say my goodbyes. They shouted and screamed, clearly offended by this slight on their hospitality. I offered money and they only screamed louder so I hurried out, regretting this small contribution to ill feeling between Muslim and Christian.

The minibus from Peshawar into the Swat valley wound up the high pass, from where Churchill once sent enthusiastic despatches to the *Daily Telegraph* on the Pathan uprising, into a gentle flat landscape butting northward into mountains that rolled in, ever higher along the horizon. Black oxen ambled slowly through streams and trees, followed by young cowherds or led on a string by shawled women. Camels passed by lazily, in the slow motion of a dream. Graveyards were marked by hundreds of small upright shales and by the occasional tomb of a wealthy man, flaunting bits of red rag on sticks. Small brickworks – nothing more than patches of red dust with two short iron chimneys set on the ground belching black smoke – produced piles of little handmade bricks. Several times the bus was stopped: by police checking for guns, drugs, anything dangerous in 'this troubled land', or by schoolboys placing stones across the road to hold up every vehicle and then jumping on it for a lift.

Accidents were frequent. Soldiers tried to pull crashed lorries off the road with what looked like bits of string. In a small bazaar town a pony trap had tipped its load of bricks across the road and a small crowd held aloft a dead old man. Whether he had collapsed while driving the cart or whether the bricks had hit him was unclear as we sped through, hooting madly.

At crossroads groups of ragged nomads congregated, their meagre possessions tied with rope, the women in satiny clothes with tattered shawls, the children in small amulet-hung dresses and helmets. They were Gujars bringing their flocks down from the high pastures before winter set in. In the wake of one group a peaceful old tramp, clad in road-stained white clothes and a resplendent green turban bestuck with straw, walked slowly by chanting gently and offering sweets. Over his shoulder he carried a rifle made of car parts – bits of exhaust, spark plugs, metal piping – lashed into shape with string and with strips of plastic and red rags.

Swat

Siraj Ahmed's gentle face was lined beyond its years. White hairs at his temple, he regretted, were due to the stress of customers complaining that his antique wooden chests, temple doors and bookrests from Swat, shipped in containers to Europe, were not perfect. Here there was a fault of carving, there of staining. And then there were his three sons, five daughters and twenty-stone wife to support, though he made no mention of her enormous size, stating only that she was a healthy woman of thirty-six and had many more babies to produce. But she had decided enough was enough, though daughters were good because bridegrooms had to buy them. He didn't mention that he would also have to buy three brides. On a simple calculation he could have given up after his first two daughters, charming creatures of seventeen and sixteen, one slim and one fat, who did all the housework and cooking. The younger ones squinted and, I surmised, would not demand such a high bride price, but his favourite five-year-old might.

Not only the domestic scene, but also the horrors of the world weighed heavily on his shoulders. His conversation returned continually to the slaughter of the Second World War, the stupidity of nuclear weapons, the greed of modern man. His own small contribution to the salvation of mankind was the possession of a room kept as a guest bedroom while the family slept outside. This he was able to offer to passing travellers in the small bazaar town of Kwazakhela where there was no other bed for the wayfarer and where the road forked between the northern route to the Swat valley and Swat Kohistan and the pass to the east that lead to the Indus valley, to Indus Kohistan and the Kara-koram Highway and thus to Gilgit, Hunza, China and the world beyond.

I had been sent from the stall he held in the bazaar of Kwazakhela to the workshop in his home down the road where old workmen were hacking woodwormed lumps out of lovely antique carved wooden chests and replacing them with rough bits of planking which they then blackened. His wife, hearing from the children that there was a foreign woman alone talking to their father, invited me into their home. She was squatting (and I then had only an inkling of her bulk) making naan. Slapping a dough of flour and water into balls she then deftly flattened them with wet hands and threw them on to the side of a hole in the ground with a fire of sticks at the bottom. I shook hands in a slippery wet grasp of mutual pleasure. 'You are to stay to lunch' became dinner and the guest room.

Dinner was a large bowl of rice taken sitting on the ground with Siraj and his three sons in the dark for the electricity, as usual, had failed. The women hovered and when we had finished ate what remained while Siraj retired to his small private bedroom, a dusty refuge full of books: worm-eaten copies of Sir Aurel Stein's *Serindia* and Kipling's *Kim*, among others.

It was about halfway up the valley, where the mountains close in and the road hugs the voracious river and Swat becomes Swat Kohistan, that I began to envelop myself more generously in shawls. It wasn't just that when they saw me babies' faces crumpled and they burst into tears or that little toddlers, walking hand in hand down the path towards me, turned tail and fled in terror, it was mostly the deftly aimed sharp stones catapulted at my feet by unseen boys or men, laming me for a while, that drove me to the strongest protection I could muster against the Muslim male's uncomprehending hatred of a woman alone – layers of gauzy cloth.

Thus wrapped I was tossed with a large bag of flour into the back of a Toyota truck and shaken along the road leading northwards to where the first jagged snowclad peaks pierced the sky. Afghan refugees with their strings of camels moved slowly up into the mountains – it was unclear why – while more Gujar, nomads of the Swat valley, moved in the opposite direction, away from the imminent winter snows, driving their silky goats, cattle, women and sheep down the valley before them. Always below was the cascading river, a tumble of froth surfacing a glacial turquoise undertow that dragged the Swat round the smooth massive rocks that littered its bed.

*

NOTICE WARNING
EACH AND EVERY PERSON
IS INFORED THAT THE AREA IS DANGEROUS ...
WANDERING HERE AND THETHER IN THE FOREST/
MOUNTAINS ALSO DANGROUS AS WELL AS PROHEBITED
ANY ONE DESIRES TO DO SO, HE SHOULD INFORM
POLICE FIRST PERSON AVOIDING THESE INSTRUCTION
WILL BE RESPONSIBLE OF ANY LOSS SUSTAIN
TO HIM. FURTHERMORE PHTOGRAPHY NEAR
HOUSES IS ALSO NOT ALLOWED.
                          BY ORDER OF
                          Asstt. Supdt. POLICE

The old brick wall, to which this notice was affixed, was being desultorily repaired by a grubby workman. 'Welcome' he said and then, when I smiled in response, spat at me and looked as if he'd rather kill me.

This was Kalam, the end of the line. As the sun set the *paseo* and *quattro passi* of Mediterranean lands was played out in an inelegant promenade of men hand in hand taking the measure of the muddy bazaar. No women, of course, were ever to be seen. Whereas the bazaar of Chitral was the hub of its valley commerce and fine-faced Afghans strode with local tribesmen up and down its stony causeway, Kalam was a desolate, no-hoper sort of place. Men hung around in the mud in disconsolate groups, surly, scowling and spitting or surveying me with penetrating hatred. The settlement itself was a huddle of plank huts on spindly pole supports, straddling the swirling river over a shaky wooden bridge, by which a couple of men were skinning a goat, its four legs rigid in the air, the front two bare flesh, the back two still hairy. Jostling the huts were innumerable half-finished grandiose concrete and brick buildings, abandoned remains of the shattered dreams of what enterprise? They looked like hotels, but for six months of the year the whole valley to thirty kilometres below Kalam lies buried under snow, cut off from the outside world. The handful of bazaar stalls stocked more biscuits, tea and candles than anything else. A few sold naan and paratha, the men at the stalls rolling, slapping and stretching the dough in their hands. At others men stitched shirts and trousers on pre-electric sewing machines of obscure make, otherwise everything was being constructed, welded, beaten, created by hand and there was not a machine in sight, bar a Heath Robinson contraption of wheels that activated a mallet, pounding some brown stuff. When I asked what it was I was told 'Hashish, brother'.

Whichever way one stepped out of Kalam there was a notice:

> WARNING: DO NOT GO BEYOND THIS POINT.
> THE AREA IS DANGEROUS AND THE FOREST
> AHEAD IS DENSE.   SWAT POLICE.

Past one such notice, across a swaying plank bridge over the boulder-bedded tumultuous river, flat wooden shacks on rickety posts huddled along the bank. As I wandered beyond the felt-makers, their fingers dyed mauve, their clothes full of fluff, a group of women waved me into their home. I entered through a tiny open-windowed reception room full of what looked like Christmas decorations which led into a main room of crumbling stone walls. In the pitch dark a small fire on the dirt floor shone on the metal pots on the walls around and dimly disclosed the sleeping area beyond. Only the woman starting to prepare tea for me was there. The others, swathed in embroidered dresses and most with a baby at a bare breast, were sitting on a verandah among the chickens, crosslegged on the earth round a metal bowl. The bowl was full of muddy water with what looked like potato peelings in it that they were in the process of wiping. It was hard to know what was in the bowl but whatever it was, with my hefty gauche European feet, I trod in it as I stepped across to admire the newest baby boy. All apologies were inadequate and I could have wept. I discovered much later that they were preparing truffles and that these were what I had been offered in the Kalash valleys when I stepped unwittingly into the 'pure' area between the hearth and back wall where no women are allowed. More stones were justifiably hurled at me as I made my way back across the river to Kalam.

I hung around the bazaar waiting in vain for a bus that never came. A jeepload of Germans refused to take me: 'No. We do not want'. The tribesman in turban and white cricketing pullover with pink stripes who had taken it upon himself to look after me and find this lift was vexed: 'Germans no good people. Germans NOTHING people' he spat vindictively. A man with a dying baby soused it with dirty water from a tin tub by the roadside. The chill in the air crisped perceptibly.

The would-be cricketer finally found some men who agreed to give me a lift to the small settlement further up the valley where I wanted to go. 'We return in half an hour. Do not walk. It is dangerous.' At the settlement the women again waved me into their homes where fourteen-year-old girls dangled their babies. The women welcomed me with tea, the girls stared, the school-boys greeted me and gave me walnuts, and, though I was a sitting duck waiting by the roadside for the lift back, no stones were thrown. My men returned me to the bazaar and refused any payment.

I met no other travellers in the Swat valley, bar a young American family working in Pakistan (the father provoking stares of incredulity from the men idling in the bazaar by walking round with his baby daughter strapped to his chest) and two large groups of Japanese who – glasses, wide teeth and cameras glimpsed at the windows – sped by in a pair of smart coaches hugging close together and labelled 'The Ultimate Travel Experience'.

Still further into this territory, where the track ends and the goat trails begin, the quest for the Kohistan I sought brought no results. In every small bazaar that flanked the one dirt road with its wood-smoked food and haggling poverty, textile traders, looking at photographs of the embroideries, always said 'Chitral' or 'Kohistan'. No women wore dresses anything like the one I was looking for. Following clues – leaping from boulder to boulder across agitated streams to remote homesteads – brought me only to the traditional Swati shift: white or black cotton kaleidoscoped with a geometric pattern in a shocking pink Schia-parelli would have sold her soul for. But never to the work of Kohistan.

Amulets round children's necks and on their caps were square or made of red rags and cowries; camels, horses and donkeys, under close inspection, wore only tassels, beads and trinkets; high-prowed Bedford lorries were decorated only with flowers, eagles killing snakes, parakeets on branches; women banged their washing on stones in the streams with laundry beaters decorated only with crosses; houses were protected from evil spirits with zigzags – an old symbol for water – and with blobs and loops; mosques were intricately, beautifully carved with intertwined Islamic blossoming; flaked marble gravestones (and I hoped not to desecrate such places by treading through them) were etched with Buddhist symbols, with the lotus and with ancient pagan motifs of the sun and the tree of life, some even with that symbol of fertility, the great earth goddess, her skirt triangular and her arms akimbo. Only tawdry local jewellery came in the shape of the triangular amulet.

This was not the right Kohistan.

Indus

❖

The Highway

If India is a land of labyrinths, of courtyards and passages, of nooks and corners, a maze that at the turning grasps the heart with a flick of sari, with an intensity of colour, with sharp musky scents, marigolds and dusty beggars, Pakistan is a corridor with violence as its walls, stained with blood like spat betel juice. Fundamentalism in Iran, lawlessness in Baluchistan, factionalism in Afghanistan, Muslim uprisings in Xinjiang, outright war in Kashmir, Sikh unrest in the Punjab, tribal terrorism in Sind: it lies closed to the world on all sides as if it were blinkered by shawls like its women. Hemmed in not only by violence but also by desert and mountain it is a defile that, in the main, follows the Indus river.

The Indus is massive, laden with silt. As its surface waters race seaward, currents beneath hold back in a counter swirl so that the river seethes with submerged waves and ripples that never break but merely marble its skin. Only where it flows through the mountains of its own Kohistan does it thrash in the deep canyon confining it. Here, hundreds of metres above its bed, it is skirted by the Karakoram Highway, the road that follows one of the ancient silk routes and spins a fragile link between Pakistan and China, over the Khunjerab Pass.

At its southernmost end in the plains the road could be said to be a road. Trucks, buses, vans, buffalo carts, donkeys and horse-traps zigzag like dodgem cars along it. Advertising billboards declare with an engaging frankness the merits of various products: 'you'll like our hammers best', 'always buy Hercules boards', 'we sell decent furniture and electronics'. Little homilies decorate roundabouts: 'Tomorrow's Projects are Today's Joys', 'Give a Child a Book', 'Trees Sustain and Beautify World', 'Smile'. Every school entrance, reminding those who attend of their privileged position, bears the device 'Enter to Learn, Leave to Serve'. Political slogans are painted on walls: 'The Most Certain and Competent Candidate. Please vote for Mr Allah Wallah'. Peeling stuccoed buildings, empty lots, rubbish tips and bazaar stalls line the road. The odd grazing camels and goats are still there as they have always been, long before the road was built.

But as it climbs into the mountains the road becomes a living thing, always evolving, never still. Uneasy fractures hold the rock face back from the highway but sudden rainstorms can split the rocks into fissures, sheering off huge slabs that fall on the road surface and lie there. Cascading streams suddenly increase in power with melting mountain snow and spread debris across its path. Glaciers melt and deposit moraine, potholes temporarily filled with stones simply remain as stony troughs, mud slides in over Tarmac and settles in tyre-ridged tracks.

The road is known affectionately as the KKH.

Alai

The three valleys of Chitral, Swat and Indus lie in a north–south direction already high above the plains, approached from the south by winding passes and butting in the north against ever higher peaks, the domain of the ibex, the markhor and psychedelic trekkers. Over the mountains between them run a complex network of small side valleys, hardly valleys but more like high plateaux streaked by streams into small communities, sometimes isolated, sometimes linked among themselves by goat trails. Some have fertile land, some stony. Some are friendly to the traveller, most are hostile. As they were perpetually at war with each other the British left them well alone. They have usually been the fiefdom of some private ruler, a nawab or mir, but more often anarchy reigned and still does. They are the traditional refuge of men on the run.

The way into them is always vertiginous. The first of the valleys off the KKH in which I searched for my embroideries was the Alai.

From an early morning bazaar on the highway, slapping back its shutters and setting out its dusty wares, an overloaded Suzuki truck, men hanging off it on all sides, set out along a roughly blasted track. This wound up the mountainside for hours until it seemed impossible to go any higher; the track was simply a notched ledge on a perpendicular slope to which whiskers of human life hung. A woman with clenched foothold sickled tufts of grass at shoulder height; a toddler led a cow along the edge of an abyss; a mud shack was spearheaded into the void; a thin terrace of maize gripped the verge. Roadmenders sat breaking stones with small hammers, their homestead tents pitched on the skirts of the road, their children gambolling with the sky at their side. Donkeys pulling tin carts tipped tar into the gaps in the road where the land fell away downward into thin air.

The Suzuki lurched upward, filling its radiator at every stream, until the flat valley – only a valley because there were yet higher

mountains around it – lay before us, clear in the intense light of
the immediate sun. Centred on a shanty bazaar of stone and tin
the valley opened into tightly manicured wheatfields serried
between rocky outcrops. Pathways led alongside them, where
men armed to the teeth hurried past and small boys crawled
home from school with wooden writing tablets. Traditional flat-
roofed mud housing squatted beside new government buildings
of sloped tin roofs, old donkeys browsed below shady new
concrete bridges. There was no sign of any embroidery.

The Communication and Works Department of the North-West
Frontier Province maintains a number of rest houses, grand
gloomy bungalows usually set in tranquil gardens beside the
river. Here official personnel on government business are expected to stay and, as only one or two a month do, outsiders may
also rent rooms. In most the electricity does not work, there is no
bedding, no hot water, no phone, no cutlery. A caretaker, the
chowkidar, runs them, shopping and cooking meals for any guests
who come. The sleaze compares with most cheap hotels but the
price is higher. However, the courtesy towards memsahibs is
traditional and you will not be grabbed as you try to pay the bill.
They may generally be regarded as safe.

At Alai I was the only guest and the chowkidar called me for
dinner. The room was in total darkness save for a hurricane light
at the head of the table where my place was laid: a plate of raw
onion and tomato, a pile of chapattis wrapped in newspaper to
keep them warm, and a metal bowl which glowed in the flicker
of the lamp. In the bowl was a small portion of vegetable curry. I
ate my meal alone at the head of the huge table surrounded by
heavy wooden chairs, barely discernible in the darkness and
peopled by the ghosts of the Forest Ranger, the Clerk of the
Works, the Officer of the Frontier Constabulary, the Public
Health Engineer and the Magistrate First Class, all of whom had
signed the visitors' book in the preceding months.

I headed back to the KKH for the next rest house, at Besham.
Two government officials in Western suits and clean shirts had
called there for lunch. They pounced on me as self-appointed
information officers, keen to answer any questions in immaculate
English. They knew nothing at all about embroidery. Nor about
marriage costumes, though on marriage itself they were well

informed. 'Yes, indeed, though parents used to choose the bride now the boy can. She can't refuse. Also here in the Northern Territories it's the boy's family who give dowry presents to the girl's, while in the rest of Pakistan it's the other way round. They usually marry at about thirteen or fourteen years old and start producing children a year later. So of course the population has doubled in fifteen years. Nobody takes any notice of birth control: "Allah will provide". Men are allowed two or three wives but that's too expensive for most of us' they said. 'We're waiting till we get to heaven' they added. 'When God destroys the world he will be there on a hilltop giving judgement. And each man will receive seventy heavenly wives called Hura, plus anything else he wants. There will be gardens and lands flowing with milk and honey and of course wine. We are waiting for the wine of heaven, that is why we take none here. It is to be hoped the vineyards are good.'

They left at dusk. 'The electricity here is nominal' they said, as it failed completely yet again. I was given their leftovers for dinner and retired by torchlight, the only person staying there. The chowkidar disappeared. Gunshot reverberated from somewhere along the highway. Shortly after midnight I was aroused by a tremendous banging on my door and the noise of someone trying to force it open. 'Let me in' some man outside bawled. 'You are just a sister to me. Only a sister.' The door was firmly bolted, though it had no lock. Even so, with some difficulty, I pushed the second bed against the door to support the bolt and then put a table on it. The rattling, turning of the door knob and heaving against the flimsy wood continued for some time. I put on my trousers, my moneybelt and my glasses, and, holding my torch in my hand, tried to go back to sleep.

A couple of hours later the man came back again. 'I just want to talk to you like a sister. Let me in.' There was still no one else around, no sign of the chowkidar, and I cowered in what I hoped I had made into a fortress. This time he tried the windows too – which I had also carefully bolted – and pressed his face against the glass. I could see every feature of his squashed brown face, his eyes and teeth glistening in the light of the hurricane lamp he held in his hand, as he peered salaciously into the pitch darkness of my room.

*

The chowkidar at the next rest house off the KKH was a fine-featured man with the usual aquiline nose, beard and squashed woolly hat. Having settled that I needed a room ('camera?' – perhaps the nose was Latin too), he enquired about dinner. 'Chicken or vegetable curry?'

'Chicken would be nice.'

An hour or so later a small boy appeared clutching a bag of tomatoes in one hand and a half-plucked scrawny chicken, struggling and squawking, in the other. 'Thirty-five rupees for the chicken, Memsahib' he said. It jerked in an effort to free itself, flapping its wings and scrabbling at the air with its sharp scaly feet. 'Only Memsahib to eat chicken. No one else here for dinner.'

While I pondered this, the chicken hung limply, staring at me with one beady eye. 'I'll stick to the veg' I said.

Indus Kohistan

Travel on the KKH was by bus or pick-up or lorry. Buses were loaded up with sacks of flour, consignments of washbasins, bolts of cloth, crowds of men and a few tourists. As they drove past, the occasional woman walking along the road would wrap her shawls more closely around her and turn her back so the men would not see her face.

I progressed from one small settlement to another looking at the children, the gravestones, the donkeys, the stalls and the doorways, but my costumes and amulet were never there. In each place as I waited at the roadside for the next ride along the highway men would try to bundle me into a back room where I was out of sight. They themselves sat in the front, fondling each other's hair and holding hands. In some places there were jams of vehicles, in others the road was almost empty – a goatherd leading home one bell-hung goat in the dusk, a few log-laden trucks lumbering by. Almost anywhere it was possible to saunter across the highway without bothering to look.

The KKH's construction had killed eight hundred and ten Pakistanis and an unknown number of Chinese, who were often hung from helicopters to blast its track. In terrain already unstable, the explosions had rendered its instability more immediate. Rock slides and glaciers skidded over it, its verge broke off and fell into the river bed below and it was often curtained by waterfalls under which the drivers stopped to rinse their buses. Scree and gravel washed over villages leaving a skin of mud.

I had now followed the KKH to Indus Kohistan. Here the Indus river cuts a slash through the mountains, a chasm so deeply incised that the opposing rock faces almost touch like the upper storeys of a medieval street. Following the river, the road in places cuts a notch between the sheer rock face below and the overhanging rock face above. In others it lies like a thin filament around the shoulders of some gaunt crag. Before the highway was built the way through the gorges was by a narrow track which ended when the rock face was too sheer. The traveller

would have to jump a couple of metres down to a narrow ledge
to pick it up again, with the possibility of a missed foothold
hurling him into the churning river far below. Here the merchants
of the Silk Road turned away and took another route.

In some places this track would be replaced by a ladder of
rope, the top rung clinging giddily to where the track could find
no foothold and dropping to where purchase for the bottom rung
and another trail could be found. When the Chinese traveller Fa-
Hsien traversed Indus Kohistan in the fourth century on his
quest to record the standing of Buddhism in western China and
India, he negotiated seven hundred such rope ladders, the terrifying 'route of the hanging chains'. In between these ladders he
progressed hesitantly along the rocks, his foot unable to find its
own width of ground to settle on and his eye confused by
perspectives lost in immensity.

Every so often the river's course widened and opened into
small level side valleys precariously cultivated. These valleys
were not strung along the river bed like a rosary but were
arbitrary and unexpected like occasional blister pearls on a fine
gold chain. They hung on the KKH by a ramshackle bazaar,
each one of which I investigated. Except, that is, for the Palas
valley and Pattan, whose bazaar lay well below the highway. The
centre of an earthquake in 1974 which destroyed the villages in
the valleys around and killed thousands of people, hurling shepherds and farmers into the raging Indus, it had been entirely
rebuilt. It seemed unpropitious for amuletic embroidered costume. What's more, the guidebook clearly said that the walk back
up to the highway was a killer. I stayed on the bus and carried on
to Dasu.

Dasu

Officer Mohammed Rashid of the police force of Dasu was a dapper little man, moustache clipped, beret set at a rakish angle. It was not his business to interrogate me – his colleagues at the police headquarters were doing that – but he had placed himself on a plastic chair opposite me and assumed an air of authority. 'What is your name?' he barked. 'You're British I see. I am telling you that British subjects have the freedom to roam anywhere in Pakistan. You have a glorious history.' It was very clear from his colleagues' conversation that I was not going to be allowed to step sideways off the KKH into the Kandia valley. 'But she is British I am telling you' Mohammed Rashid shouted at them. 'Where's your passport?' He grabbed it and waved it at the other police, becoming more and more excited. 'This exempts you from all civilians' he shouted. 'The British deserve our respect. They never do anything below dignity.' The officers seemed unimpressed. He turned to me and in confiding tones announced: 'One of my ancestors, the nawab, was knighted by Queen Victoria's son. Knighted, you understand.' He puffed himself up and opened my passport.

His expression changed. He smiled, then laughed. 'Not possible. Not possible. Sixty-two years and the lady is wandering the world alone.' This seemed in his mind to cast some cloud on my sanity. He leant across: 'You have relations in Australia? Descendants of the criminals expatriated?' I shook my head. 'In the time of India Colonel Nohr was here. Are you knowing where he is living in England?' I shook my head again. 'I was educated as lawyer' he announced proudly and then, as if to stress that this entitled him to the truth, carefully spelt it out letter by letter: L-A-W-Y-E-R.

The question of where my Kohistani embroidered dress came from met with the same suggestions as it had everywhere else. It was always over one mountain further. Here in Dasu it was from Chilas. In Chilas it would be from Gilgit and Hunza, further north. Chitral and Kalash were always mentioned. 'Non-believers

41

you know, not like our ladies.' But wandering around Jalkot, a wild village near Dasu, I had seen women wearing the helmets I was looking for. They were not embroidered but were a simple everyday version, hanging in a flap at the nape and peaked at the crown. The height of the peak, the ethnographer at the Museum of Basel had said, depended on the number of sons the woman had borne. Though I saw none with the soothsayer's horned silver amulet stitched on, they were the right shape and I decided to hang around in Dasu.

The Indus Waves Hotel, 'Flush Attached', was set back from the road on a dirty parking lot for lorries. A small repair workshop, consisting of a shack constructed of planks and piled with fire-wood, old tyres and bits of ironmongery, and a dark cookhouse with a smoking chimney and a bucket of water for washing-up outside shared the premises. The hotel itself was a decorative ensemble of bits of rubble, two storeys high. Grimy wooden doors with scrawled numbers denoted the rooms, all leading straight on to the parking lot and the road, though the upstairs ones had a verandah in front of them, approached by a rickety iron ladder. It was one of these I was given. The toilet – a hole in the ground with a cistern that didn't work hanging by a couple of rawlplugs off the crumbling wall – served the four rooms of the upper storey and was kept carefully locked day and night; the key was obtained from the hotel owner.

Service at the hotel and restaurant was assured by a young boy with a savagely slashed face and one eye missing and the owner of the premises who had a gunshot hole clean through his right ear. The restaurant – a shambles of charpoys and wobbly wooden tables – was busy with wayfarers from dawn onwards, the boy rushing around with chapattis draped over his arm, little metal dishes of food and cracked cups of sloshing tea. The owner joked and smiled and collected the money. He was a charmer whose friendly bearded face hardened quickly when he thought he was not observed or when he was busy counting the wad of rupees he kept in his shirt pocket.

I had gone upstairs and installed myself on the verandah with my book and my small evening glass of vodka, when two men came and lounged on the charpoy next to me. After a decent lapse of time they engaged me in conversation: 'We are police assistants. You are alone and we come to notify you that the police are alert. Where is your husband? Is he in service? How many children? Four sons indeed. [It would never occur to them that I might include girls in the count.] Where is the nearest police station to your home? What drink is that we can smell? We wish to taste. Where did you spend last night? Where are you heading? How much a year do you earn? Your eyesight is weak but you read without glasses, why?'

Having survived this grilling, vodka intact, I was then advised that I must notify the police immediately if there was any trouble in the night, though it was not clear how I was to do so as there was nothing like a phone anywhere. I assured them the owner of the hotel had already indicated to me that I was to lock my door tightly and open it to no one.

They left and I had hardly stepped into my room when suddenly half a dozen policemen piled in, installing themselves on the bed and completely filling the place.

'We are police officers' they said, though the uniforms made that clear. 'It is natural for the Pakistani police to look at isolated women. These embroideries of yours that you seek are not in our valleys, they do not come from our valleys. Of course you can look. You are free to look for them. People are free to roam anywhere in Pakistan but not in our valleys. Is hleetrain.' This turned out to be 'hilly terrain' which, as most of the surrounding peaks were over five thousand metres, was something of an understatement. 'We cannot offer you our security. We will not go to our valleys for your protection. You must leave in the morning for Shatial. These embroideries are from Shatial. And Chilas. And Gilgit.' They named all the points north on the Karakoram Highway outside their jurisdiction. 'Maybe just the shawl is from Jalkot. Yes, we saw you walk there today, yes indeed. You will leave on the morning bus to Shatial. We expect you on it. We shall be there to see.'

I went to bed, bolting the door firmly and piling behind it the only furnishings of the room, bar the bed: one chair and some very large stones that were unaccountably on the floor. I left Dasu at dawn on the back of a truck and wondered how the police spent their day.

Chilas

The boulders lay on the gravelly bed of the Indus, a few metres from the river itself, lumpen, glossy, like beached whales. They lay along the dry valley where the river flows westward before veering south into the clamp of its gorges. Not everywhere. Here and there. At Shatial, Chilas, icy names of cruel settlements that for travellers from the north preceded the menace of the path ahead and for those from the south gave no respite from terrors past.

Massive hunks of basic igneous rock, polished by water-borne debris, the boulders had a dark presence that must have been arresting for all who passed. Their patina, burnished blue and brown, as rich as old copper, had been incised from prehistoric times on with petroglyphs, with symbols of ritual cult, of the magic of the hunt, of sun worship and of the Buddhist faith. From the thin, scrunchy, cracked wheat valley track of the wanderer their primordial solidity, chiselled with the spirit of man, must have beckoned.

Those at Shatial lay between the highway and the river, just beyond the ramshackle wooden bazaar where men glower at passers-by and where a murder a day is normal. An ancient ferry crossing of the Indus, it was probably the men of the garrisons guarding it who had scratched out the prehistoric hunting scenes – the same animals as those of Lascaux and Ancient Europe – the tribal tokens and the fire altars, shouting their beliefs for the gods to hear. Today just taxi touts shouted menacingly when their services were refused.

'Now the TGV goes to Orléans' said the group of French tourists in the Chilas Shangri-La Hotel, where a cup of coffee costs the same as dinner and bed and breakfast anywhere else, 'Paris will be empty and everyone will be commuting.'

'Paris is so cultural,' said another 'I don't think that will ever happen.' The Indus swirled by, below the terrace of roses and bright plastic garden furniture on which they sat with their

44

evening drinks: Coke, lemonade, tea. 'The provincials will never understand – peasants. There'll never be anything but Paris.'

The boulders lay a short distance away from the hotel, below the police check on the highway where a wooden barrier counter-balanced by a bag of stones was raised and lowered to let vehicles pass. The police lay around on charpoys in their tent and waved vaguely towards the river lower down. 'There's a signpost for tourists anyway' they said. It all seemed quite cosy compared to Shatial but, out of earshot of the French and then of the police, in the deepening twilight the eerie power of the place chilled the bones. The boulders were immense, hunched, their graffiti hugger-mugger in the gloom.

Chiselled on them were the names of Sogdians – traders along the Silk Roads – the lion as the heraldic animal of clans, Buddhist stupas, Buddhist legends, Chinese names marking the starting point of the travellers' dangerous winter journey through the gorges, and then the anti-Buddhists, the hooligans scratching illiterate squiggles alongside, with sun symbols, horns from the magic of the hunt, axes, deities, mythical figures. All who passed had succumbed to the power of the boulders.

For the early peoples Chilas was an imposed stopover. Autumn and winter were the best time for travel in the north: the rivers were fordable on foot, snowfall in the valleys was low. But, heading south, early snow then closed all the passes. Travellers were obliged to hang around for a season in Chilas. It was a natural hub. An easy route led down the valley of the Kiner-Gah from Gilgit, another over the passes from Kashmir, another south through the Kaghan valley. Even as late as the British occupation the routes to their isolated Residency in Gilgit – protecting India from the threat of the Russians – were through the Kashmir and Kaghan routes. They knew that in the gorges of Kohistan they would constantly be in a hornets' nest but that they could safely get to Gilgit by the Kashmir route from India or by the Kaghan one to Chilas from the south. They prohibited their men from going right or left of these imposed routes and left Indus Kohistan well alone.

The people of Chilas were wild. They were austere Sunni: 'assaulting infidels was accounted as a twofold righteousness in this and the next world – slashing at their heads and other limbs'. They were continually fighting. They regularly sent marauding

parties down the valley to plunder Astor, unprovoked and bringing in men from other valleys – Darel, Tangir, Palas and Jalkot.
On one sortie they brought back hundreds of slaves and eight
kettles, on another sixty prisoners and 'eight hundred goats
which they ate with glee, as being lawful property taken from
Shias'. They were tyrants who sold their women, indulged in
slavery and allowed no music, dancing or polo. As elsewhere the
sexes were separated from May to September while the women
did all the agricultural work. Their women were renowned for
fighting with iron wristbands, 'a custom confined to Chilasi
women, who bring them over their fists which they are said to
use with effect'.

The whole region had barely been tamed by Islam. In pagan
times the fine for seducing a woman had been one head of cattle
and there were women reputed to have enriched their husbands
with a herd. And nudging north to the steppelands a man who
lusted after a woman simply hung his bow on her cart and slept
with her. Those who inscribed the boulders had need of their
gods. But the amulet was not among their symbols. Not even the
plain triangle.

The crowded bus rattled along, turning all the passengers off
whenever a landslide across the road left only a perilously narrow
passage between the rock face on one side and the sheer drop to
the Indus hundreds of metres below on the other. Rocks were
shovelled, wheels spun back and forward, warnings were shouted.
Once the hazards were safely negotiated the passengers climbed
back in again. They were all men, bar a smart American couple
maybe in their late thirties. Been working on a research programme
in the Middle East, they said, and were now taking a trip before
going back to the States, partly as a holiday and partly to buy
Persian and Afghan carpets at Quetta. They had a few galleries
back home lined up to buy them, a good way to make a fast buck.
We were passing Nanga Parbat – eighth highest mountain in the
world, rising seven thousand metres from the river and crowned,
in the local people's belief, by a crystal kingdom of fairy spirits,
mythical snow creatures and a garden with just one tree, exception-
ally tall, guarded by serpents and made of pearls and coral – when
the conductor came round collecting the fares. The American
produced a student card and asked for a reduced fare.

'Only the first four students who get on the bus.'

'You mean to tell me I've got to push and shove to be first on the bus to get the student rate. That's crazy. I'm not paying.'

The row then escalated to such an extent that the bus driver stopped. The American grew pink with rage but had to pay. He carried on swearing as the bus set off again. He would have saved three rupees and Nanga Parbat slipped by, outside his mental vision.

We skirted along more dizzying heights and then the valley fanned out into a dry dun plateau strewn with lunar boulders and rimmed with sliced shales, fractured slabs that piled up from the side of the road against the flanks of the encircling mountains. Nothing lived but the hurrying river.

On into more valleys where bridges with little stone Chinese lions carved on each parapet – homesick whimsies of the construction engineers and now mostly defaced – linked across the river small isolated patches of level land. These were just wide enough to hold crumbling stone villages, cemeteries, tiny terraced wheatfields with bent toiling women, apricot orchards and pools the colour of mint sauce.

As we moved further north police barriers across the highway became more frequent, passengers were frisked. By the time we reached Gilgit there began to be an accumulation of tourists. Some had flown in, others had come rapidly up the KKH in one long bus haul or by private coaches that carried on over the Khunjerab Pass to Kashgar and on to Beijing. Australian backpackers used the road as a route through Asia and back home, or into Russia and then on to the Trans-Siberian Railway. Smart tour operators whisked people through to the Sunday market at Kashgar and the Buddhist caves of Dunhuang. But there were riots in Kashgar and the Chinese were keeping the pass closed, no one knew for how long. So the expensive tours stayed away and marooned Australians, trekkers and trans-Asian tourists wandered aimlessly around Gilgit.

Gilgit

André was Swiss and for some years past had regularly left his home in Zürich, accompanied by his silent girlfriend, to embark on lengthy periods of travelling, interposed on his return with short highly paid job contracts which financed the next trip.

His conversation, broadened by travel, ranged lightly over the vices and virtues of the whole of mankind. He reserved his highest praise for the dignity of the Tibetans and for the trains and lavatory cisterns of the Japanese, whereas the behaviour of Australians, the pollution of Taipei, the bus drivers of Peru and the late hour of dinner in Nepal made him blow his cheeks out with exasperation. This facial gesture, accompanied by a downward sweep of the hand, larded his conversation to such an extent that it became addictive to the listener and I found myself watching for the next display rather than paying attention to what he was saying.

His travel was always meticulously planned, but the unexpected closure of the Khunjerab Pass was forcing him to revise his itinerary completely. He brought out his map of China. On it he had carefully marked with red dotted lines the routes he would fly over, with blue highlighter he had picked out a possible river trip, while rail and road itineraries were defined in pink and green. In each case he had printed neatly beside every lap of the journey the dates of the year when such a trip would be at its best, when feasible and when to be avoided. Consulting this for some considerable time he decided on a revised plan for the next couple of weeks, announcing that he would fly instead to Hong Kong but would first cut his losses and go right away to Peshawar. He took out the relevant guide from among his papers to look for a suitable hotel. I promptly recommended one that was mentioned in it that I knew, rather seedy but acceptable, next door to the Gulf Air office and near the old city. He decided to head for it.

The next day – I heard later – it was blown up by a bomb.

In Gilgit itself tempers sharpened. Fighting had broken out

between Shia and Sunni. Several people had been killed and the army were whizzing up and down the long main street pointing their guns menacingly at the populace. Tourists began to move back down south.

The news whipped round the town in seconds. Two American brothers, converted to Islam – Charles and Daniel Boyd – had been charged with armed robbery and sentenced to a fine of 50,000 rupees each, five years in prison, then deportation. But first of all their right hand and left foot were to be amputated. More people moved out.

Etched into the mountainside above Gilgit was a water channel, running for kilometres from the glacier to the town and visible from below as a thin green line. A walk along it passed small settlements, stony groups of windowless houses, where clusters of men stood staring. Centuries of inbreeding had left their eyes vacant and their mouths drooping with spittle. Boys sat astride tree branches eating mulberries. Women and girls, doubled up under laden baskets strapped to their backs, walked by dumbly. Others, more alert, rushed up and invited me into their homes. No knowledge of the local language was necessary: gestures sufficed and the questions were always the same. The first was where my husband was, the second the number of my children.

In one house where an old woman narrowed her eyes, tapped me on the knee and indicated that she had ten sons, my humble contribution of one was well received. My girls were as usual of no interest whatsoever. Warming to the theme of my children I raised my arm to indicate that they were all now tall and grown up, whereupon the old woman suddenly leaned across and grabbed my breasts. Though she clucked approvingly it rather ended the niceties of conversation. Tea was then offered and, as a diversion, gratefully accepted. It was immensely salty, in the Tibetan custom.

Moving north towards the border the valleys opened into little frilled terraces. They were deeply green, a sharp intense green, a distillation of spinach, emeralds and frozen peas. Golden poplars pierced them here and there. Unveiled women in flat caps embroidered with the same solar symbols as on the boulders at Chilas stared at the passing bus. Nothing came in the other direction save one lone Chinese cyclist carrying mail.

It was from the Hunza valley that the unveiled women came.

It had always been an old custom there to lend your wife to a guest and to kidnap good-looking strangers to improve the race. Such customs must have been destroyed by the KKH and the virile backpackers it brought, but the women still kowtowed less to Islam than in other valleys.

The ruler of Hunza had abandoned his palace, a simple Tibetan-style fort commanding the valley, whose shutters now unhinged let a dusty light into empty rooms interconnected by ladders and recesses, and had built himself a bungalow down by the tourists' hotels. His second old fort at Altit on a defensive crag above the Indus, facing his old enemies the Nagyr across the rift, was approached through the village. Here in the evening light men, boys and women had gathered in an open space by a stagnant pool, reminiscent of a village green and duckpond. Though they sat in rigidly separated groups, the sight of the sexes out together in the open was traumatic. '*Kalam, Kalam.* Pen, pen' they said. 'One rupee, one rupee.'

The hotel door was plastered with stickers of adventure tour operators from every European country. But it was empty. Or almost. In the dusk I discerned two familiar figures on the balcony of their room, tripods angled towards Rakaposhi mountain behind which the moon was about to rise. They waved: 'Took it today at f11. Then you leave the camera still and superimpose the night shot. Magazines love it.'

At the border post of Sust, a bleak row of concrete beach huts set along the river bed, backpacking Australians had piled up, penned and corralled like sheep at the beck of a whistle and a dog. The border stayed closed; there was nowhere to go but back. Some decided to sit it out – it was in the end a full three months before it reopened – others headed on the gruesome bus ride back to Islamabad. For me there remained, as a last hope, only Pattan and the Palas valley. Maybe I should look at them after all.

Palas

Palas lay on the east side of the river, a low ridge like a sleeping ox with a sharp backbone separating it from the Indus and beyond that a narrow valley between hills that gripped each other from either side of the rift, like lovers' hands. High up near the sunlight was a patch of light green, perhaps green enough to graze a few goats, perhaps space enough to grow a family's maize. Would this be my valley?

'Yes, these are our costumes' said the government official at Pattan. 'Of course you did not find them in Chitral or Kalash or Swat or Chilas. They are here. From Palas. But these are wild people. They do terrible things I would not mention to you. We will have to arrange the formalities with the police here. You have time? It will take a few days. You can stay at the rest house.'

'And transport?'

'There is none. You will have to hire a Suzuki. Then there is the police roadblock into Palas – they have to give you an NOC and then they are responsible for you. But you cannot go alone. We will find a man who can take you.'

The man in question appeared an hour or so later. 'It is regretted the police will not provide an escort for you. They will not allow you to go. These are tribal lands. Men are killed all the time. Women, all women, stay indoors all the time. No man will let his own women out. Terrible things happen.'

'How far can I go up the valley before I have to have police protection?'

'You can go nowhere, Madam.'

Jared had a soft submissive face, all round contours and shades of brown, which burst easily into smiles. He came from Abbottabad, a town of the old Raj somewhat further south. He had spent eight years in this isolated posting, where for most government officers the assignment was for two at the most. He knew the valley well, as there were times when the violence subsided or when many of the men had taken their goats up into the high meadows to escape the summer heat and it was more or less safe for officials to venture in. It was true, he said, that the doctor living in the small settlement on the opposite bank of the Indus just below Palas had one or two of these embroidered dresses, but he would know nothing of the women. He would not be allowed to look at them or speak to them, let alone examine them. They were left without any medical care whatsoever, apart from a female health visitor with a minimal training in nursing who occasionally managed to get into the valley.

The women were kept carefully imprisoned in their homes, he explained, so that none but their own menfolk should see them. Outside those walls they were fair booty for any man, and for their own protection many carried guns. They were not too keen on modern weapons in the valley, no Kalashnikovs or anything like that. Both men and women preferred old 7mm rifles.

The dresses and helmets, he said, they embroidered for themselves while they were young girls, their menfolk buying the silks and buttons in Pattan bazaar. They liked buttons because they banged together and made a tinkly noise as they moved. It frightened the bad spirits away. So did the amulets. They looked beautiful and went up and down with the air. As for the six hundred and forty-seven tiny godets of black fabric they stitched around the bottom of the skirt, that was simply to enable them to sit modestly in front of their men. So that made the skirt flare out like a Greek royal guard's tunic, did it? He had never realized that. An interesting connection. The men are, it's true, sometimes obliged to sell their wives' precious dresses, which they wear just at the time of marriage, but then they are very poor people and the money enables them to buy food and materials to make a new dress. And guns. But you will never see a man selling his wife's trousers. He might sell the embroidered cuffs but only after he has cut them off the intimate bit and only if he is really desperate. No, it would not be possible for me to see any of the women nor the dresses nor the amulets nor the children nor the men.

'The men,' he continued 'all have beards and moustaches. One hundred per cent. I questioned residents about why they have these beards and, you won't mind my telling you, Madam, they say because our women like. From my point I can't say how, I don't know why women like this beard' he coyly added. It flashed across my mind that maybe he had had no wife here to share those eight miserable years. No, he had no wife. He reverted to the matter in hand and stiffened: 'It is impossible, actually impossible. Nobody will allow you to cross the river'. I looked close to tears. 'It's because of their traditions, Madam, the traditions of these bloody bullshit.'

The valleys of the west bank around Pattan had once been ruled by the Wali of Swat and had had some semblance of civil obedience, but those on the east, such as Palas, had never been ruled or governed by anyone, had never submitted to any laws, or paid any taxes, or taken any kind of part in any society outside their own small valley. 'Where did they come from?' They might have been Shin, the dominant local tribe. Or they might have been Afghan. Or it was even claimed that they might have been people of the Quresh tribe – to whom Mohammed also belonged – who had migrated here from Arabia. This was a theory first put forward in 1895 by Abdur Rahman, Amir of Afghanistan, in an attempt to speed the conversion of all the local population to Islam. They were, in fact, like Afghans. Men and women ate and worked together. And though men from other valleys bought wives with good money from anywhere in Pakistan, the men of Palas never took a wife except from their own valley. So it had always been and so, sighed Jared, it would always be. 'How long will I stay here? God knows, Madam.'

There was still the Assistant Commissioner, newly arrived from Lahore and in the job only two days. At first he was enthusiastic and flexed his authority. 'We will certainly accompany you into the Palas valley, Madam. Call back tomorrow.'

His deputy took me to the rest house. 'When the men have finished eating you will be alone in this building for the night, Madam. I shall call later and confirm that all the outside doors are locked.' The men caroused by hurricane lamp, eating platefuls of curry; a small portion was brought to my room and I was locked in with a thin candle for light.

I called on the Assistant Commissioner the next morning, but it was no good. 'We can do nothing with these people. They kidnap and the victims are never found. The police have the inability to protect you – they won't even go there themselves. We had not long ago a Frenchwoman separated from her companions and so cycling along the KKH at night alone. Three culprits did to her, did a thing I cannot tell you, Madam. We found them months later in those faraway hills. Ten years, ten years, ten years they got. They were wrong but she was wrong too. Why cycling alone at night? And Palas is worse. Much worse. If you are killed over the river we can do nothing, Madam. And if you're kidnapped we never find you in those hills.

'This is a bad place. All of us come from other places – Abbottabad, Mansehra, Lahore – the men here won't work. They only want women and land. And guns. It's a terrible place for us. The phones don't work; the electricity doesn't work. At least there's a road now where there used to be just a track and rafts across the river, but the road is our only link and sometimes you can be stuck on it for four or five days with landslides ahead and behind. You get sick of the same eight to ten people here. Even the tiffins, Madam, must come from Abbottabad.'

As the light faded I glowered through my binoculars across to the Palas valley. The stone fort was catching the last rays of the sun ('there will be two men in there, always guarding the valley') and the darkening hills were tightening their lovers' clench. Between us the river glinted and tumbled southward.

Mohenjo-daro

The Indus was by now, in its southern reaches, wide and limpid, spilling over into flood plains and reflecting on its waters the small town of Sukkur; low flat mud houses blurred into ikat on its still surface. Huge wooden boats, standing high out of the water, glided slowly along at the pace of the small figures of men atop them, paddling them by hand. They slipped by silently, seeming hardly to disturb the river's gentle flow.

Away from the Indus the road to Mohenjo-daro passed through a watery landscape of stagnant malarial pools pierced by reeds and grasses, a mirrored landscape of pink and white water lilies, white crane-like birds, canals, palm trees and mud shacks. Men sat embroidering caps with shisha glass or stood flailing rice. Everywhere there were glinting rice paddies, save where the land was not irrigated and remained a scrubby desert. Herds of camels swayed by indolently.

A night in a train had taken me to Sukkur. From there a bus to nearby Larkana and then an hour or so in an auto rickshaw had brought me to Mohenjo-daro, site of one of mankind's earliest civilizations, where I might find the pattern of the amulet. The costume itself I was now certain came from Palas, though it still angered me that it had been almost within my grasp but that I hadn't seen it with my own eyes. Now I was still, as ever, looking for the amulet in the form of an embroidered pattern or as the amulet itself. Maybe here among the ancient carved seals and goddesses of Mohenjo-daro I would have better luck.

'Great place, Adelaide. Nice and warm in the summer, not too cold in the winter. But got seasons, yes, proper seasons. And libraries and bookshops. Then there's a shady park you can sit in. Read and whatever. Just wonder what I'm doing in this hole. It was India really that I was going to, but it just seemed like a good idea to see Mohenjo-daro. Thought it would be interesting but, my God, I've been here three days, cooped up in this prison and I've only seen the ruins for half an hour. You have to go with two armed guards, at gun point, but mostly they refuse to take you.'

Three Japanese students had been kidnapped and held for a month, the Australian explained. Not here but somewhere around Chaukhandi, that windswept burial site in the desert of lower Sind. Because of that Japan had threatened to stop investing in Pakistan until it got its act together. 'So they watch us like hawks. Say it's for our own good, but it's a real bore. And you can't leave the site. You can't get away. They won't let you. I've got a ticket for tomorrow's plane to Karachi and they wouldn't let me change it. Otherwise I'd have gone yonks ago. Geez, when I think of dear old Adelaide.'

Mohenjo-daro is a listed World Heritage Site, the ruins of one of the major towns of the Harappan civilization that flourished between 3000 and 1500 BC. Laid out in grids, it had a shopping mall, a working-class suburb and a wealthy residential area where the houses had bricked bathrooms, separate lavatories and rubbish chutes. The great ritual bath remained, along with the store where grain taken as tax was hoarded, a few alleyways between high walls, a complex drainage system and a great number of bricks which a woman employee of the government Department of Archaeology had been given the task of counting. One by one in intense heat. Apart from her and the Australian there was no one there.

The site consisted of a barricaded tourist complex, surrounded by barbed wire and guarded by a Beau Geste-style police post. In the compound was a good museum displaying seals of the merchants of the Indus who traded with Egypt and Mesopotamia, intricately carved with bulls, elephants and crocodiles and with deities and devils. There were fertility goddesses fashioned in clay but, alas, no triangular amulets. Between the police post and the museum were a couple of souvenir shops and a bank that never opened. A rundown hotel completed the facilities. There was no phone. A nearby airstrip welcomed daily flights from Karachi but no one came.

The hotel had small simple rooms with fans and no curtains, so that a posse of men and boys was soon stationed outside my window. A few men slaved away in a dirty dark cavern of a kitchen preparing food on an open fire. It was served, pursued by mewling cats, in a pretentious dining room furnished with a table of peeling plastic wood and Louis XVI-type painted wooden chairs, upholstered in faded brocade. There was no electricity.

The police interview was brief. 'How could you have got here from Larkana on an auto rickshaw? That's a city vehicle. And you didn't report to us. What if you'd been kidnapped? You will leave tomorrow morning. There's a bus to Larkana at six. There you will go to the PIA office and buy a ticket for the flight to Karachi.'

Silhouetted in the gold of dawn a shawled figure on the roof of the police post shifted his rifle and pointed it at me. 'STOP!' he yelled. The gates of the compound were locked, but it was early yet and I waited. Around six o'clock a camel loped by, but no bus came. 'No bus, the police said 'only a police van to Larkana. You can't go. What if you go in the jungle? The Japanese men were taken in the jungle. And yesterday four teachers were kidnapped from their school about a kilometre from here. You can't go.'

In the kitchen I sat down on a wooden bench with an old man and three cats, hoping for tea. The room, I could now see, was walled with white tiles, cracked and yellowed with age. The floor was of earth and the ceiling, painted black, looked menacingly like earth too. The cook, his dirty blue shirt and fag dangling out of the corner of his mouth giving him the vague look of a thirties' French film star, was stirring metal pots and adding measures of spices, then chopping onions on a filthy slab. His 'stove' was a stone cupboard with bricks on top. Between them were large branches of trees burning under his pots which he pushed and pulled, like an organist his stops, to control the cooking heat. He stirred some thick whitish substance boiling in a black cauldron with a soup ladle and then served it. It was our tea. Made certainly from water I had seen the old man pump up from a rusty well behind the hotel. There had been no water in the taps that morning.

At intervals vehicles could be heard at the gate. Each time I rushed out, followed by the manager of the hotel with his Departure Book for me to sign. Each time I was detained by the police.

Then the gardener arrived. He wore an embroidered cap, a brown shirt and wraparound sarong and blue flipflops. Over his shoulder, like a waiter's dishcloth, hung a scarf edged with gaudy woollen tassels. He had come by bike.

This marvellous vehicle had its chassis entirely wrapped in mottled pink vinyl. Above the handlebars rose a superstructure of yellow plastic with sequins, holding two metal domes that served as wing mirrors. A small brown scarf edged with tinsel and bits of green plastic tied the contraption together. On the front lamp attachment there was no lamp but two mirrors with gold crowns and pink tassels bouncing up and down on gold-covered springs. On the front brake cords was an erection of green plastic leaves culminating in two dirty white plastic flower pots bearing plants made of gold and green sticks. From each handlebar hung a blue tassel, each brake was wound in tinsel and pink, and in between the spokes were brilliantly coloured fluffy balls. The final touch was a fur saddlecover. Seldom have I coveted such a symbol of freedom so much. But my admiration and desire met only pride: the owner adjusted his shawl and remarked that such a bicycle was 'very practical for seeing behind'.

In the event it was on a police van that I left. For the PIA office in Larkana. The arrangement was that I was to book my flight and then spend six hours walking round the town – a hot, dusty dive with nothing to do – carrying my bag and escorted by an armed guard until the police took me to the airstrip for the afternoon flight.

My guard duly appeared – a policeman about six feet five inches tall, as thin as a rod and clasping a long thin gun. He left me in the PIA office. 'Back in fifteen minutes' he said, but he didn't return. After about half an hour another armed policeman appeared. 'Come' he said. I followed. 'Bus stand Mohenjo-daro?' It seemed the best solution to return there and wait for the flight. We got a rickshaw and I paid. At the bus stand there was time for tea but I was unsure of the protocol. Is it normal to pay for tea for one's bodyguard? I did and he drank it out of the saucer. And what about his bus fare? I forked out six rupees. The bus passengers were almost entirely women in burqas and children, most of them dirty and sick. They didn't appear to constitute a danger but the guard glowered at them, clutching his rifle.

Suddenly the bus lurched to a halt and my guard and I were bustled off. There, in their police van, were my original attendants. 'You're suspended' the police officer shouted at my guard. 'Suspended, do you hear? You're not allowed out of the city premises. Suspended, do you hear?' His ire was then directed at me. 'I told you to wait. You're my responsibility. This man is only in charge of tourists arriving in the town. Just because there aren't any he thinks he can take you away from us and look after you. He's suspended.' I pleaded on the man's behalf and admired the officer's gun. 'This?' he said. 'It's a sub-machine gun with a thousand-metre range. Even at a thousand metres it kills.'

It was thrust behind me as I was escorted back to the Mohenjo-daro complex. I was not allowed out to visit the ruins again but was watched over until the Australian and I were marched along for a kilometre or so to the airstrip, escorted by two armed guards. On the route was a half-built tourist hotel bearing a large plaque honouring the politician who had thought its construction a good idea.

Makran

❖❖❖

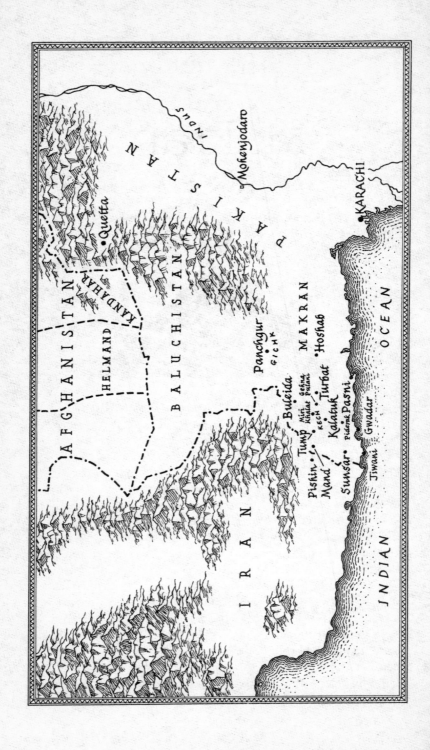

The Trail

The doorbell of my home is obscured by a creeper, red in the autumn sun, so it was in response to a diffident rap of the knuckles that I opened the door to a grey-haired lady in a beige mac. 'I'm so sorry to call on you out of the blue like this' she apologized 'but I understand you can tell me about Baluchi embroidery.'

A quirky chain of events fraught with odd coincidences and fostered by unexpected mutual acquaintances – specialists in indigo and Foreign Office Arabists – had brought this stranger to my doorstep. It was a chain that was to lead me back to the trail of the amulet.

The trail had petered out in Sind, first among the zigzags and intertwined circles, goddesses and bulls of Mohenjo-daro, and then finally in the desert a little inland from the Indian Ocean among the bracelets, turbans and solar motifs of the carved stone tombs of Chaukhandi. There had been nowhere else to go.

Eastward was not my route. Westward there was no passage. The abrupt wall of violence surrounding Pakistan halted any progress: Afghanistan, after thirteen years of Russian occupation, had been embroiled for a further year in internecine warfare. The puppet government was about to be pushed out, the vacuum was disputed by mujahed fighters, by fundamentalist and moderate, by Pathan and Tajik, by Hazara and Uzbek and Turkmen, by Shia and Sunni. Frontiers were firmly closed. Even aid workers faced enormous difficulties in getting in and then were sometimes killed for their pains.

To the south, Iran gave no visas to Western travellers and in any case between Sind and Iran lay the bizarre territory of Makran, totally closed to outsiders, including Pakistanis. But here a group of Italian archaeologists had been given permission – and guaranteed No Objection Certificates for its work in Makran by the Pakistani government – to do annual fieldwork on the history of the Baluch. For six years they had been going to Makran each winter and with them, researching handicrafts and traditions, went the lady at my door who, it turned out, was also called Sheila.

It had become apparent to the Italians over the years that, though the archaeology of Makran, the westernmost reach of the Indus valley civilization, was interesting, many other aspects of the territory were even more fascinating. Its isolation from the rest of the world had left it in the Dark Ages. The Italian Archaeological Mission to Makran, the project of a Catholic university in Italy, staffed by eminent specialists in various disciplines, thus became the Italian Historical, Ecological and Archaeological Mission to Makran. Within its widened scope fell the carved wooden chests of the Indian Ocean region in which my visitor was an acknowledged expert and ultimately the embroidery. This was not her speciality and, though on previous visits she had carefully noted the stitches and patterns, she was happy to arrange for the brief to be given to me. She handed over her notes in the expectation that I would find them helpful.

Once Sheila and I were in Makran she became our communicator: she soothed relationships within the team and safeguarded our goodwill with the locals. Over the years she had built up a stock of small notebooks in which she jotted down the names of cooks, drivers, farmers, heads of families and their children (which ones were naughty and which sweet), the uncles (which ones bald, which bearded), the daughters (which ones marriageable, which pregnant). They all loved her.

Taller and older than I am, she took precedence and was dubbed 'Sheila One' while I was 'Sheila Two'. Disliking the hierarchical situation this entailed she suggested the team look for an alternative. The only one possible was 'Big Sheila' and 'Little Sheila'. Modest and gentle, her hair in a soft bun, Big Sheila had a rather regal air and, with her long experience of Makran, was held in great respect. She had five times as much luggage as I did but looked five times smarter and thought to travel with Marmite and clothes-pegs and a short-wave radio.

The territory in which the Italian Mission worked was confined to the Pakistani part of Makran, but Makran is split by the Pakistan/Iran border and the Baluch live on both sides. To research their embroidery seriously, and to have more opportunities of finding the amulet, I needed to get over into Iran. It would be a pity, after all, to stop at a barrier that was merely political. A visa seemed hopeless but in the end the Iranians granted me one. My intention, once the Italians finished their work and went home, was to cross into Iran on my own and make my way back through Turkey.

Quetta

Until Sister Virginia took orders and donned her black habit – 'Looks great, kid. Who's your undertaker?' – she must surely always have worn a shirtwaister. She still had that 'prunes and prisms' look, sitting in the warm paraffin fumes of St Joseph's Convent, Quetta, dressed in a mauve embroidered Pakistani outfit under her black. An incongruous cardigan, carefully chosen in the same shade of mauve and thrown around her shoulders, warmed her sparrow-like frame. She chased her lunch, a tough minuscule lamb chop, around her plate with a fork, making no concessions to its intractability by using a knife, nor to her presence in Pakistan by using her fingers. Her manners were as neat as her stiffly crimped fair hair and her peach-rimmed glasses. New York and California must be as alien to her as Pakistan.

She hated Pakistan. Hated every minute of her five years there. It had been a great relief to her to be repatriated to her teasing brother in the Mid-West when the Gulf War broke out and she had been pleased to see that her fellow Americans were sent back to Karachi, Lahore and Islamabad long before Quetta was considered safe. But now she had come back to St Joseph's to finish the last few months of her assignment with the sisters of St Joseph of Chambéry. This teaching order of nuns had been established in 1812 in the Savoyard town of Chambéry, site of an old Roman station where routes from France, Switzerland and Italy meet. The nuns had spread, in the wake of increasing European affluence, from the orphanages and schools of Chambéry to establish others in poorer parts of the world, of which the school and convent of St Joseph's in Quetta was one.

Here, sharing their meals and helping ourselves to a full teaspoon each from the small jar of Nescafé by Sister Virginia's plate, the three of us from the Mission were clearly cuckoos in the nest. Whether we had been placed in the care of the nuns, rather than in a local hotel, through parsimony or fervent Catholicism was hard to determine. Certainly it was at Bishop Lobo's instigation.

Bishop Lobo worked with the Mission as a kind of on-the-spot head of HQ in Pakistan; his assistant, Maurice, arranged flights for us and dealt with all the bureaucracy. We had met Bishop Lobo in Karachi presiding over the cathedral and the school of St Patrick's, where many of Pakistan's politicians had received their education. A large bearded man with an aura of bonhomie, he had engaged us in conversation while Maurice busied himself carefully hiding the plastic bag concealing the whisky that Sheila had given him and making out a bill overcharging us for our onward air tickets to Quetta.

'A plot of land in Gwadar' the Bishop had said. 'I have been given a plot in Gwadar to erect an English-medium school.' He waved an official letter at us: 'Such an honour. Gwadar is the future. You must understand' – he tucked his thumb into the draperies spreading over his corpulent frame – 'now that the Soviet Union is crumbling, all those Central Asian republics, they look elsewhere. And they have no port. Tajikstan, Turkmenistan, Kazakhstan, Khirgizstan, Uzbekistan, all of them. And even Afghanistan when its problems are over. All landlocked. All look to a port on the Indian Ocean. Gwadar it will be and there I shall have my school. You have architects in your Mission? They can design it for me with the old traditional patterns of that region. We have a new future there.'

We took our leave of him, Sheila handing him one of the gifts she had brought out for the locals. Apart from the whisky these seemed mostly to be packets of Suttons broad bean seeds and pictorial calendars for 1992 of her home county: 'Scenic Devon. Gems of the West Country'. This one depicted 'Visitors Enjoying some Good Weather on the Seafront at Sidmouth'. 'Thank you' said the Bishop. 'More of those ancient mansions, I see' as he thumbed over idyllic thatched cottages under intensely blue skies. He seemed a worldly rather than a holy man.

The nuns answered to him and accepted us at St Joseph's. Though the school thrived and parents cheated and bribed to get their children into it, the convent itself was somewhat run down. It had obviously seen better days. In the corridor little boards slid in and out of a wooden slate to show visitors – though none came – the staffing schedule: Sister Virginia 'In', Sister Ursula 'Out', Sister Nasreen 'In', Sister Carmeline 'In'. A further series of blank wooden boards indicated that in former times a considerable

number of sisters had enlivened the rooms of the convent. A
rusting playground now stood empty. The long low institutional
buildings, animated by green painted doors, fretted stone screens
and a smell of leaking gas, occupied a prime site in the centre of
town, having been overtaken by unexpected urban growth. Rapa-
cious developers eyed its wide gravel drives, endless corridors
and dusty gardens.

The sisters were strengthened in their faith by uplifting prayers
printed on shiny posters with curling edges pinned along the
walls:

A prayer
to be said
when the world
has gotten you down and you feel rotten,
and you're too doggone tired to pray
and you're in a big hurry and besides you're mad at everybody.
Help.

The author of this piece modestly omitted to sign his name, but
another homily:

'Living is an everyday want.
Coming to life is strange and beautiful'

printed below a picture of a nest of birds' eggs in a snowy
Christmas tree, turned blue with exposure to light, was attributed
in large letters to J. Conteh-Morgan.

Each sister's cell was a small dark but cosy room. Ours were
the same. In the middle, standing on a tin base and connected to
the wall by a flue pipe, was a wobbly gas stove that had to be lit
with tapers of newspaper to prevent our hands from being
burnt. Gas lamps and intermittent electricity provided lighting. A
metal bed, a small wooden desk and chair, a cupboard full of
spare pillows and packets of soft biscuits completed the décor.
Each room had its own bathroom equipped with erratic plumbing
and a pink loo roll with Chinese characters, imported into
Pakistan via the Khunjerab Pass over the Karakoram, penetrable
only in the summer months.

There were three of us: Sheila, myself and Ugo, an Italian
putto of middle age whose cherubic face surrounded by curly
locks would lapse into Eeyore-like gloom whenever a decision

had to be made or a burst of effort was required. We were delayed in Quetta for almost a week waiting for our No Objection Certificates. It seemed that they would only be issued in person to Genoveffa, as the professor in charge of the Italian Mission. Of Genoveffa there was no sign and no news. Ugo went off to phone his wife in Italy and returned looking like Eeyore confronted with news of an expedition to the North Pole with Piglet. 'Genoveffa's mother has been put down by a car in Rome' he said gloomily and, before we could enquire into the exact state of her health, he added 'and her sister. By a motorbike in Milan.'

We accepted this rather surprising juxtaposition of disasters without question and continued to wait. Quetta was a rootless, shiftless place built on an unstable earthquake fault. In a haze of acrid exhaust smoke the roads eddied with donkey carts, goats, men, auto rickshaws and immaculate white four-wheel-drive vans labelled UNICEF, Immunization Programme for Afghan Refugees, UNHCR. Aid workers and refugees mingled in a temporary homeless restlessness, a medley of faces – proud aquiline-profiled Afghan, Asian Mongoloid, soft brown Indian – all men, all capped, turbaned, scarfed. Only indoors were these exotic headcoverings removed.

Thrown together but not interacting, the men held conversations that eddied around each other like the traffic. 'I gave my coat to my son, but not my gun' said Ibrahim, a freedom fighter from Kandahar, smoothing back his slick grey hair. 'Inshallah I shall be back home soon.' We all sat barefoot and crosslegged around a beautiful carpet laden with food, Muslim and Christian alike drinking whisky and neat gin.

'Pakistan gets a bad press abroad, all fundamentalists and nuclear weapons.'

'Have nothing to do with charity organizations' said Roger, an aid worker from Sydney, the shoulder pad of his blue jacket slipping forward as he gesticulated limply. 'I've told my family not to buy UNICEF cards. Save the Children are OK but as for WHO they've never done any good. A bunch of administrators.'

'When I'm thinking of pretty girls,' volunteered the manager of the local Serena Hotel 'I think in English. If it's farming I think in Pushtu and for everyday things it's Urdu.' We moved on to a bottle of Montepulciano d'Abruzzo. 'You can get smuggled whisky in Makran, very cheap' he added. 'That's all I know about the place. We're never allowed there.'

We passed our time with such evenings. Sheila and Ugo whiled away the afternoons in the smoky vaguely Art Deco tearoom of the Farah Hotel, where I would join them later. The old waiter in a smutty shalwar kameez would shuffle up with a faded menu to tell us there was only tea and mutton patties. They haunted bookshops, where Ugo would buy such things as *The Days and Times of a Brahui* or *On Alexander's Track to the Indus*, while I spent most days in the convent working hard on a book on Afghan embroidery that one of the aid organizations had thrown me to translate from French into English.

We called at UNICEF's headquarters, a rather smart building on the edge of town. We were ushered into a boardroom littered with piles of badly printed pamphlets in recycled paper: broadsheets, reviews, results of seminars, a report on 'The Year of the Girl Child'. The latter carefully analysed the situation of girls in Pakistan: 'they only get scraps of food, all the protein goes to the boys, there are only one third as many schools as for the same number of boys, the male population of Pakistan, unlike almost anywhere else in the world, is significantly higher in all age groups than the female, a high proportion of girls die of malnutrition and neglect, six out of a thousand women die in childbirth.' That figure seemed on the low side.

The director, Dr Rami, a very short plump lady in exceedingly high heels, came in and sat down opposite us. She looked like a bird of paradise with her floaty scarves, wide flowery trousers and Chanel-style jacket lavishly trimmed with gold and fastened with huge gold buttons that matched her earrings. 'I think Israelis are wonderful people' she enthused. 'I mean the Arab Jews not those coming from Russia and everywhere else; they have nothing to do with the culture. When I go to Tunisia I feel the same, when I go to Iraq I feel the same. It is the Mediterranean, Semitic upbringing but these people don't understand, how can they think they belong there?' she continued, warming to her theme and failing to explain that she was Jordanian.

'I collect money for UNICEF' interrupted Sheila 'but we send most of it to Africa.'

'Perhaps now you've been here you'll send it to us instead' suggested Dr Rami, twiddling her gold earring. In the silence that followed while she waited for Sheila's reply I put my travel bag on the table and opened it. Out staggered – bemused by the flight from Karachi and its week-long incarceration in the bag – a Jabees Hotel cockroach. It headed rapidly for the kitchens.

Finally one morning there was a kerfuffle at the gates of St Joseph's and we were called out. There on the pavement surrounded by a mountain of luggage stood Genoveffa. 'I am your leader' she shouted. 'Why was I not met?' She had a strong Italian accent, adding an 'e' after every consonant so that 'not met' came over as 'not-e met-e' and her conversation sounded like bursts of sporadic machine-gun fire. 'As leader of this Mission I looked for a welcome at the airport.' We hung our heads and the next day, leaving Genoveffa to a round of administrative and social duties, Sheila, Ugo and I were on standby at the airport waiting for a Fokker Friendship to fly us to Makran.

Turbat

'If we were strangers in Quetta,' said Ugo 'here we're from Mars.'

'They're from Iran' someone whispered, as we walked through the bazaar of Turbat. An old policeman, terrified, saluted us and retreated backwards as fast as he could, treading on the people crowding behind him, his hand still on his cap. The throng, we noted, consisted only of men and boys. There was not a woman to be seen, not even veiled.

A few goats and cows ambled along the dusty road, eating bits of cardboard and wrappings thrown out from the stalls. To reach this land of paper-eating cattle we had flown over an extraordinary landscape of flat dun desert crossed and cut east to west by stacked mountain ranges pleated and goffered like the frills of Victorian bonnets. 'Not exhilarating' wrote Sir Thomas Holdich in 1901 'a dead monotony of laminated clay backbones where even that ubiquitous nuisance, the common fly, finds existence insupportable.' Here and there a valley knifed through, always east to west and never cutting a pass from north to south across the ridges. They too marched resolutely from east to west so that the territory was a sandwich of three horizontal bands. Alexander the Great had crossed the coastal band and found it peopled only by fish-eating savages he called ichthyophagi, for of fish they even made their bread.

In the central band was Turbat, where we were to be based. Almost a century ago it had been a lonely outpost of British administration, a small village, one of only a hundred and twenty-five in the entire territory, for these were tribal lands devoid of towns, where settlements consisted of hovels made of matting that could be quickly whipped on to the back of a camel or donkey and transported elsewhere if danger threatened. The transient dwellings of Turbat sheltered around the castle which now lay ruined and served as the town lavatory. Of the fragile British rule there remained a mud fort in French Foreign Legion style, now the police headquarters, and the trees in the old garden of the Political Agent. The hold of the present administration on the territory was just as tenuous as British rule had been.

Most of the matting and reed heart of Turbat had now been destroyed and replaced by buildings of mud and shoddy breeze-block. The bazaar was a shambles of these ephemeral materials and offered a very thin choice of produce for sale, of which smuggled apples, tins of tomatoes and pistachio nuts from Iran were the highlights. Of the artisans who must once have worked in the bazaar only the halwa man and the brothers decorating cradles and low chairs with lac remained. Apart, that is, from the Luries, gypsy knaves, always regarded as gypsy knaves, 'impudent and immodest adulterers, addicted to every species of vice and gross sensuality, adorning themselves with feathers, skins, berries, shells and other baubles.' They didn't have stalls but sat on the pavement forging steel knives and setting them in hooked carved handles. The men looked harmless enough, though the knives were lethal.

Along the rough main highway straggled what might be termed Turbat's motor industry: a few open-fronted workshops where tyres worn and new lay piled up and where small boys, welding together bits of old trucks, sent sparks flying. At the end of the highway the town was fringed by the oasis to which it owed its existence and by a long low bridge built by American aid. This spanned the now dry river and ended in an imposing gateway manned by armed guards and leading to an empty landscape. Here no more than a kilometre or so of tarred road turned westwards towards Iran before petering out and a dirt track forked north to Quetta.

On the waste land to the south of the town a sprawl of low modern buildings, a maze of hard concrete walls in a stony land, had sprung up. Official establishments provided services new to the territory: a polytechnic, a social welfare office, a building spoken of reverentially as the Government Diggery College, settlements for doctors, paramedics, an American aid depot where no Americans were to be seen but where people played tennis by floodlight every night to the hum of the generator. Then, just opposite the illuminated tennis courts, the only two-storey build-ing in town, the government rest house for visiting officials, referred to as Circus House. Now that the old Keshm Hotel, of which Captain Abdul Khalid once was owner and guiding spirit, had been converted into an insalubrious hospital, it was at Circuit House that we were to stay.

The three of us who arrived from Quetta ahead of the rest of the group had instructions from Genoveffa to find Captain Khalid immediately on our arrival and present him with the compliments of our leader. 'A very important man' she had said 'a Gichki. Owns a fishing business.' We found him standing in a stall in the bazaar, which he also appeared to own, surrounded by bolts of fabric. He was a rotund fellow, paunch straining against his shalwar kameez and a pudgy face encircled by jet black curls. He had a winning smile. 'He's got fatter since last year' said Sheila. 'It's the whisky.' We told him, as promised, that our leader would be on the next day's flight. Captain Khalid received this news with obvious pleasure and offered us tea.

'And you must let the District Commissioner know' Genoveffa had said 'that your leader has allowed you to come on ahead. Announce to him my arrival.' We trooped into the office marked 'Secretary to the District Commissioner'.

Mr Mohmin was a very small thin man dressed in white, with large ears on which rested a woolly Chitrali cap, several sizes too big. He was very important, Genoveffa had said. He put his hands out towards us as if in benediction and then crossed them on his chest, bowing obsequiously. 'I am very much glad to see you people. Yes, feeling very good, very happy. All my bad feelings all gone seeing you people. Ah, Scenic Devon, thank you – how very good. No, here many things different since you good people here last year. But always my ring remains the same. Old is gold but gold is never old. We pride it, our oldness. But now my son has lied. Only an official lie – what do you say? – a white lie, but with such a thing in this today time our character is lost.'

'I heard about your misfortunes' Sheila said. 'I am very sorry. How many deceased?'

He smiled wanly and gave a Popish gesture of blessing. 'Life goes on its way.' A few months before a bomb had been thrown at his house, killing several of his family.

In anticipation of Genoveffa's arrival the next day Ugo took himself off to the small village of Kalatuk where, as a social anthropologist, he had set himself the task of studying the hierarchy of the villagers and the means whereby invading peoples – employing the theories and cunning of Machiavelli and coopting freebooters and mercenaries – always managed to set themselves up in control of the indigenous. We visited him there a week or so later. He came down to greet us from the castle – the smell of which announced that it too was used as the communal latrine – a *bella figura* dressed entirely in white. When he departed before the rest of us to spend Christmas with his family in Italy he left us a box of dates given to him by the villagers and a half-finished tin of Cherry Blossom neutral shoe polish.

Though Sheila and I made certain we were at the airport to meet our leader this time, we were brushed aside and it was Captain Khalid who gathered up Genoveffa and her luggage and escorted her in his car to Circuit House. 'Where is my Mercedes? The leader of the Mission has the Mercedes. Where is it?' screamed Genoveffa, the second she arrived. It was being driven from Karachi, bringing the last two members of the group, Gianni and Gionata, young architects specializing in the restoration of ancient monuments, whom we called 'the boys'. They had not arrived when expected the night before and we had been watchful and worried. What with two punctures and a pitted dirt road they had taken two days to cover the few hundred kilometres.

The journey had been horrendous, they said. The parallel rows of mountains that traverse Makran from east to west veer north at its easterly end, so that once across the desert west of Karachi and over the border into Makran, instead of following one straight valley the track switchbacked like some lunatic fairground. Each ridge had to be crossed, one after another, at twenty kilometres an hour. The boys' driver, loaned by the Italian Consulate, had never been outside Karachi before. He headed due west and kept going, veering right at the only fork in the road, when they should have gone left. Fortunately they had been warned that if they couldn't make it in a day there was only one possible place to stay *en route*, a dilapidated rest house at the tiny village of Hoshab. Here they were received by a government officer, a short young man who sat in a dark room, a Kalashnikov propped up in each corner, recording official business and translating Persian poetry into Baluch for the benefit of the local tribesmen.

*

'What do you mean, no spare wheel? The Mercedes is meant for the leader of the Mission and now I'm expected to walk to the town.' Some placatory words and a new spare wheel later – fixed by the twelve-year-old mechanics – the Mercedes and driver were assigned to Genoveffa and the boys. Another vehicle was still needed for Sheila and me. A driver the Mission had used on previous visits, Jan Mohammed, was sought out.

He presented a truck for our inspection. The number plate was blue. 'Omani Export' it said, with some Arabic squiggles, whereas the rougher pick-ups of Turbat had only simple dusty numbers like TR125. Jan Mohammed had some lengthy and suspect tale explaining why his own vehicle wasn't available and what a good deal he had found for us in hiring this one. He pointed out its obvious merits: brand new, with a shiny trim of hearts and stars made in Muscat set around the open back, though 'not with the four wheels going, so on road Zamram we stay in sand'. So it wasn't a four-wheel drive and there would be areas we wouldn't be able to visit, but it looked a good reliable vehicle. The owner, a smiling modest man, stood proudly by, fingering the shawl crumpled across his right shoulder. It seemed, JM explained, that this owner, Mr Khodedad, was happy to hire out his pick-up to us but was not prepared to let it out of his sight for a second. JM was one of those tall rigid men of military aspect who never incline their ear to listen but pause before repeating their opinion, so that our protestations of one extra person to house and feed and one seat fewer in the truck for us were passed over and the two simply waited for our assent.

And so it was that all our journeying around Makran was in the company of these two old friends from the same small village, JM stiffly manning the driving position and Mr Khodedad in the front passenger seat with his pair of rifles cocked at the ready and his bandoleer on his knees. Every time JM stopped Mr Khodedad would step out and carefully dust down the vehicle, using his shoulder scarf to rub and flick the sand off every surface and then blowing his nose heartily in it as soon as he'd finished this satisfying task. On one occasion, when my own shawl got trapped in the door lock, he gallantly lent me this same piece of cloth to wear so that I could step out of the truck without giving offence to the local male populace by being unswathed.

The Villages

The Makran Levy Corps had been organized in 1904 under two British officers; it replaced an earlier force of levies the army had left behind to maintain order, escort prisoners and generally make themselves useful. The members of the corps were tribesmen armed with Martini-Henry rifles and carbines. Whether their arms were those given to the levies in 1904 I could not say, but it seemed likely that they were. There were garrisons of levies in all the major villages of Makran and we were not allowed to go anywhere without two of them escorting us. It was always JM who chose them for Sheila and me. He would stride into the Turbat depot, a low mud-walled building where groups of men – idle turbaned fellows with shabby coats and long rifles – hung around. The barking chap in charge wore a semblance of uniform, of leftover Brit style: a khaki sweater with epaulettes and tilted beret with vague insignia. And he carried a stick. With this he would strut around and designate the men to be assigned to us. They often seemed to be rather old and always were anything but alert so their usefulness under possible attack was suspect. But they sat resignedly enough in the back of the truck and lurked behind us at archaeological digs, or hovered outside when we entered women's houses. We gradually overcame our first reticence about going into a village protected by armed guards and forgot about them after a while. If we stopped anywhere overnight we would be issued with new ones from that village's garrison, giving the old ones a few pennies to find their way back home, though they never left before a good meal of rice had been offered.

Chaperoned by the levies, JM and Mr Khodedad, Big Sheila and I covered most of Makran looking for embroideries, for amulets and wooden chests, for weavings and baskets, for lac and jewellery, sallying forth from Turbat and returning at night to Circuit House, or staying several nights elsewhere. The country we covered was arid in the extreme: nothing but rock, stone, gravel, sand, dust. The roads were rough tracks. Everywhere between and around the villages panniered donkeys struggled for an even foothold in the stones, hobbled camels grazed in the thin bushes, pye-dogs skulked and women and girls walked by carrying water on their heads, always wearing beautiful vividly embroidered dresses.

Date palms were everywhere. It was the main crop of Makran. Dates saved the remnants of Alexander's troops as they struggled back home from the Indus; boiled dates were given to newborn babies. Small date groves along a fertile valley would denote a village. Sometimes it was hard to see where any water could be found to sustain the people until a pile of rubble like the edge of roadworks betrayed an underground water course, a keraz. I saw no rice growing but it certainly used to be cultivated in the Kech valley in irrigated fields enriched with human manure and tamarisk branches as fertilizer. The worse the field smelt the better it was considered for rice cultivation and best of all were those fields where the frogs died of the stench.

The villages had no roads but were a jigsaw of open spaces and mud walls. Each wall would enclose land belonging to a family and within this encircling boundary an encampment of homes would gradually grow. The walls themselves were like beautiful strips of basketry or Fair Isle knitting: an intricate sloping pattern of smoothed pebbles at the base, interwoven in zigzags and diagonals, topped by handmade mud bricks in straight lines. Within these walls was an open space through which goats, sheep, chickens, women and children wandered. In the centre was a small thatched shelter, where women cooked and goatskins of water hung, which was surrounded by individual mud buildings of one windowless room with a central door opening. Their hand-rendered mud walls appeared to grow from the ground. Below their flat roofs, capped by small chimneys like rounded dice, were carved friezes of triangles and rosettes and jutting wood conduits to lead off rainwater. Each room would have a different purpose and the homestead would house an extended family of grandparents, cousins, daughters-in-law.

In some villages, and in hamlets of nomads, the homes were of matting. Matting made from the pish dwarf desert palm had been the major building material throughout Makran. It was eminently transportable in the face of danger. But mud was the superlative material. It was solid, protective, deflected the intense rays of the

sun and insulated from the cold. Mosques were built of mud:
they were like sandcastles or children's drawings of Bethlehem
and three small mud turrets announced their function. But people
were beginning to learn to make concrete bricks. When mud was
replaced by these bricks, they said, everyone caught flu and
pneumonia. The concrete mix was not reassuring: they hadn't
understood that concrete bricks are hollow and industrially made,
so cheaper. They resolutely used the old wooden moulds with
which they had made mud bricks, filling them instead with
cement bought in Iran, so that the concrete bricks were terribly
heavy. They were also unhealthy, difficult to replace, didn't
breathe and were bad thermally. It was the wrong technique used
on the wrong material. But the use of concrete was gradually
becoming more extensive. Maybe the definition of a town was a
settlement of concrete bricks, a village one of mud and a hamlet,
especially a nomadic hamlet, one of matting. Or in winter of
woven black goathair. All these materials were found in juxtaposition: it was a matter of expediency.

The village homesteads were all very similar. In many the old
watchtowers at the corners of the enclosing walls were now used
as lavatories. Stone steps led up through a doorless opening into
a tiny room with peepholes in the wall. The floor was a mud
platform with, rather surprisingly, a pair of hole-in-the-ground
latrines with a foothold on either side of each one so that two
people could use the place together. Bits of dried shit hung from
these holes above a drop of about a metre to the ground below,
where a pile of mixed ordure lay hygienically drying in the sun.

The interior of the living rooms was consistent. They were
dark, lit only by a shaft of sunlight through the doorway, supple-
mented in the richer homes by a fluorescent strip bulb on the
opposite wall, though electricity was often wanting. Ceilings
were very high and made of matting and twigs supported by
beams of halved trunks of date palms. Floors were of concrete,
linoleum or dried mud, covered by carpets. The reception room,
reserved for men, would be bare except for political posters
showing 'Martyrs of the Baluch Students' Organisation' sporting
the bloom of youthful moustaches. Or 'Long Live Struggle of
the People of Baluchistan against Imperialism Colonialism Neo-
Colonialism and Facism'.

In the room that served as a kitchen women squatted over fires of sticks and plastic buckets of rice, while goats wandered in and were shooed out. A few metal pots and supplies of tea and sugar lined the walls. There was nothing else.

The bedroom of the head of the household and his wife, furnished with a high double bed and a cradle swathed with so much embroidered fabric that it was impossible to see whether there was a baby inside or not, usually adjoined the room that formed the women's quarters, though sometimes it was in these quarters that bed and cradle had to take their place.

This was the room, the domain of the women and forbidden to any man outside the immediate family, where I was always taken to see the women's embroideries. It was such a privilege to be there, to be invited into the intimacy of their lives, to be recording what no one else had recorded, that it was often impossible not to draw breath and just murmur to myself 'what a privilege to be here'. It would be a windowless carpeted room with the wall opposite the doorway reserved for a display of the treasures of the household. On the ground would be a row of locked tin trunks, in which the women's store of embroidered clothing was kept, dresses and pieces – bodice fronts, sleeve cuffs, skirt pockets and trouser hems – ready to have made up into garments by the bazaar tailor when the women could afford it.

Above the trunks would be two glazed cupboards displaying precious objects such as half-finished bottles of nail polish, miniature china animals of the seaside souvenir variety, tins of talcum powder and photographs of small boys. Around them, hanging on the walls, were more photographs of young men, or sometimes of Saddam Hussein or Rambo. The mosque at Mecca was another favourite or Technicolor pictures that evoked the West: a blond couple in a daffodil field or some chamois in the Alps. Mirrors and works of art, such as a picture of a chalet made of twigs with a garden of shells, entitled 'God Bless Our Home', also found a place. But the glory of the display came above all these. It was a shelf that ran the full length of the wall at just below ceiling height. On it teetered piles of cups and saucers – maybe three or four stacked on top of each other – teapots, bowls, plastic buckets and vacuum flasks, all arranged symmetrically and untouched.

To the side of the room, piled to the ceiling, were the family's quilts. They rested on cases covered with kilims and protecting this treasury of textiles was a cloth made of strips of fabric set with tiny shisha mirrors and hung with rows and rows of the amuletic triangle I was looking for. Each triangle glinted with three circles of shisha that would clearly frighten away the djinn and the evil eye. 'No, we don't think it means anything. It comes from Afghanistan or Iran or somewhere.' It was deflating to find that it didn't come from here or that people vaguely believed that it was from somewhere else.

Paree was a wonderful embroiderer, they said, as I noted for the Mission all the details of her stitches and patterns. A Zikri. You could see where she lived from Circuit House, at Koh-e-Murad – that mound beyond the American tennis courts. To hell with Mecca the Zikris had declared, our Mahdi has vowed pilgrimages to Koh-e-Murad instead, this small hillock by Turbat surrounded by a white wall. Here is our Haj. And prayer: we have done away with all those prayers. Now we chant incantations instead.

To the Sunni Muslims of Makran the Zikris were heretics. Outsiders. They had come from Makran with the Buleidais perhaps, people who had arrived in the fifteenth century either from Helmand in southern Afghanistan or from Muscat. No one really knows. They didn't hold with fasting so they were even more anathema to orthodox Sunnis. Known to the Brahui people of northern Makran as 'Dai', which was an ancient Scythian tribe, they seemed disappointingly to be of Indian origin. As part of our research we went into their homes too. They were arranged in the same way as the others we had visited in Makran with cups and saucers, thermos flasks and kilims. And Paree's embroideries were exactly the same as the Sunnis'.

Gwadar

Back at Circuit House we gradually slipped into a routine. Nobody manned or managed the establishment and almost nobody stayed there so we took the place over as our own. It was an imposing jerry-built construction turning its back on the town and facing the open country with heavy iron gates and a wide circular drive set in bare earth. A well-worn footpath led across its land in the opposite direction from the drive. The official approach was up a flight of stone steps under an impressive portico, where a white-gloved flunkey would not have looked out of place. These steps led to two high wooden doors labelled Drawing Hall, Dinning Hall. Beyond these gaunt chandeliered rooms with stained carpets – boasting grandiose furniture and an unconnected telephone – noisy swing doors led to the ramshackle rear of the building. This was the kitchen, domain of the cooks Gul Mohammed and Ashgar, the one small and glum, the other a tall dashing fellow in a red scarf. They cooked on a concrete bench over small fires of sticks laid between three rows of bricks and nonchalantly hurled vegetable peelings, eggshells, empty milk cartons and tea leaves on to the floor around them. A ring of old rice circled the drain in the floor.

Our meals seldom varied. Breakfast was always chapatti and fried egg until one morning Genoveffa could stand it no longer. From then on it was chapatti and an omelette – somewhat easier to eat with the fingers. For the evening meal Gul Mohammed would gloomily take orders in the morning but in any case would produce more or less the same thing: rice and chapatti, augmented by scrawny chicken and a curried vegetable which might have been turnip, potato or aubergine, though it was so deeply slurped in sharp sauce that it could have been anything. Makranis had never cared much for vegetables anyway, referring to them all as 'grass'. Gul Mohammed's shopping bill, neatly itemized in Arabic script, usually came to about forty rupees for all of us.

JM had a few fingers in the smuggling trade and managed to

get us whisky and gin brought over from Dubai. The brands were dubious and the labels distressed by seawater. We made cocktails of them with mango juice, which we drank at sunset. This was always a spectacular affair when the dry sunny day exploded into crimson dust, silhouetting the mountains around us, and then faded into a chill starry night.

Genoveffa organized our social life. Captain Khalid was a frequent caller, a bottle of Black Dog or Smugglers whisky tucked under his arm. A Mr Imdadali came to discuss providing a house for the Mission's visit next year. He was a fat cheery fellow with several blubbery chins redeemed by gleaming white teeth and black curly hair. He plonked himself down on one of the beds, swung his foot on to his knee and relaxed. 'You want four bedrooms, I give you four bedrooms. No problem!'

'I'm sorry we can't offer you any whisky' said Sheila.

His face lit up only to fall rapidly once the full import of the words hit him. 'You need house. I construct. You want lawn, I make lawn.' He picked up a packet of biscuits lying in front of him and started to munch them, detailing all the 'no problem' aspects of the house he could provide. He scratched his crotch, fiddled with his penis, munched a biscuit. 'I protect you too.'

'Very good,' said Genoveffa 'when we refused protection before, our house was plundered.' He finished our biscuits, screwed the packet into a ball and was clearly about to throw it across the room when he remembered where he was and placed it on the table. Nothing further being offered he left. 'He's very important' said Genoveffa. 'A Gichki.'

We met other Gichkis too. They were the so-called aristocrats of Makran, people who had probably come from India and had settled in the Gichk valley at Panchgur and then gradually moved over the territory building up a power base for themselves. They claimed not to be landowners, though in fact they had lands that others worked for them, but to base their power on sending their men to be educated in different parts of the world – Russia, America, England – and then when they came back to spread them around Makran in positions of influence. 'That's how we rule.'

They were now an ethnic mix that was typical of the shores of the Indian Ocean. The three brothers of one family we spent an evening with looked ill-matched though ostensibly of the same parents: one Indian, one African, one Persian. The Persian-looking fellow seemed to have kept the home fires burning while the African one spent seven years in Odessa training in marine engineering and the Indian one studied surgery and psychology in the States. Imprisoned at the age of fifteen, three weeks after his marriage, he was kept handcuffed until released on amnesty at the festival of Eid which ends Ramadan, the Muslim month of fasting, and has the power of Christmas. Now he was active in human rights and ran the local health service, working with drug addicts. Another relative, a thin aesthete wearing large sunglasses in the dark smoky room, sat with his legs crossed and feet turned up, drawing deeply on a cigarette and drinking Black Dog.

There were thirty-seven in the family and they lived in a compound of two old adobe houses with an arched terrace, belonging to the father and an uncle, and a series of new concrete bungalows built along the inside of the walls. The women served the men and us as we ate dinner and drank whisky. They wore embroidered dresses – machine-made and bought in Karachi – and were laden with wonderful gold jewellery, solid bangles, dangling pendants, earrings so heavy they had to be held by a chain over the head. Most were fat, many had eye disease, all giggled at Sheila and me.

Sometimes Genoveffa went out alone – not telling us where – dressed up in one of the half-dozen fetching embroidered Baluchi costumes she owned, a diaphanous shawl over her head. In the daytime she rarely bothered to cover her short curly hair and usually dressed in trousers and shirt. Among women all wearing embroidered dresses this outfit gave her a boyish vaguely busy look. Sometimes she took us along with her when she socialized. It was very important, she said, for us to be introduced to the District Commissioner. Our qualifications and credentials were presented, followed by Genoveffa's own. 'As you know, District Commissioner, I am an Islamic historian, speaking Farsi, a professor of the University of the Sacred Heart, many years experience in Makran, as leader I . . .'

'You are coming by air?'

'As your Department of Antiquities and your Department of Archaeology know this part of Makran is the westernmost point of the Harappan culture, as excavations at Miri Khalat . . .'

'Tea?' He clasped his plump hands together, heavy with turquoise rings. 'You must go nowhere without two levies.'

It didn't strike me as odd at the time but none were available when we set off with Captain Khalid to cross the moonscape desert that lay between Turbat and the port of Gwadar.

It was a desert not of sand but of stones. They lay glazed in a mosaic embedded in the ground, petrified by wind and dust, a floor across which yet more stones had been scattered, strewn, hurled around. They heaped together along the roadside, they dusted the river bed like thin snow, they cascaded down rocky slopes. They were piled into small cairns on the hilltops, silhouetted like crouching men against the bleached sky; they were set in circles as places of prayer.

Never as dark as black, never as light as white, they were mottled and brindled, they seemed made of charcoal, burnt mud and clay, bone and alabaster. Only along the edges of the road did the pall of dust obscure them to the uniform colourlessness of lunar ash. Some were smoothly rounded pebbles, others were sawtoothed stickleback combs; some were nodules clutched icily in twisted strata, others were scratched and jagged flints. A man's hand could cradle some; a man's stride would be curtailed by others.

Breaking this stony waste were high bare outcrops, bones of sharp hillocks assembled in crowded ridges or tangled into mazes. Though they rose not many metres from their bed, their shales and chips, the broken boulders lying around them, their serried ranks presented an impenetrable barrier. They were like the scaly backbones of sleeping dragons and it was easy to understand the myths of local tribesmen. These hundreds of flaked upright flags, explained JM, were Turkish soldiers defeated in battle in an alien land and turned to stone.

'"You must not to come here. This our land" our tribal priest, he tell Turkey soldiers. But the Turkey king he kill priest's son. "Must all be turned to black stone" say priest "even the flour and the sugar, from white they to be turned black stone also." But then the Turkey queen, pain in stomach, starting delivery, baby coming outside. "Stop" say priest. "Not know life, turn also stone."' So the three monoliths on that towering crag were the Turkish king, the queen in parturition and the midwife who delivered the head of her stillborn child. Black stone sealed as in amber in a setting of flour and sugar.

It seemed impossible that there should be yet more razor-sharpened ranges, more zigzagged horizons, more slanting cliffs pleated by the lowering sun, but for kilometres the dusty track wound through them, until suddenly they tumbled into creamier, more rounded mounds, a landscape of dirty whipped egg white sprinkled with gravel, that itself softened and spread into a plain of bare sand dotted with wispy tamarisk. This scrubby desert rolled on over the last kilometres to the paired massive peaks that marked the isthmus of Gwadar, where it then subsided into a long naked beach – naked, that is, except for piles of rotting fishheads, the odd donkey cart and laden camel, and a few keen footballers in red and green jerseys.

Bishop Lobo's enthusiasm seemed misplaced: it was an unlikely route for the container lorries of Uzbekistan.

Bishop Lobo was contemplating a large expanse of sand in the hinterland of Gwadar. He stood, ecclesiastical gowns billowing, facing the rocky isthmus, one sweep of the Indian Ocean to his left and another to his right, the desert and Central Asia behind him. 'Here will be my school' he declaimed, then fingered his cross. There were few buildings in Gwadar and none near his piece of land.

Gwadar had never been much of a port. British India steamships had called occasionally before the First World War but had been forced to anchor several kilometres offshore because of dangerous shoals. Mud volcanoes erupted regularly under the sea, causing such a stench that even the British telegraph officer had abandoned the place. The half-empty Ismaili quarter – an Indian Ocean settlement of vertically squashed buildings with carved doors and balconies such as used to thrive around the seashore from Kutch to Zanzibar – hugged the coast. Only forty-six Ismaili families sheltered in its ramshackle buildings: the rest had long since left for Karachi. The fish market, a few old mud houses, a shrine known to the Portuguese and a main square full of stacked firewood and camels wearing blue beads comprised the town before investment came in to develop a new port. Now there were a few harbour installations, a small hostel where a handful of foreign engineers got drunk every night and a number of large moneyed bungalows concealed behind fancy concrete walls, one of which – surprisingly, as he maintained an impressive establishment of women and children in his home village in the hinterland – belonged to Captain Khalid.

Clustering at one end of the bare crescent of the western beach were half a dozen clinker boats being painstakingly put together by hand, one curved wooden plank placed on another with the only tool being a primitive drill like a violin. On the eastern beach men waded out to the fishing boats carrying large mats which they then dragged back laden with rays, gurnards, sharks, throwing them down on the sand. The auctioneer, a small man with a notebook, stood over them while a crowd gathered round in the morass of sand, blood, fresh fish, rotting fish, flies, old fishbones, litter and rubbish that formed the 'dunes' on the edge of the beach. Eight thousand rupees the two sharks fetched. 'They'll go to Singapore' someone said, and their livers were cut out then and there, spewing more blood on to the sand.

There were two government rest houses in Gwadar. One, on the eastern beach, had been the old British residency but was closed for repair work. Near it a small stone column surmounted by a cross stood in a little paved garden. 'The British used to drink whisky here' the locals said. Two nineteenth-century gravestones nearby, worn and barely legible as the resting place of Fanny and, years later, Ann – whose mournful lives can only be guessed at – seemed to indicate that it was more likely communion wine that had been sipped quietly.

The other rest house was out of town by the empty western beach, a modern bungalow with leaking pipes, failing electricity and a Bengali cook who had got as far as Gwadar in his endeavour to reach the Gulf and a new life. He served us rice and curried chicken and longed for a visa to England.

The Minder

Dr Kholiq was a very small man who spoke in a high-pitched nasal whine through clenched teeth. He was very important in the Department of Archaeology for Baluchistan, said Genoveffa, and she had already sent us to pay our respects to him in Quetta. Now – when the boys were having a night out with the foreign engineers, Genoveffa was absent in her Baluchi regalia on some nocturnal assignation, and only Sheila and I were being served our dinner and vainly asking whether fish would be possible for a change – into the rest house at Gwadar walked a flustered Dr Kholiq. He had followed us from Quetta to Turbat, he explained and, not finding us there, had carried on to Jiwani where it was rumoured we had gone. After a chase of several days he had found us and seemed confused. His instructions, from the Director of Archaeology for Baluchistan, his immediate boss whom he obeyed with servile uncritical attention, were to tail us everywhere we went and not let us out of his sight for a moment.

It was unclear why, but the assumption was that the government was afraid the Mission was removing valuable archaeological material from the country and taking it to Italy. He doggedly stuck to us, sitting in the back of the Mercedes shrouded in dust, hovering outside village women's quarters waiting, alert to any wandering away by any of us. As I walked alone from the rest house one evening along the beach in the setting sun, through a watercolour wash of sea, strand and desert that stretched empty and immense to the horizon and the Persian Gulf and beyond, he spotted my absence and rushed down the beach in pursuit, but unfortunately took the opposite direction towards Gwadar. Our mutual dislike deepened over subsequent days. 'He says of course' said Sheila 'that he resents following some woman around the country looking at embroidery when he's an important government official. It isn't his role.'

His task was impossible and he attached himself finally to Genoveffa and the boys, clinging to them as they made neat architectural sketches of crumbling castles and ruined shrines and argued in Italian. 'There is nothing to be done' said the boys. 'You could have seen that before you brought us here. All these buildings are beyond restoration and anyway the attitude of the locals would quickly bring them back to ruins again. Look at Mohenjo-daro. A World Heritage Site and the international money poured into it goes straight into the pocket of the directors.'

'I am your leader' Genoveffa shouted. 'I say what we will do, not you. You will catch the first plane back to Karachi.' Voices were raised and lowered again and the meticulous drawings continued.

Kholiq was happiest when we stuck together as a group, descending on some small unsuspecting village, the boys and Genoveffa looking at ruins, me at the women's embroidered dresses and Sheila quizzing the snake charmer with JM interpreting. 'Dangerous snake. If he eat you must be die. But joghi will be giving you snake and talking some words from Koran and then when snake eat you, nothing will do. Joghi catching snake in desert, making bag and putting snake in. Snake eating milk and after one month changing leather. Again coming new. Joghi sitting on sand and putting line round himself on ground with finger and snake not coming into this circle because joghi keeping Koran in head and thinking of it. Saying to snake you is my servant, you agree to go anywhere. Then teaching dancing, playing music to snake and when going villages he putting snake with some sand in bag and when come bazaar he saying to all peoples and snake: I am joghi.'

Kholiq was at his most miserable when we split and he couldn't keep tabs on all of us, such as when I left on my own for the village of Sunsar near the Iranian border, where there were no old buildings and no snake charmer. The arrival here of a lone woman, accompanied only by a levy, rifle at the ready, caused considerable agitation. We called first at the Assistant Commissioner's office, a dreary little room which, it crossed my mind, would be greatly cheered by a calendar depicting Plymouth Hoe. The petty official sitting on the floor combing his hair, surrounded by toiletries and half-empty packets of medicines, leapt to his feet, shouted orders and then dived down to the old black telephone on the floor, winding up its handle and asking to speak to someone. From behind a closed door – a dirty pair of men's rubber sandals on the mat outside it – came sounds of hasty sweeping and mopping. A broomstick was heard to bang twice on the inside of the door and the official then stood and bowed: 'Bathroom, Madam. You want take bath?'

The village was a small cluster of twenty or so huts made of poles and matting with a couple of concrete buildings that served as offices for those involved in the frontier trade: customs officers, forwarding agents. It was an exceedingly poor place with scruffy goats, children and women carrying babies milling around. All the females wore beautifully embroidered dresses and most had some eye disease; they stared at me with one eye half closed, with one eyeball missing or with one good brown eye and one glazed with blue.

They were in dire need of amuletic devices to ward off sickness and disease. Maybe here the women's clothes would be decorated with the Afghan amulet, maybe their jewellery would be of that distinctive triangular shape, hung with gewgaws, for the old Brahui of Baluchistan used to 'dabble in dark and unholy charms' though by the early years of this century 'the knowledge of such has all but died out of the country, and the man that would seek them out had best go seeking in far-off Bengal.' In the whole of Makran there was not a single triangular amulet to be seen; the embroidery on the dresses of the women offered no amuletic protection against the evil eye or the djinn, no tassels, no bits of mirror, no blue beads, nor any patterns of triangles. The embroidery was rigidly linear and restricted to six colours only: red first, then burgundy and small touches of black, white, dark green and royal blue. It was the same in every village and had not changed in living memory.

The women embroidered first the bodice of the dresses they wore every day. A line of red chain stitch, one of cross-stitch patterns, three lines of chain in red, green, burgundy, a narrow line of black and white, another red chain, a band of satin stitch finely worked from the back, red chain again, black and white, three lines of chain in burgundy, green and red. Only then was any variation possible. Either a rough crisscross stitch called *jalar* or, if the dress was very special, a time-consuming complicated interlacing stitch which was believed to have reached here from Saxony, followed by a line of bottle shapes called *tanab*. Over the breasts were wonderful patterns of chicken's feet, diamonds or arrows and then the lines would begin again. The cuffs were worked in the same way, as was a long deep pocket up the front of the skirt, which ended in a triangle protecting the woman's sex. But it was not like the triangle of the Afghan amulet. It contained no neatly folded piece of paper with a text from the Koran prescribed by the mullah, nor did tassels dangle from it.

As for widows and old women, they were entitled only to a few discreet lines of embroidery while 'a mother who has lost an only son will have no *chat* or *lar* or *niam-tik* on her shift. And the shift of a widow who has lost her eldest son will be embroidered with plain thread. But a widow who is the mother of children will keep the *niam-tik* and the *gul-gulchik* on her shift, in token that she is the mother of some sons despite her widowhood.' No one seemed to know any longer what these patterns were but widows still allowed themselves only two narrow bands of embroidery down the front of their dress.

Perhaps the amulet might be found in the jewellery: in every village silversmiths squatted in small dark stalls in the bazaar, concentrating over sparking anvils. When a customer appeared they would shake an old cocoa tin, tumbling its contents on to the dusty floor. But the amulet was never among them. Only in the tawdry modern goldsmiths could it be found: pendants, earrings, each a filigree triangle hung with chains and bells. The amulet did not belong to the old jewellery, the heavy turquoise nose rings and the intolerably weighty bunches of gold and turquoise that coiled round the women's ears. Each baby girl had her ears pierced in a series of holes all around the sides and lobes, which were left threaded with blue cotton. It was then so painful for the baby to turn that she lay still on her pillow of millet and her head, it was hoped, would grow perfectly round. Baby boys slept freely.

'You give me a report on all this' said Kholiq. 'What you are doing in Makran', as we set off to JM and Mr Khodedad's village of Gehna Pulani, a few kilometres west of Turbat.

Mr Khodedad's young wife was beautiful and hung with gold. She sat modestly on the floor of their reception room in front of a photo of him in a jaunty cap, officer's jacket and lean cuffed trousers, taken when he had served as a young man in the Omani Army and had had another wife. With considerable pride Mr

Khodedad showed us this photo, his wife, his son, a cradle, somewhere under whose hangings a baby lay sleeping, and his cow. This tethered creature with soft brown eyes represented five thousand rupees of his retirement pay and clearly, like his truck, was an investment to secure his old age and his young family. JM's five thousand had been invested not in a cow but in a fighting cock with spurs that was to perform tomorrow as part of a marriage ceremony. 'Ten thousand if he wins' he said, clinching it by the wings as it struggled.

JM's garden, like Mr Khodedad's, was a patch of the oasis of their village, divided by irrigation channels into small sections, but it was all much bigger and better than his friend's. 'This is mango tree. This lemon. Here lucerne.'

'Try these broad beans' said Sheila.

JM took the packet, nodded and proceeded with his tour. 'This date. Male.' Pointing to the flower on the date palm, an upwardly growing cluster next to the trunk, he continued 'We cut this and put it into female date tree. Then we are getting baby.' He gave us a knowing look. Mr Khodedad had ventured no such remark concerning his date palms.

'Water from keraz' JM continued. These channels, known in Persia as *qanat*, brought water many kilometres from some underground source, feeding it along a gentle downward gradient, sometimes very deep below the surface of the earth. Every so often there would be a well into which a leather bucket, hung on a spoked wooden wheel counterbalanced by stones, could be lowered. Or there would be stone steps leading down to the water where the women would take their washing, immersing it among suds and fishes and then laying it on the stones to dry. The water was at the same time the drinking supply for the village and around the countryside groups of Pathans from Afghanistan could be seen camped around some keraz where they had been paid to clear out the stones and snakes.

The system of the keraz, JM explained, was that several men shared the cost of construction and then were entitled to use the water in proportion to their investment. This share appeared to be measured by floating a clean cup with a hole in its base on the water and seeing how long it took to sink. The time taken would be the time they would be allowed to have the water flowing through their land. This of course was only for measuring at night and on cloudy days. When the sun was up a system of dials and a man's shadow was used. Though JM seemed rather unclear about precisely how the system worked, he had ensured an ample supply for his garden and his womenfolk.

From Mr Khodedad and JM's village we were to continue west to our last port of call, Mand, just half an hour away from the Iranian border. Here I intended to stay for a while and then continue on my planned journey alone into Iran, as the Italians had completed their work for the year in Pakistani Makran and had no brief to operate over the border in Iranian Makran. There was no true road but a track and a border post and I had already arranged a lift across. 'I will not allow it' screamed Kholiq. 'It is absolutely forbidden. You are not to go to Iran. If you disobey me the Italian Mission will never get another permit to work here.'

'Yes, yes, as your leader I forbid it' chipped in Genoveffa who had known for ages that that was my intention.

Kholiq grew quite apoplectic: 'Iran is closed,' he shrieked 'you will be killed there. Or taken hostage. It will be bad for the Department of Archaeology. I will not allow it.' From then on he never let me out of his sight.

Mand

The embroidery teacher sat crosslegged on the earth, her shrouded head bent over her work. Her fine-boned face, the olive of her skin, spoke of Somaliland and Yemen and of ancestors carried in dhows by the monsoon from the coasts of eastern Africa and southern Arabia to this godforsaken desert land. She had a quiet dignified air and was dressed plainly below the black that entirely enveloped her, as befitted a widow. She had seen her husband stricken with some sort of fever, no one knew what. He had left for Karachi some years before in the hope of treatment and had never returned, leaving her homeless with five children. Now, in her late thirties, she taught embroidery to support them and lived with her parents-in-law. With her long-boned shell-nailed fingers she threaded her needle with white cotton, stuck it in the hole through her nose and began my instruction.

My fellow students, destitute girls and women, sat on the earth around her, while Kholiq, not allowed into this female compound, paced up and down outside. The girls – orphans, widows and abandoned females – were given a hundred and fifty rupees by the government for a year's instruction and then provided with a sewing machine. With this skill and equipment it was hoped they would be able to earn their own living and provide for their families. It was the only social welfare available to them.

I slowly mastered the interlacing stitch while Kholiq watched for me to escape to Iran.

The embroidery school was housed within the family domain of Jalal Khan, as indeed was the school for girls, the only one in the whole of rural Baluchistan. This kindly man, who wandered regally around the compound of his home supervising its domestic life, had brought his family from a high-powered prosperous life in Kuwait back to his ancestral terrain when, on the death of his father, he inherited these primeval lands and the people who lived on them. His six daughters and three sons quickly moved back to the Gulf or to Karachi and considered the old man's

94

quest for his roots a mental aberration. Except, that is, for
Zobaida, the unmarried daughter, plain where the others were
beauties, intelligent where they were shallow, motivated where
they were led. Taken at seventeen from a sophisticated Western
life she had found herself in this backwater. 'Why sit around?'
said her father. 'Look at all those girls in the street, tending goats,
washing clothes in the keraz, kicking their heels. Why not start a
school?'

Seventy-five girls had turned up, increasing in number as the
years passed to five hundred, and Zobaida had tried to employ
teachers. There were none. But now her old students were
becoming available as teachers and the future was assured. The
government had even offered land in Turbat for Zobaida and her
father to start a girls' school there. But news had reached them
that the Minister for Revenue was giving it away behind their
backs to his cousin in a private deal as building land for houses.
He was hoping to hurry the papers through before Jalal Khan
heard of it. A few days later Zobaida and her father flew to
Quetta to plead for the school.

The girls' school at Mand was held in the mornings. It was in
the afternoons, in front of the same chalked blackboard but
understanding nothing of what was written on it, that the embroidery women met. They worked for two hours – the most
their eyesight could stand and they could spare from domestic
duties – to build a future for themselves.

There was a magical quality to Mand that was hard to
pinpoint. Wide open dusty spaces separated the small one-
roomed houses; so wide and open were they that the light across
them became strangely bleached and the goats and women
walked as in a mirage. The southerly aspect of the compound of
Jalal Khan's house, facing plumb in the night sky to the stars of
the southern horizon, meant that in the cold pre-dawn light a
rosy glow would appear over the kitchen to the east, silhouetting
this small room with its flower-pot chimney. The first light in
the home was always the candle of the woman who rose before
anyone else and laid the fire of sticks in the kitchen to make the
breakfast chapattis and tea. Jalal Khan would then invariably be
the first to emerge from the bedrooms, sniffing the air as undis-
puted top dog of the tribe.

The centre of his compound was a small fenced garden, a

dusty enclosure of date palms, lime, guava and fig trees and patches of coriander. At a distance, against the westerly wall, was the bathroom where a system of tanks and pipes provided the ultimate refinement of hot water from a loose tap in the wall. The family's toothpaste and brushes fitted neatly between the pipes and the wall. There was a hole in the floor, but nothing else. From this small building a patch of damp sand spread into the dry dust that formed the soil of the rest of the compound.

The bedrooms were ranged along the northern wall. The door of the main one still had 'Happy Wedding' in sparkly tinsel across it, above the shoes left outside. Here Zobaida and I took our meals. A goat rested on the large double bed and an important dressing table which lacked a mirror in its ornate frame – three attempts had been made to bring one from Karachi but none had survived the road – completed the décor of the room.

The other bedrooms were full of quilts and the ramifications of the family who slept on them. All were there: the son who had worked for eleven years in Bahrain, only to be made redundant, and who was now taking stock before returning to the Gulf; the married daughters on holiday from Karachi, their ten children in psychedelic track suits ornate with Mutant Turtles and dinosaurs, watched by the servants' scruffy children in traditional embroidered Baluchi dress, while they whizzed about on rainbow plastic bicycles labelled BMW 3ND CHERUB. Jalal Khan supervised all. 'Why are you scolding that child? Did I bring you up in such a way?' They had brought cherry cakes from Karachi, an unheard of luxury in Makran, and spices: cumin, caraway and turmeric.

The rhythm of the day was immutable. Just as the sun rose over the kitchen, so it set over the bathroom on the opposite wall of the compound, an intense glow of cloudless dusty red each morning and evening. Herders brought the goats home to rest, and camels – laden with sticks of firewood they carried maybe a couple of hundred kilometres to sell, one load for a hundred rupees – moved into the security of the village.

The servant women set about making the evening naan. Three of them, one my embroidery teacher, squatted in the light of the setting sun on a pile of palm leaves waiting to be woven into baskets. They made the naan with a rhythm that was as slick as it was uncontrived. The first woman finger-pressed the pads of dough into flatter dimpled discs which she handed to the next. This woman placed them on a round wooden plate and with a regular beat rolled them with a wooden rolling pin, then quarter-turned them, a repetitive sequence of pin, hand, pin, hand that was mesmeric. When the rounds of dough were flattened to the perimeter of the board she passed them to the embroidery teacher who threw them back and forward on a padded cushion with all the delicacy and precision she had applied to her stitchery, and then slapped them down one at a time on to the sides of the oven – a circular well cut about one metre deep into the ground with a fire of sticks in the bottom. This flared in the night air rather more than was desired, as the children had helped by throwing on more sticks.

As night fell the generator would churn noisily for an hour or two and then peter out, plunging everything, both indoors and out, into a darkness that lasted again till dawn.

A lost, end-of-the-line feeling permeated Mand. The road there from Turbat had followed the wide, flat and stony valley of the Kech, winding through the middle of date oases and switch-backing up slopes of gravel as it approached the mountains to the west. There was a clear feeling of the proximity of a different people and a different land. Already there were words of Persian, new terms for the same embroidery, a refining of faces, touches of a subtle complexity in the simple architecture: extra furbelows crowning the mud houses, always with the slight wobble of the handmade; just a few more turrets on the mosques, some shockingly painted turquoise, pale pink and white. Instead of in tents of matting and goathair the semi-nomadic people around Mand lived in circular mud huts roofed with tree branches that were held together by nothing but tied palms. Inside the women's reception rooms instead of the cups and saucers and thermos flasks of the rest of Makran were Persian copper bowls and instead of quilts, piles of carpets. Embroidered dresses were still stored in trunks, balanced on old tins of baby milk powder.

Almost nothing appeared to cross the nearby border: no vehicles came through, nothing was in transit. The locals themselves, nomadic or settled, were allowed to go across to see relatives and a small trickle would cross in the summer months when jaundice, hepatitis and malaria were rife, for no medical treatment was available in Makran. Three widely scattered GPs served forty thousand people, but they had heard that on the Iranian side there were mobile malarial treatment centres and drugs and medicines. Apart from this movement of people a small amount of smuggling went on but it was claimed to be small beer compared to Dubai and the Makran ports. A bit of rice crossed westward to Iran, a few apples and pistachio nuts eastward. As far as anyone was saying.

While nights in Makran were spent in total darkness, in the near distance just across the border the lights of the Shah's rural electrification programme twinkled. It was going to be easy for me to get there in Zobaida's van. 'You can't go' shrieked Kholiq. 'I have my instructions. You are to fly to Quetta with me. Then you must fly to Mashad. It's a place of pilgrimage so there will be transport southwards.'

This enlightened itinerary – three boneshaking hours on a truck to Turbat, two thousand kilometres as the crow flies to Quetta and on to Mashad in northern Iran, then one thousand five hundred kilometres of road by bus, just to get back to where I now stood – was dreamt up by Nabi Khan, Director of Archaeology for Baluchistan, and insisted upon under threat of evicting the Italians. I protested violently and continued to protest. The scheme was supported by Genoveffa. 'Otherwise you'll catch the first plane back to Karachi. I am the leader.'

'Dr Kholiq doesn't like you' Sheila patiently explained. 'He thinks you're too strong for a woman.'

And so the Mitsubishi van, labelled 'From the Governor of Baluchistan for the Teachers of Govt Girls', bumped at top speed back eastwards along the rutted road past the flying flags of the bastion of Tump, past the hooded falcons of hunters from the Gulf, past the goathair tents of nomads seeking grazing for their herds, back to Circuit House.

It was Christmas.

Christmas

'No chance of any wine, I suppose, JM?'

'Wine? No. No wine. Whisky. Black Dog.'

'Not for Christmas. What about cognac?'

'What's that?'

'Brandy.'

'Write it down.'

I wrote 'Cognac Grande Fine Napoléon' and drew a few stars.

JM returned, flushed with success, a newspaper packet under his arm. 'Cognac Napoléon. Made in France' the label said and the screw top didn't appear to have been tampered with, though it didn't taste quite right. We had it with almonds the boys had cracked with stones on the verandah of Circuit House.

Rashly I had offered to produce a Christmas dinner and ferreted around the bazaar to see what there was to buy. It wasn't promising. Some fruit and a few vegetables and nuts were available but the grocers had only tea, sugar, baby milk, washing powder, eggs, rice, flour, lentils, spices, coconut oil, small cartons of milk, tinned peas, biscuits and absolutely nothing else. Gul Mohammed could produce a chicken. There were the dates that Ugo had left behind and Zobaida had given us one of the cherry cakes from Karachi. I whipped round to see what the others had brought with them from home, what they had thought essential in this wild outpost. Sheila contributed Marmite and a tape of carols; the boys had celery salt, Sasso olive oil, black cherry jam, Elli coffee and some spaghetti they wouldn't part with. Kholiq had procured a packet of Kraft processed cheese. 'And' said Sheila 'you have to be very careful. Even with the rubbish they have to put up with here these Italians can be very fussy when it comes to something European. They won't eat things like ready-grated Parmesan. You should have heard Ugo. "*Parmeggiano? Già preparato? Impossibile. Non mangio.*"'

We hung tinsel stars bought at the marriage shop on a branch of tamarisk, so that we had a Christmas tree, and made little trees to eat, cut out of green halwa. In honour of the Italians we ate on Christmas Eve.

The boys had kept their spaghetti to serve us for Christmas Day lunch. Enough for five, they said, but there were to be ten of us. Genoveffa had invited some Gichkis and hadn't told Gianni, who was having a fit in the kitchen when Captain Khalid arrived with three bottles of Smugglers. 'This is our national dish' said Genoveffa proudly, indicating the spaghetti. She had not only omitted to tell anybody about the extra guests she had invited but had also done nothing about the meal. The bowl of spaghetti was never going to play the role of five fishes. We rushed out to the back to rescue the leftovers from the night before but the cooks had eaten everything, even the whole cherry cake. It was a solemn meal, with the Captain ruefully eyeing his small portion and swigging his own whisky.

Ashgar the cook came and whispered in my ear. 'There's a man in room seven who wants to meet you. You must go and see him.'

There were two men there. They bombarded me with questions. Why had I not gone into Iran from Mand? Was I going to? Would I stay on after the rest of the team had left? In response to my protestations that I wasn't allowed to do any of these things they simply said they would make it possible, 'though we must see your papers'.

'Who are you?'

'I'm Sayel el Haq, social anthropologist from the Ministry of Defence. We will get you across the border from Mand.' There was something very unpleasant about the man and his questioning. I got up to leave. 'I'll be back for you again at eight tonight' he said, threateningly.

The boys left immediately afterwards for the flight to Karachi and home but returned half an hour later. The airport was locked up and there was no one there. The flight must have been cancelled, they said. Gianni looked glum.

Just before eight we came down for dinner only to find no table laid, no food in the kitchen, no fire lit and no one around. We discovered the cooks had eaten all the food again. They made us a chapatti or two and one minute dish of curried vegetable for the six of us. Gianni left and locked himself in his room. 'He was invited to a reception at the Italian consulate in Karachi tonight' said Gionata. 'Chianti. Prosciutto. Tagliatelle. Panettone.' He looked pensive.

Ashgar came to the table and whispered again in my ear. I went outside. Sayel el Haq was standing by a car. 'Get in' he said.

I ran away. He shouted that he would be back in fifteen minutes. He returned, looking for me in my room. Gionata found him and brought him into the dining room. He had expected to be taken to room seven and was surprised to find himself confronted by a group of people.

He was grilled by Kholiq. 'I'm a social anthropologist' he replied. 'I met Genoveffa two days ago. She will tell you I'm from the Ministry of Defence.'

'I *am* Genoveffa' said our leader.

He looked discomforted. He continued by making some amazing claims of what he thought I had been doing or intended to do. Then he tried to make polite conversation. 'You should investigate the big mound at Mand' he suggested.

'There is no mound at Mand.'

'You should look at Miri Khalat.'

'We've been looking at it for six years.'

'What about the graves at Buleida?'

'There are no graves at Buleida' Kholiq said icily.

'To which university do you good people belong?'

That finished Kholiq and he rose to the occasion magnificently. 'You must know the Department of Archaeology is a government organization and not a university. And you clearly know nothing about social anthropology. You have told a lot of lies about this embroidery lady of ours. I know she is telling the truth and you're not. What's more you don't approach a member of our scientific team by getting one of the cooks to whisper in her ear.'

'No' shouted Genoveffa, feeling usurped. 'I am the leader. You do not approach one of my team like that.' He left quietly.

'Let's go for a stroll' said Gionata 'and walk our dinner off.'

The next morning the entire team, apart from Kholiq and me, were to leave Makran. It was only ten minutes to the airport and my colleagues were sitting in Mr Khodedad's pick-up ready to go, JM at the wheel. Our leader, who had a slight cold, was sitting next to him, clutching her brow and moaning 'I shall be dead of fever before I get to Rome. *Morta di febbre.*' The other three were squashed in behind and the mountain of luggage was piled on the back. It was all too much for Mr Khodedad who had been twiddling his scarf as he watched his beautiful truck about to depart. As JM turned the ignition he slid into the driver's seat beside him, forcing him half on to the gear lever. The boys waved goodbye and the truck set off down the road in first gear.

'You are not to move from Circuit House,' said Kholiq 'not to take one step outside your room.'

'House arrest then?' I suggested. 'You could call it that. I'm going out.'

He returned a few hours later looking rather flushed. 'There's only one bastard round here' he said, finding some rather unexpected vocabulary 'and I've sent him packing. That man. He wasn't a social anthropologist at all. He was a secret agent from our intelligence service. And I sent him packing.'

'He didn't seem very intelligent' I commented.

'He was supposed to have taken you away for close interrogation. And I sent him packing.' I had to feel grateful.

'Could we walk down to the bazaar? I need a torch' I asked, hoping to profit from his sense of well-being.

Now that the others had left we had no vehicle, so we set off down the road on foot, Kholiq lost in thought. 'Why was Captain Khalid with you at Gwadar?'

'We gave him a lift.'

'And what was Bishop Lobo doing there? Why was he there the same day as you?'

'I don't know. I think he hoped to see the boys and ask them to design a school for him.'

'Why did you go without any levies?'

'We were told there were none available.'

'There are always levies. You went everywhere else with them.' We continued in rather frosty silence.

'It wasn't just my director who said you couldn't go across the frontier into Iran. It was Genoveffa too. She told me first of all that she had already arranged for Jalal Khan to take you across, but when I said I'd have to tell my director she backed out and said she would forbid you to go as it might harm the Mission.'

'It wasn't Genoveffa who arranged it' I replied. 'It was me. I arranged it with Zobaida.'

'I know. Genoveffa lied. I checked with Jalal Khan and he knew nothing about it. And I don't believe a word of the story about her mother and her sister.'

I pondered on the implications of this, when Kholiq took up the theme again. 'What do you think of the way this Mission is run?'

'It's very unprofessional. Not the people on it. The way it's run.'

'Exactly. Big Sheila was complaining too. They've been coming for seven years and we have no results, no reports. I always felt there was something wrong, but now I see what goes on I'm horrified. Genoveffa changing her mind every minute, socializing, not doing anything serious. And does that simple honest man Jalal Khan know how she's taking him for a ride?'

'And the nuns?'

'Them too. And she's had three or four affairs. One with Captain Khalid.'

'So I heard.'

'And with the Frenchman Robert.'

'Yes, I heard about that too. Now she just keeps saying how stupid he is, but they're supposed to be running the next Mission together.'

'I shall report it all to my director. We will let them come again in January because the permit is already arranged but then after that never again unless they have a new leader. It all stops at the second millennium BC too. They have no Islamic expert. That is terrible.' He looked at me for approbation.

'Very bad.'

'And I understand she has paid the boys sixty thousand dollars. Each. Though they're both doing the same work and I can't see why she had to have two. And you and Sheila nothing.'

'No, only our expenses.'

'It's incorrect. It isn't professional. I am only a small man, but I can see what's going on. And the people higher up, the government, they know. They have been watching for some time and there are a lot of things behind this Mission. They know what's going on. It isn't just a Mission, there are things it is hiding. It is, what do you call it?'

'A cover.'

'A cover, that's exactly it. There are people here using it as a cover.' He paused and looked sideways at me, weighing his words carefully.

'Captain Khalid is a known international heroin smuggler.'

Iran

❖ ❖ ❖

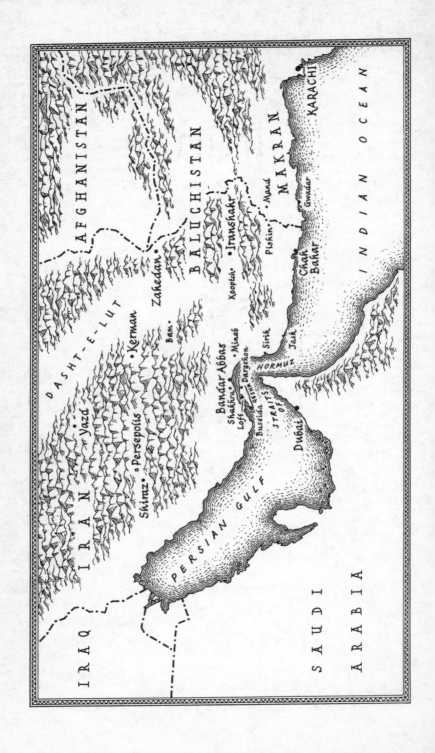

Zahedan

'You can eat the chicken and the bread. They're Iranian. But don't touch the chapatti. It's Pakistani and it's filthy. Use it as a plate.' The two men who had followed their wives into my compartment to stare at me had offered some of their own supper, explaining that there was nothing on the train, no water, no food, nothing. An old man at some halt had sold scummy tea in chipped glasses and at another a small boy had held up a basket of hard-boiled eggs to the passengers leaning out of the train windows. Otherwise it had been nothing since Turbat.

Kholiq had almost lost me there. For a few worrying moments he had stood alone at the foot of the aircraft steps with all the other passengers safely on. Left carefully in the women's waiting room, I had been held up while the woman frisking me had opened the plastic bottle in my bag, smelt it and called an official. He had taken a deep sniff of the vodka, raised his eyebrows and had then said categorically 'Water'. But it had been enough to delay me and convince Kholiq that I had escaped him and was again heading westward to the Iranian border. He shepherded me on to the plane and in Quetta hired a rickshaw for us. 'St Joseph's.' He escorted me in and delivered me into the hands of Sister Virginia. 'You'll be safe here.' A few minutes later a rickshaw was hurtling to the station, winding through lorry fumes, whipping past trucks, braking behind cows. There was a train to Zahedan in Iran in twenty minutes and not another one for four days, by which time Kholiq would have seen me on to a plane for Mashad.

The train trundled south-westward for most of a day and all night through an arid plain that skirted the mountains bordering Afghanistan. A shepherd in a wide-shouldered felt cape watched over his flock, a camel pulled a plough across a dry wasteland. At wayside halts groups of boys would gather to stare. 'Hello, Grandmother Miss. What's your religion?' Women – Pathan, Hazara, Baluch – would crowd into the compartment, sit and gaze intently for a while, then leave, followed by others waiting in the corridor to do the same. All were shrouded in black chadors. As darkness fell the compartment seemed like a cavern full of black ghosts, its dim bulb eclipsed by the light of the ticket collector's match. It was bereft of any fittings and the freezing night air seeped in through the broken wooden windows. It seemed a joke even to have imagined that sleeper bedding might be provided.

The train ground to a halt in an uneasy pre-dawn light that sketched the outlines of a huddle of small houses in the distance and, close to the train, a platform in the sand. There was no station, only a hut lit by a hurricane lamp where three uniformed men checked the passports of the passengers already milling round. I jumped down the two-metre drop from the train steps into the sand and joined them. The men glanced cursorily at my passport and motioned me back on to the train. Pick-up trucks came and went, families and baggage loaded on the back. The brightening light revealed a mud army fort emblazoned with the device 'Live with dignidty, die with honour'. A little old man came into the compartment bringing a grimy cracked cup of tea, a fried egg swimming in ghee and a piece of soft dirty toast. Daylight came quickly and with it the realization that there was nobody else left on the train. 'Well' the officials in the hut said 'it's quicker to get off the train and walk to Iran.'

I set off along the edge of the railway track and then across a wide expanse of sand towards a huddle of buildings. Someone passed. 'Is this the way to Iran?'

He waved into the distance. 'Yes. Go that way. You'll see Khomeini.' The path across the sand, hardened by footsteps, rounded a group of hovels where pye-dogs lurked and then led alongside a high metal fence. Ahead, looming in the sky, disproportionate as Canary Wharf or the Eiffel Tower, was a massive portrait of a dyspeptic, scowling Ayatollah Khomeini. Below it a small iron gate led into Iran.

Armed guards were everywhere. On walls leading from Police to Money Exchange to Customs to Passports chalked messages extolled the virtues of Islam while other, more splashed, larger daubs, shrieked 'Down With USA', 'Down With America', 'Down With The US' and on the long path to the Medical Centre 'Down With The America'. Here a kindly man sat surrounded by packets and bottles of medicines such as they never see in

Makran and offered me malarial tablets. At every check I was given tea and welcomed. My vodka was simply shaken and replaced in my bag.

The bus to Zahedan passed through another dozen checkpoints before entering the town. 'You don't want to go there' Kholiq had said. 'It's just like Turbat.' It was, in fact, nothing like Turbat. The roads were tarred; there were pavements – fountains even – no goats, no cows, no piles of festering rubbish, no muddy quagmires, no people working on the streets shaving customers or polishing boots. And there were women wearing glasses. Its grid of low concrete buildings, badly stocked shops and cracked Tarmac were reminiscent of modern developments of Eastern Europe. The women were all wrapped in chadors, the men wore Western dress and turbans, or shalwar kameez.

At the bus station a man offered to share his lunch of kebabs and rice, found a taxi, ensured I had the right change and instructed the driver to take me to the eye hospital.

The door of Dr Arrish's consulting room was besieged by about twenty people with bandaged, missing or squiffy eyes, the ones in front pounding it with raised fists, the ones behind pummelling the others' backs. The hospital itself was a collection of shabby buildings that looked like some social security office. Here Dr Arrish, a distant relative of Zobaida's, carried out operations and held his clinic. I waved Zobaida's card of introduction at some white-coated men and was ushered into a side room full of journals on ophthalmology. They were all American and looked as though they had been donated. An old man followed me in, clutching a small notebook. 'Is it cheaper to live in the north or south of England? Or Scotland? Is Glasgow cheap? Where's the best place to buy a house? What are the best investments? What rate of interest?' Dr Arrish mercifully walked in and suggested lunch.

A fretted wood screen separated the 'family room' from the rest of the restaurant, shielding the one or two women sitting there with their husbands from the gaze of the men filling the main room and attended more readily by the waiters. Dr Arrish and I faced each other over a vase of red plastic flowers that enmeshed one or two dead flies. Our lunch of rice and kebabs, small plate of raw sliced onion, cucumber and tomato, and bread in the shape of – and tasting like – a folded paper napkin, was brought as Dr Arrish talked about Baluchistan.

'We're Baluch above all, whether we live in Iran, Afghanistan or Pakistan. In the end it comes down to being Baluch. So we've been terribly oppressed just because we want our own country. Under the Shah no Baluchi boys were educated beyond primary level, they were never allowed to go to university. It was only by going to the Gulf that any education was possible. That's where my parents took me. Then I qualified as a FRCS in Edinburgh. But I always felt I had to come back to serve my own people. There's a paediatrician here and the two of us are the only qualified specialists in the whole of Baluchistan for oh' – he waved his delicate hands in the air – 'I don't know how many million Baluch. They keep offering me money to go to Tehran or Isfahan but I won't. I belong with my people. We have no money for anything here – the rural electrification programme was too little too late. Since the revolution it's been even worse as the rulers are Shia and we're Sunni. But things have improved a bit under Rafsanjani. Baluchi people are now allowed to move between the Pakistani and Iranian parts of Baluchistan, but not if they're educated.'

Remembering the mobile malarial unit the Pakistani Baluch hoped might also serve them, I asked Dr Arrish whether he carried out operations across the border as well. He looked pensive. 'I'm not allowed to leave Iran at all. But maybe there'll be elections soon and some of Rafsanjani's moderates might win. Then there could be a few changes: the country opening up, more international contacts, maybe even tourism again.'

We ploughed through the plain unflavoured rice and scrunched the onion. 'Islam is a good religion. It reaches the truth before science does. We know now that fasting strengthens the body, helps us survive in tough circumstances. Then alcohol, science tells us it's bad for the liver and brain but our fathers and grandfathers knew that instinctively. They protected us. And homosexuality. We were right to make it illegal. Look how it's keeping us safe from AIDS. Our grandfathers just sensed what was right. They knew it was right that men and women should be kept separate. They are not equal.'

Challenged by the suggestion that his religion might be throwing away the talents and potential of half the population, let alone depriving everyone of real relationships, he reflected for a while on the matter before giving his considered reply: 'Men and women are different'. He paused, savouring the truth of this remark, before continuing: 'Women are better living differently. They have other talents, mostly kindness and patience, so they make good telephone operators and teachers. It's best to keep things that way'.

The problem of a chador became urgent. I wandered round the bazaar but none were on sale. It gradually dawned on me, seeing stall after stall of bolts of dreary fabric – black with beige patterns, plain black, navy with beige patterns, beige with black patterns, plain navy – that the material had to be bought to be made up by the bazaar tailor. I stopped at a stall. Black chiffons, black Japanese polyesters, black satins, black viscose, plain black, black pattern on black were presented. 'Something warmer. Tabriz.' I tried to convey the cold north by a shiver. By this time a crowd of about thirty men had gathered. The old stallholder, a puzzled look on his thin brown face, wielded a huge pair of scissors over a bolt of thicker black stuff while the men argued.

A fat man burst in, out of breath. 'Do you speak English?' he asked.

'I *am* English' I replied with Victorian pomp and possessive patriotism.

The man had clearly been fetched in a hurry to help. 'Old man say five metres not enough, must be six. Six for chador not five.'

'Fine' I said with a cheerfulness that belied my feelings at having to spend every waking hour from then on shrouded in six metres of black fabric. The stallholder sliced away.

'My friend take home' the fat man continued. 'Make chador. You here at old man eight o'clock morning for chador.'

'Thank you. How much for making chador?'

'No how much. Is nothings.'

The next morning I collected my chador, enveloped myself in it and sallied forth into the busy morning bazaar. It felt like driving a Volvo.

My early mastery of this shroud was not to last. It continually slipped back from my forehead and if a whisker of hair showed someone would point at me and scream 'Islam! Islam!' At least it never actually came off completely as my dupatta – that immensely long, drifting shawl – had done in Makran, when I stepped forward into the crowd only to find a donkey standing on one end of it. But whereas just slung over the head and shoulders the chador appeared quite a fetching garment, once an outlet had to be found for glasses on a chain, a free hand to cope with shoulder bag and, worse, a travelling bag when on the move, the whole scenario became impossible. It disintegrated into a tangle of forbidden hair, trapped hands, slipping black fabric, uncontrollable bags and lost glasses, smugly surveyed by grinning small boys. Though never known to swear, I found myself – arms flailing in acres of black – muttering under my breath 'Bloody thing'.

I finally relinquished my ownership of this garment a month or so later on a bus in Turkey when a man was sick on it.

Chah Bahar

Moving south was rumoured to be difficult – 'they won't sell bus tickets to foreigners' – but Dr Arrish sent along a ticket for Iranshahr and the next morning at six the bus trundled out of the bus station of Zahedan with two drivers in front of me and a gaggle of men behind. We passed a queue of people at a baker's and the bus braked. The drivers leapt out and returned with slabs of hot naan under their arms. They tore off a large piece and handed it to me with a glass – carefully wiped first on their grubby kameez – filled with tea from their thermos. We circuited the town and fifteen minutes later were back at the bus station. Setting off again we repeated the same circuit, this time stopping at a checkpoint where soldiers boarded the bus, looked at the men's faces and asked a few of them for their papers. Next we halted at a roadside stand where the drivers bought packets of butter for their bread. This was also offered to me and more tea was poured as the driver headed back for the bus station. Some time later we started off again.

The landscape we drove through was a scrubby plain and rolling hills topped with mud watchtowers like toy forts. Soldiers stood on them surveying the road below, while others pounded up and down stopping vehicles. It was a landscape that became increasingly more disagreeable, especially as we approached towns. Telegraph poles, electricity pylons, barbed wire enclosures and green metal fencing littered the scene. Villages of mud houses were aligned in streets, towns were like abandoned building sites titivated with pompous civic sculptures of a political nature and motorway street lighting. They had all the allure of the Nissen hut back-end of the Wantage Trading Estate.

The poverty of Makran, if you were not part of it, had been picturesque. It was medieval. It was man and animal surviving together: a man following his goats where they could find grazing, or driving his camels where firewood could be sold. Hundreds of kilometres for a pittance. And it was a poverty that drove man back to his hands to make everything he needed. Curing a

113

goatskin to fashion it into a water carrier, weaving goathair to roof his shelter, plaiting palm to make mats to sit on and baskets to hold dates. And man in most instances meant woman. But the poverty of Iran was a bureaucratic poverty, a poverty of soul and imagination that unified everything into a drab gloom. Even the lunch I had eaten with Dr Arrish turned out to be the standard menu – kebabs alternating only with chicken – in every single restaurant and hotel throughout Iran. There was never anything else. It was Communism without the name.

The main street of the port of Chah Bahar must always have resembled nothing more than a line of lock-up garages, even before the bombardment of Iran's eight-year war with Iraq scarred and ruptured it. The walk along it was nearly two kilometres from where the bus had dumped its passengers on the highway, past flaking concrete and rusting blue roll-up doors, to the shabby white hotel on the seafront.

'Dollari' muttered the swarthy manager out of the side of his mouth to his assistant as soon as I walked in, presuming I wouldn't understand. He turned out to be one of the very few hoteliers who imposed the law requiring that foreigners pay in dollars. This immediately booted the price of a room up from the usual two pounds to more like twenty.

It was a spacious jerry-built hotel, mouldy and peeling at every ceiling joint and heavy with the usual salt-incrusted shagreenous decay of buildings close to warm tropical seas. Great cracks fissured the walls and loose wires hung about. Rusty old-fashioned air-conditioning units had been seized up for some time, scaled hot water taps gurgled but produced no water and obviously never had. But blown-up engravings everywhere of David Roberts' Middle Eastern scenes and the small balcony for each room overlooking the bay redeemed it entirely.

The bay was a beautiful arc of golden sand where herons and cormorants walked longlegged and small boys carried by their wings gulls they had somehow been fleet enough to capture. Fishermen worked at their nets and men perched on wooden frames built clinker boats by hand, as they had at Gwadar. A few youngsters swam and a couple of women sat in the warm sun encased in chadors. Around the edge of the beach was a settlement of fishermen's huts of matting and a little village dominated by a mosque. In many parts of the world concrete hotels and tourist effluvia would have fringed such a bay but here all new development had been on the further seashore – reduced to blackened twisted girders by bombing – and along the shabby strip of main road leading away from the port into the hinterland.

I set off along this road, past half-finished buildings and empty lots, to look for the bank. There seemed to be no rhyme or reason behind the many building sites: they began anywhere and ended anywhere and cows roamed about them at will. Every building gave the impression – as the bank did – that the contractor had made off with the money before it was finished. The bank staff, all men, were busy working on old cash registers of the kind children have as toys. They looked up to stare. The customers were all also men and stared even more intently. I was shown into a side room while my dollars were changed. I had, of course, both here and in Makran, to carry them in cash.

As I came out of the bank the young man who earlier had directed me to the hotel from the bus sprang from behind the building. He lay his hands together by his ear and rested his head on them in semblance of sleep. 'Hotel room two' he then added, holding up two fingers – a gesture I resisted reciprocating.

At half-past six in the morning the old shopkeeper, looking tired and dejected, unlocked the padlock on the rusty blue doors that formed the front of his shop – as other shopkeepers did all along the main street of Chah Bahar. I walked in to buy biscuits for the bus journey ahead. He was listening to the BBC World News on a small receiver, stroking his beard as he concentrated: Shamar had had to make some concessions. He considered this thoughtfully, taking more biscuits from his stock for his own breakfast. Bush had had some confrontation with American farmers. Listening together I waited for some less controversial country to be mentioned before engaging in discussion. Serbs were busy slaughtering Croats and Croats Serbs. As we chatted I photographed the mosque opposite and the dilapidated buildings around it. Suddenly the little shop was full of armed police. 'English' the old man said, standing close to me. Then, proud of the linguistic skill he had acquired solely from listening to the World Service, he interpreted for the police.

'Passport. Visa' they demanded. 'What are you doing here?'

The reply that I was only here for the embroidery provoked disbelief, until I rattled off in Farsi and Baluch the names of twenty or so stitches and the word for embroidery, which changed when the stitch used was chain or when the patterns were floral. They scrutinized my visa very closely. 'You are here to take photographs of this town. That is why you are here.'

'No, no. I was just taking the pretty patterns on the turrets of the mosque. They're the same as the patterns embroidered on the women's dresses.' The police were visibly disconcerted.

'She's catching the seven o'clock bus back to Iranshahr' the old man said. They looked relieved and handed back my passport. With my packet of biscuits I hurried away to the bus stand and waited quietly till seven.

They sat me on the bus next to a very plain young woman with a heavy black moustache and beard, displacing her husband to the seat behind. I wondered whether she had been a bride concealed by her chador until the wedding night.

The bus sped along and in the middle of nowhere an old man stood by the roadside holding up his begging bowl to the traffic whizzing past.

The envy of those who viewed Iranian Makran from across the border was hardly justified. Tarred roads and electric pylons there might be, but they marched across a landscape that barely differed from the Pakistani side. The geology was less lunatic, the desert flatter and more tedious, there were perhaps just a few more oases, a few more villages, but those scattered to the south and west of Iranshahr were still of matting, of wattle and palm. And mud was still the material of the mosques. Water was still stored in hanging goatskins and rice in handmade palm baskets left in an unattended line, with no fear of thieves, in the sand at the edge of the village. There were the same camels and goats, the same small settlements of nomads' tents and beehive huts. The Shah of one such community, they said, had left for a new life in America.

Access to the women was not as easy as it had been in Pakistan. With the women in the streets of the towns there was virtually no contact. They were so overcome by my presence and so totally uncomprehending as to where I came from and why I had no man that after the first expression of shock they simply lowered their heads and looked away. Even the men revealed their unfamiliarity with the outside world by asking many times, in spite of my Nordic looks, whether I were Japanese.

The village women invited me less readily into their homes, but brought their embroideries out into the courtyards to show me. When I did go inside, the interiors were plainer than in Pakistani Makran. There were no shelves of wobbly china, no piles of quilts, but instead a curtained niche on each side of the central door, concealing all their treasures. As in Pakistan there were no windows, only the shaft of bright light coming through the door and a fluorescent strip bulb on the opposite wall.

The women wore the same embroidered dresses as on the other side of the border, the stitches and their sequence still exactly the same. But here and there the traditional six colours had been modernized: orange had replaced red, purple blue, and even a little yellow had crept in, upsetting the original balance completely. Then, whereas in Pakistani Makran the women walked ablaze with colour in a bleached landscape, here they moved in the obscurity of covering black. Even a baby girl with a dummy in her mouth wore a black veil.

There was no sign of the Afghan amulet in their dress, no triangles in the embroidery nor in the jewellery. Only their headscarves, embroidered in the same patterns, colours and stitches as the dresses of Swat, had a motif that probably derived from the fertility goddess. The connection between this desolate hinterland of the Indian Ocean and the high mountain valley of the Swat far to the north was curious, and though the goddess motif was often to be found together with the triangular amulet in the embroideries of other parts of the world, here I had drawn a blank.

The next possibility was the Zoroastrian community of Kerman, some six hundred kilometres inland on the edge of the Dasht-e-Lut, the Great Salt Desert, and that of Yazd somewhat further north. The Zoroastrians had tended their holy fire, it was said, for fifteen hundred and twenty-one years, had laid their dead on temples of silence for the vultures to pick and had embroidered their clothes with strange small animals, with peacocks and solar discs.

The Zoroastrians

The departure of the night bus to Kerman was considerably delayed by the bubble gum. There were boxes and boxes and boxes of it – almost a container lorryload. The men it belonged to shinnied up and down loading it on to the roof of the bus and when that was completely full they moved into the bus, blowing the stuff between their teeth. They stacked up the luggage racks, then they started stowing boxes under the seats, under the passengers' feet and along the aisle. The bus was filled with a pervasive sickly sweet smell.

It finally set off, only to grind to a halt a little further on. A young policeman got on, watched over the tops of their raised knees by the passengers. He was followed by a score of dark-skinned men, veritable rapscallions they looked, scowling at the passengers from under their voluminous tie-dyed turbans. As they moved along the aisle we could see that they were hand-cuffed together in twos and threes. The young policeman sat them down towards the back of the bus, those shackled in threes being obliged to hold hands across the aisle.

At midnight the bus stopped at a roadside café for dinner. Long tables were laid with a line of large red plastic buckets down the centre, each with a smaller red plastic water jug and saltcellar by its side. The handcuffed men were each given a glass of water which they spat into the buckets. While all the other bus passengers sat at the tables in front of the buckets eating a supper of stewed chicken and rice, the men sat shackled together on the floor, each with a glass of tea and a packet of biscuits. The policeman then marched them out to the loo, though it was not clear how they could manage.

I tried to find out from the fellow sitting opposite me who they were, by pointing discreetly in their direction and indicating my wrist. 'Ah' he said 'Greenwich Mean Time. Persian Programme. London calling.' I tried again. 'Ah' he said, saluting and indicating epaulettes, 'officers.'

Kerman was the nadir of my journey. In the chittering days of mid-January icy sleet whipped down the wide vacant roads. The main highways were tarred along only half their width; the other half was surfaced by mud, holes and stones. Streets leading off them were puddled in slushy mud. Between the roads and the unmade pavements lay a wide ditch that had to be jumped over – pushchairs and wheelchairs, which would have been impossible to move, were utterly non-existent. Buildings of yellowed lavatory bricks, when not fronted by lock-up garage doors, were grilled like prisons. Most had no second storey, instead rusty iron pipes stuck up like chimneys, waiting to be set in concrete. Between the buildings were waste lots, half-built walls, piles of oil cans, heaps of earth, bags of cement, cardboard boxes. It was an urban scene mystifying to the uninformed observer.

My chador had overpowered me to screaming point: it hung soaking wet round my ankles, flapped in the cutting wind, tripped me as I jumped the ditches. I had managed to stop it slipping off my head by hanging my bag round my neck, though this tended to pitch me forward as I walked, making me look like some blanketed horse with a bag of oats. Other women had problems too, I noted. They passed, pushing it forward on their forehead, or clenching it in their teeth like a yashmak as their eyes swivelled sideways to watch my progress. Even to eat in the hotel restaurant I was obliged to keep it on. There was no respite from its weight on my head and my hair became more and more tangled and electric.

There was no respite either from rice, chicken, rice, kebab, Pepsi and yet more rice. Only the Pepsi had changed since travellers commented on the diet a hundred years ago: 'Supplies are only bread, eggs and fowls or fowls, bread and eggs.' 'The Persian chicken is a standing joke.' 'Lamb and mutton appear with exceeding regularity.' 'Nothing was forthcoming but the grisliest of fowls served upon a piece of chapatti instead of a plate with a lot of half-smoked and half-burnt rice in a bowl.'

Everywhere I looked – even as I ate, struggling with my chador – posters of Ayatollah Khomeini scowled down at me, left eye drooping, thin moustache, white beard, and an air of disdain, scorn and cruelty. It was a relief when the electricity went off, as it always did at nine in the evening.

'You missed Bam' the man at the hotel said. 'Three hours back on road from Iranshahr. Old walled city. When Shah, tourists visit.'

I dressed in total darkness before the electricity resumed, and caught the dawn bus.

'Maps of the old telegraph line?' the custodian of the Royal Geographical Society's map room had said. 'Never been asked for that before.' Now, as daylight broke and the bus resumed its journey after a break for tea, old wooden posts were clearly there by the roadside, some with a little white china disc numbering them, as drawers of butterflies are numbered in old museums. First they were to the left of the road, then to the right and towards Bam on the left again, just as the 1914 map of the Surveyor General of India, Southern Persia sheet, showed them.

Constructing the line 'through desolate countries and among semi-barbarous people' had not been easy. In Persia it had to cross salt deserts and mountain passes, one known locally as the Ass's Pass 'because a donkey had once been ass enough to go that way.' Rocks fell on the line, camels knocked down the posts, lions were troublesome and in 1872 the starving populace destroyed it, stole the material and murdered one of the telegraph officers.

Inspectors maintaining it had a hard life. They could 'hope for no shady tree nor for a single stream of water'. They slept in wretched caravanserai or hovels, often infected by ticks. They led a lonely existence. One, a simple signaller, was described as 'valuable material wasted by the Telegraph Department' for he had learnt the language and studied the customs of the country. This caused him to be much admired by the locals. He was, indeed, 'striking proof of the homage which Asiatics are always willing to pay to the sterling qualities of a good, honest Englishman.'

Bam was an unprepossessing place, neither ancient nor walled, but rather deserving of its name. Sketches I made of crumbling buildings – I was none too sure whether I should be drawing palaces or hovels – and waved at the inhabitants brought an enthusiastic response, 'Arg! Arg!', except from one man who spoke English and who simply narrowed his eyes at me and muttered 'Hard dollar'.

She had offered cake, tangerines, biscuits, oranges, water, nuts, dates, the woman behind me on the bus. Meeting me in the street again, she found a taxi for herself, her daughter and me. 'Arg' she said and when the driver pulled up at an immense barbicaned gateway, she waved me towards it, insisted on paying the fare and returned with her daughter to nearby Bam.

The fortifications of Arg were breathtaking. A perimeter of fosse was surmounted by earth ramparts and then topped by a vast curtain of stone wall that circled away to right and left, an unbroken sweep of battlements, embrasures and parapets that bulged at each angle in a massive bastion. A cobbled bridge led over the moat through a soaring gateway into the inner stronghold. Here the complete ring of the bulwark could be seen, the crumbling edge of the ancient town clinging to its rim like mouldering fruit flesh to tough peel. On the far side the battlements rose to extraordinary heights, capped by a castle that dominated the valley beyond the oasis. Held in the encircling grip of the strong stone walls the town was a huddled labyrinth of disintegrating mud walls, enclosures, domes, roofs and arches. Most were built of an amalgamation of mud and straw, embedded with small stones. A few were of mortared handmade mud bricks. Between them ran main streets of multi-coloured, rutted cobblestones, gouged by a central drainage channel, while side streets were of earth.

Four workmen lay fast asleep in one enclosure, otherwise there was no one to be seen. The man in the little office by the gateway, selling tickets for 10p, had no leaflets, no information and could tell me nothing. And so I wandered through the streets and buildings having no idea of when it was built, nor by whom or why, nor of when it was abandoned or why. Though tourists had come when the Shah was in power, now that Iran was so isolated from contact with the rest of the world Arg had been abandoned again. It felt like stumbling alone into some ancient site long lost to outsiders: Petra, Tikal, Dunhuang.

Later I discovered that arg meant citadel and that this one – though much of what remained dated from the Safavid period of the sixteenth century – was originally built in the tenth century on one of the invasion routes into Persia, sited on an oasis at the edge of the dreaded salt desert. Maybe it was depopulated at the time of one of the Afghan attacks on it, maybe it was just left to fall down like so many Persian towns and villages whose houses have 'domed roofs made of sun-dried bricks. These domes are

built with the greatest ingenuity and would be capable of lasting
for years if repaired occasionally, but this the people are too lazy
to do.' With a severe winter or heavy fall of rain they collapse
and 'in the case of the domes of the greater part of a village
falling in, the inhabitants build an entirely new village upon a
site nearby.'

'This is the direct drug route from Pakistan' they said, so that
was why, on the return journey from Bam to Kerman, everyone
was turned out of the bus and searched. In an old roadside
watchtower, warmed by a charcoal brazier, a uniformed black-
hooded woman emptied my bags, my pockets and moneybelt, riffling through my address book and turning credit cards
round and round and upside-down, like a monkey investigating
unfamiliar booty. . . .

'Arabic and the Koran I teach' said the young night watchman
at the hotel desk in Kerman. 'There is nothing else to teach.
From seven thirty in the morning to four. For that I am paid
eighty-five thousand rials a month. Rials not toman. Then I go
home and sleep till eight or nine. For the house I pay three
thousand rials a month. Then at ten I am here in hotel. Till six
thirty. For this thirty thousand rials. My father dead. I must pay
all money my mother needs. It is good I have no sisters.'

Currency in Iran seemed designed to trip the unwary foreigner.
Bank notes were in rials but everybody spoke in tomans, worth
only one-tenth: rather in the way that Frenchmen of a certain
age, when switching from the price of wine and steak to that of
houses and yachts convert automatically back into old francs.
Though banks also quoted sterling rates for rials – two thousand
five hundred to the pound – they were not interested in the
slightest in changing pounds, nor even German marks or Swiss
francs, or anything in travellers' cheques. Only dollars and only
cash, so I travelled with a loaded moneybelt.

The man who came into the hotel at half-past five in the
morning to collect a list of the guests also needed two jobs. 'List
for police' the night watchman said. 'He gets one from all five
hotels of Kerman early in morning. We give him five hundred
rials.'

At six a.m. the bus left for Yazd. Kerman had been miserable.
Even the Zoroastrians had left.

*

'Questionnaire from the police' said the hotel manager in Yazd. 'Where have you come from?'

'Kerman.'

'Where are you going to?'

'Shiraz.'

'How old are you?'

'Sixty-two.'

'What is your religion?'

I hesitated. If I said 'Christian' he would presume it dominated my life as Islam did his. It would not occur to him that State and Church could be separated, that Jesus had said 'Render therefore unto Caesar the things which be Caesar's and unto God the things which be God's.'

'Not really anything in particular, sort of agnostic, tolerant' I tried.

He snapped. 'The police always want to know your religion. Usually it's the first question they ask.'

'Christian' I said.

'Why are you alone?'

'I always travel alone.' A quizzical raising of the eyebrows. 'I'm a widow' I tried, though that had little relevance to my presence alone at his desk.

He continued reading the questionnaire. 'What are you doing here?'

'Looking at the embroidery.'

'Why have you come to Yazd?'

'Because of the Zoroastrians.'

'How did you get a visa?'

'I applied for it.'

'Who from?'

'The Iranian consulate in London.'

'Do you speak Farsi?'

'No.'

'Are you in touch with the British Embassy?'

'Yes.'

'Any other embassy?'

'No.'

'Do you know anyone in Yazd?'

'No.'

'Have you had any problems?'

'No, on the contrary. People have been very kind. Really helpful' I enthused 'very sweet, totally honest.' I stopped there and resisted adding that it wasn't at all what I had expected. Pity about the politicians and religious fanatics.

'You have seen this?' he asked and pushed towards me an official leaflet. It told women how they must dress and a drawing showed the only acceptable alternative to a chador. A roundish figure, like a Russian doll, was enveloped in a black hood, ankle-length coat with padded shoulders, trousers and dumpy shoes. All dark colours, it said. And to be worn everywhere outside the privacy of the home. It might have proved a better choice now that I was out of the sticks.

The large portrait of Sir Dinsham Marockjee Petit Baronet – an obese figure in fine Indian clothing, benefactor, with his father, of the Zoroastrian community of Yazd – hung on the wall of the temple. Beside it was a small fairground print of a hirsute Zarathustra with kitsch halo and white robes, pointing one finger up to God, and then a picture of the fire temple in Baku, a domed building full of flames with fire belching from its four corner chimneys. I asked whether it still stood. The guide droned on, ignoring all interruption. 'This holy fire has been burning for fifteen hundred and twenty-one years, kept alight by priests. Zarathustra was born six thousand years ago and we have fifty thousand followers. When we pray we must stand in sunlight, or moonlight and starlight. If we can't see the sun or the moon or stars we must stand under an electric lamp or by a fire.' They used, of course, to site their fire temples over natural vents where petroleum gas escaped. To insistent questioning about small animals on Zoroastrian embroidery he replied only: 'Zoroastrians do not kill sheep and not hen birds.'

Visits to the homes of some of the fifty thousand followers, who actually seemed a rather small community, were equally unrewarding. From narrow streets between high adobe walls heavy wooden doors led into a maze of passageways with pebble floors, here and there domed and open to the sky, in other places leading into large empty rooms. Towers above the roofs caught the passing breezes in the intense heat of summer and filtered them down to cool the rooms below. Homes at the end of these passageways would be furnished with armchairs, sofas, low coffee tables and pictures of Zarathustra on the walls. The women wore headscarves, short dresses over knickerbockers that came to just below the knee, woolly stockings and slippers. There was no sign of animals on their clothing though they still dressed in the alternating pink and green they used to embroider on. 'I used to embroider animals like that' one old woman said 'but not any more. I don't know what they meant.' They were all busy knitting jumpers from English patterns in *Woman's Own*.

Dr Arrish had greatly admired Saddam Hussein: he was honest, had the courage to stand by his own convictions against the rest of the world. Now another Iranian, staying at the same Yazd hotel – he spoke German and was a specialist in analysing data from satellites – was discussing Saddam's disastrous effect on the ecology of the Gulf. A pity the United Nations hadn't bumped him off, he thought, and expressed the fervent hope that someone might do so soon. As for our revolution it was only since then that women were covered up in all these dark clothes – 'before our women were like Germany and England.' He complimented me on the small bits of anatomy visible outside my chador and invited me to join him later in room twenty-one. I reverted to the conversation in hand. Schoolgirls at a bus stop, I suggested, might look like a gathering of rooks, but at least they were going to school. Yes, the revolution had reduced illiteracy, from seventy-five to thirty per cent. And most of those people were in rural areas. No, he knew nothing of Arg. He was most familiar with the area around the port of Bandar Abbas where he had worked. Did he perhaps know something of a tribe of red-masked women from somewhere in that region? I'd been longing to see them ever since Ugo had shown me photographs. The masks were unlike those of Muslim women and were eerily pagan. Possibly such a tribe would also wear pagan amulets or embroider them on their clothes, but I had been unable to locate them. Yes, he knew them. They were from the desert near Minab. My visa hardly allowed me time to backtrack and I was already booked on the night bus to Shiraz. 'Why not fly? There are a couple of flights a week from Shiraz.'

Shiraz

The air ticket was priced in rials and not in toman – that much was certain. Conversions into dollars: rials into dollars, toman into dollars – both into sterling – sterling into dollars, every acrobatic twist brought the same result. Old admonishments, such as 'calculators never make mistakes, only the fools who use them', resurfaced. In the end, the total fare for the flights from Shiraz south to Bandar Abbas on the coast of the Persian Gulf and from Bandar Abbas north to Isfahan – approximately the distance from Manchester to Paris and Paris to Edinburgh – added up to £5.32 or $9.43. And that indeed was what it cost.

It would in any case be a relief to escape from the interminable hours journeying on buses through a desert landscape, spiced only by the telegraph poles and pylons and by the odd round-abouts, big dippers and giant wheels that inexplicably appeared in the middle of nowhere, as if half the country were a fairground site; from night buses on which I was the only woman and the only foreigner; from breaks for food and rest at roadside pull-ins that neither expected nor catered for a woman.

Meanwhile the night bus from Yazd was scheduled to arrive in Shiraz at four in the morning at a modern bus station where passengers could wait until the town awoke. In fact, it arrived two hours early in a terminus that clearly attracted, and was designed to exclude, the local riff-raff and thus was empty and firmly padlocked. Envisaging the plight of the genuine traveller the company had installed a small kiosk at the exit of the bus station on the edge of the highway where a man, on duty twenty-four hours a day, sold taxi vouchers. These, bought at a reasonable rate, obliged the taxi driver to take you to the centre of town. There, of course, he was perfectly entitled to drop you. Which he did.

The kitchen knife I always carry prised off the wooden slats closing the glass doors of what seemed to be the only hotel in town. At the noise this created the night watchman hove into view shouting obscenities, but at least he returned the knife.

With extraordinary luck I found a lit door a few hundred metres on. The next day when I discovered the paucity of hotel accommodation in Shiraz (they have all been taken for student accommodation I was told), I realized even more what amazing luck it had been. I banged on the glass door of this next hotel and was despatched with gestures clear in any language. Then a portly businessman, with smart luggage bearing labels from the Gulf, who had obviously also just arrived, insisted they open up.

'We have no room.'

'I am happy to sleep on the floor, anywhere except in the street at three in the morning.' There was an indisputable feeling that the men on duty were afraid, that I disconcerted them in some way.

'Man? Where's your man?'

'No man.'

They argued among themselves and then seemed to relent. They showed me to a warm room which had breadcrumbs and bits of food in the bed and pubic hair in the soap, but for which I was most grateful.

'In our coming and going what is the use?
And of the woof of our lifetime where is the warp?'

Shiraz, a city of roses and nightingales and Omar Khayyám, offered only orange trees and rooks, and bookshops that yielded one single copy of *The Rubáiyát*, published eighteen years previously 'On the 25th Anniversary of the Glorious Reign of H.I.M. Mohammad-Reza Shah Pahlavi, on the occasion of the 2500th Anniversary of Establishment of Iranian Empire by Cyrus The Great'. Its price in pennies embossed on the cover in gold was still unchanged.

Shiraz was the first Iranian city I had seen and it appeared vaguely cosmopolitan. Bookshops – albeit stocked only with the Koran, Farsi novels in recycled softback covers like the French ones of early postwar years, English language aids and no international literature – did at least exist. No foreign newspapers or magazines were available anywhere. The buildings carried hoardings with huge cinema posters advertising films, though the female stars all wore headscarves, a particular aspect of censorship that must preclude all foreign films being shown in Iran.

'Down With America' was emblazoned on a large banner hung across the foyer of a smart hotel that could have been a Sheraton. 'Islamic Revolution is Everlasting as a Volcano' proclaimed another in the street.

A vast bazaar – whose dark side alleys, lit by shafts of light from gaps in the roof, were crowded with dealers warming themselves round burning cardboard boxes in open braziers – was piled with wondrous carpets. The people who whispered *'feranghi'* as I walked past were dressed in more Western styles than in the south. The men all wore cheap trousers creased around the crotch and shabby anoraks, never a turban or shalwar kameez and never a tie or suit. More women were to be seen in long coats and enveloping scarves in place of the chador, though there were gypsies wearing their chadors with élan, thrown over long flouncy frilly skirts in brilliant colours.

There was no sign of any embroidery or of any amulets except for the talismanic fertility goddesses and ibexes from the first millennium BC displayed in the city museum. But no triangles.

A short bus ride away on the sunlit plain lay Persepolis, Darius's magnificent ceremonial capital, through which successive empires had passed. Alexander, and the Brits, had been and gone, their military and administrative strength visible in what they had destroyed or left behind. The glorious entranceway of Xerxes, carved with kings and still standing after nearly two thousand five hundred years, bore graffiti that was a legacy of the British Empire.

39th K.G.O. Central India Horse

was carved deep into the golden stone. And:

Lt Col Malcolm J Meade
H.B.M. Consul General 1898
& Mrs Meade

At the airport departure hour came and went, nobody moved. No announcements seemed to have been made. A small fellow with receding hair approached me: 'The plane's an hour late, which means at least two.'

'Oh my God, it'll be the same as in Shiraz, wandering the streets at two in the morning looking for somewhere to stay.'

'Don't worry. I belong to a business consortium in Dubai. We have property in Bandar Abbas, plenty of rooms. We can offer you a room for the night.'

I thanked him gratefully and chatted about red-masked tribal women. 'Oh yes. In the market at Minab. Thursday morning. Tomorrow.' I couldn't believe my luck. Usually everything happened last Tuesday. 'My friend here will be staying with us and is going into town early in the morning. He can take you to the bus station for the bus to Minab.' He introduced us and I held out my hand. There was a ghastly moment as I remembered Dr Arrish saying: 'You'll find in Iran we don't shake hands.' They do, of course they do, but not with a woman. I withdrew my hand.

At Bandar Abbas the few people on the plane cleared quickly, met by friends, leaving the fellow from Dubai and me alone. He grabbed a taxi and we got in. 'Where's your friend?' I asked.

'I lied about him. I thought you wouldn't come with me otherwise.' The car drove down dark side streets and winding alleys, past rubbish tips and piles of sand.

'Silly idiot, stupid fool, don't you ever learn? Aren't you old enough to have some sense?' I castigated myself under my breath and was aware that my moneybelt felt extraordinarily full of dollar notes.

At the end of the last dark alleyway we came to a big iron gate in a high wall. My 'friend', Manucher from Dubai, leapt out and rang the bell. 'This is the house of my brother-in-law, Majeed.' Lights came on, a bell clicked, the door opened and a young man in pyjamas stood there. The two embraced. I felt greatly relieved. We drove into the compound, the young man in pyjamas went into the house and shouted up the stairs. 'Atefeh, we have a guest and it's a woman.'

Bandar Abbas

'Lockerbie was us, the people around Bandar Abbas. It was for the Iranian airbus. Atefeh's mother was killed on it, so were lots of others from round here. Mothers going to see their sons in Dubai, ordinary families.'

'She was young and beautiful' Atefeh quietly whispered. 'We got her body from the sea. They said it was a mistake.'

'We never believed that' continued Manucher. 'We never believed it was an accident. We warned the Americans and your Consul General in Dubai that there'd be a bomb on an American plane within two weeks, told him we would take our revenge. And we did. At Lockerbie.'

This was a claim I was to hear over and over again. And if I asked why they hated the Americans so, the answer was always the airbus. Plus the fact that they had ordered and paid for new aircraft – at the moment Iran Air had only twenty-three to cover all its domestic and international operations – and the Americans had neither delivered their planes nor given them their money back. 'Animals' said one man. 'But we're told to hate the American government, not the American people' said another.

Atefeh's breakfast table was reassuring: a tin of Ovaltine, a packet of Anchor butter. The fitted kitchen with its table and three fridges could have come from any Western magazine. It was unlike any others I had seen recently and was a world away from Gul Mohammed's in Turbat. It was a wealthy home with air conditioners everywhere – in use for eight months of the year – but apart from the kitchen and two television sets there was little furniture. We slept and ate on the floor. In traditional style each large room was covered with carpets and the walls lined with cushions. When relations came – no friends ever did – they sat around leaning on the cushions and a large plastic cloth for food would be placed on the carpet before them.

Their relations came in droves to meet me and take tea, nougat and oranges. They invited me back to their homes in equal droves. Gone were the kebabs, skinny chicken legs and plain rice; instead old Persian dishes – *faisanjan*, bowls of fresh herbs, chicken stuffed with prunes and apricots, hot milk with cardamom and doughnuts – were set before me. And on one occasion illicit alcohol which, as always, meant whisky. The warmth of their hospitality made a mockery of the sour international relationships promoted officially with such fervour.

'I believe in freedom for the people in everything' said Atefeh, inclining her shrouded black head. 'Since the revolution things have changed. But I don't mind the chador. It's practical, though we used to wear pretty dresses like Paris ones. Before the revolution I was studying chemical engineering at university – that's how I speak English. Under the Shah all university education was in English. Then at the revolution they closed down the universities for two years and when they opened them again all the teaching was in Farsi. It's only now that schools are beginning to teach English again. Also we now have drinking water, electricity. But nothing works and nothing's cleaned. We know it's better in Dubai, so people live there when they can get away. They have everything, Philippino servants, everything. And it's all clean and it all works.'

The routine of the household continued around me. Majeed was to be seen ironing his shirts on the floor. The three children came and went from school. It was a disparate family, which traced its origins to the countries round the Indian Ocean rather than Iran: Majeed looked Indian, the twelve-year-old boy African, the six-year-old European – and was teased at school for his thin lips – and the little girl, like Atefeh, classic Persian.

They insisted I stay and kept finding reasons to detain me, delighting in episodes they took for granted but which were novel for me. Early one morning we woke to find the waste ground in front of their house full of men. 'Shia fundamentalists' said Atefeh.

Four huge black cauldrons had been set over fires of wood and the men stirred the steaming food for hours. 'It's a funeral' said Majeed. 'Anyone, especially the poor, can come and eat.' A herd of goats wandered through, then came in by the gate inadvertently left open and ate Atefeh's roses. By lunchtime the men, cauldrons and goats had all vanished.

*

The small town of Minab, dominated by a ruined fort, was once a more important trading place than Bandar Abbas but its isolation from the tentacles of government had led to its decline in favour of the more accessible port: as there were no bridges over the rivers between the two it was often impossible to collect any taxes, so Minab was left to its own devices. The people who settled there were dark-skinned, like many along this coast of the Indian Ocean, and had been brought as slaves from Africa.

The Thursday morning market brings the desert women from kilometres around into the small town. No doubt they arrive before dawn, but the bus from Bandar Abbas waited an hour beyond departure time to fill up before leaving, so that it was mid-morning before it arrived and the dogs were already skulking into the shade. In the narrow lanes between the stalls, in the open spaces around the edge of the bazaar, against the railings and walls separating market areas sat the red-masked women, wrapped in black chadors. They sat behind the baskets and brushes they had made from the date palms of their oases, behind the bowls of henna they had ground, behind the braids they had woven from gold and cotton threads bought at the same market on some earlier occasion. They looked utterly alien. Creatures from another planet. Their masks were a brilliant scarlet with a central ridge that protruded several centimetres in front of their nose. Nothing of their face was visible. The slit for their eyes was like the slit in a red pillarbox. Their heads turned and followed me.

'I can't understand what they say' said Atefeh. 'They come from the desert round Sirik.'

It was impossible to see whether the dresses under their chadors were embroidered, though they probably were: a man in the bazaar sold threads in the six colours of Makran, but couldn't say who used them. He tried to give me some. The unmasked local women wore bonnets embroidered in gold and trousers with gold braid. One of the women lowered her chador to show me the bonnet underneath and then tried to give it to me, finally accepting the meagre price of a new one in exchange. Another man sold at his stall the gold threads the women wove into braids to sew on to the bottom of their satin trousers. The gold was Japanese. All the fabrics sold in the bazaar were Japanese, as they had been in Makran. All the plain black stuffs, all the dull printed

A woman wearing the Kohistani helmet. Her son has the amulet on his chest. Dasu, Indus Kohistan.

Homesteads clinging on to fractured hillsides above the Indus. Indus Kohistan.

The courtyard of a Baluchi family home, showing the shelter where the women cook. Kalatuk, Makran.

Opposite: A girl in traditional embroidered dress. Piderak, Makran.

Wooden boats being built by hand on the beach. Gwadar, Makran. (DR GIONATA RIZZI)

Itinerant firewood
vendors. Makran.
(ANDERSON BAKEWELL)

A mountain and deser
scene between Turbat
Gwadar, Makran.
(PROF. UGO FABIETTI)

The embroidery teache
with a needle and threa
through her nose. Man
Makran.

The home of semi-nomadic
Baluchi rugmakers. Mand,
Makran.

Mujahedin in embroidered shirts
and caps hang up their
Kalashnikovs to play bridge.
Kandahar, Afghanistan.

The bazaar at Sher Khabat.
Afghanistan.

Smugglers silhouetted at dawn.
Bandar Abbas beach, S. Iran.

Old basketmaker. Kooptcl
village, S. Iran.

Kurdish woman making
bread. Zakho, N.Iraq.

Yezidi woman.
N. Iraq.

Yezidi fire temples near
Sharnuk. N. Iraq.

Rizvaniye mosque and its pool of sacred carp. Urfa, Anatolia.

A corn amulet tied with rags, hung over a doorway Harran, Anatolia.

stuffs for chadors, all the shiny, stripy, satiny polyester stuffs, all the sparkly stuffs, everything the women used to make their costume throughout Baluchistan and southern Iran was Japanese.

I glanced around but saw only dealers and masked women. No Japanese market researchers.

The agricultural research station, under the shadow of the fort and only about a kilometre and a half from the hustle of the bazaar, was an ordered oasis of green calm. A long dusty drive led from the entrance gates to a small unprepossessing building from where the station was administered. Posters of roots, stems, buds, stamens, blossoms and fruit lined its walls.

Atefeh's cousin, an agricultural engineer working there, lived in a simple house separated from her office by a low fence and a bed of unkempt grass. She welcomed us first with lunch, laying a plastic cloth on the carpet and bringing in dishes of meats and rice, bowls of leaves, and sweets made of dates and walnuts. Huge round black dates lay in a sticky honey that comes from the palm, and were to be dipped into sesame paste.

'We have sixty varieties of date here' she enthused, as we walked along the ruts between stocky palms, 'and it takes us twelve years to find out which is the best variety for any area.' Other experiments were being tried too: hybrids between grapefruit or pomelos and different types of tangerine. We walked past laden trees while a man shook fruit down for us to taste. 'These are our Tangelos. This is Orlando.' Then there was Miniola and Wikiwa, some loose skinned, some tighter, some pulpy, some dry, most rather tasteless. 'We've been told to try avocado too.'

'What's that?' asked Atefeh.

'I don't really know, but it's a kind of fruit. We've been told it could grow well in Iran.'

The next day Majeed organized a family outing to Shakhru, a small village to the west of Bandar Abbas. He had cousins there and, though he had lost touch with them, there had recently been a marriage in the family and he felt the ceremony of congratulating the bride would interest me. So we all, four adults and three children, piled into their old bull-nosed car and set off.

As we passed gateways in the village there were glimpses of women in courtyards washing dishes, making braid. There were old men wearing white turbans and green sarongs – 'that's how they dress here' – and women in indigo masks, huge loads of firewood balanced on their head. There was even an old lady whose shift bore the Afghan amulet pattern embroidered in gold over her stomach. She didn't know whether it had any meaning, it was just an old pattern they had always used. It was to be the only place in Iran that I found the amulet.

We drove round and round the village. Majeed had forgotten his cousin's name and didn't know where their home was. It was a widely scattered village, an expanse of sand and dust with the odd house here and there. In the courtyard of one house sat another wedding party, where an old man played a saroz. The bride stood in her finery in a room decorated as for Christmas, in the company of several women and a small boy – no doubt to ensure she produced sons – but there was no sign of the husband. Though we were invited to join in the festivities, she wasn't the right bride. We continued circuiting the village.

An hour or so later we picnicked off the bonnet of the car on tinned tuna, bread and water. 'Majeed is a bit cross' said Atefeh, though he showed no sign of it. It struck me that a Western family would have been at each others' throats by now, but they remained placidly good-tempered. We finished the picnic, throwing cans and plastic bags all over the place. I suggested we might put all the rubbish in a bag to save it littering the countryside, and leave just the food for the animals. They agreed, but obviously saw no reason why, and we drove away leaving behind a large plastic bag full of sharp tins for the next goat to find.

During the drive back, Farhad, the six-year-old, became very agitated and pointed to my mouth. 'What's the matter?'

'You've got lipstick on' Atefeh explained.

'The pick-up truck that's just gone by is the same as the ones the Islamic Guards use.'

'Who are they?'

'They drive round towns and they're always in the bazaars looking for women who break Islamic law.'

'What law?'

'You mustn't show any hair or wear any make-up and men mustn't wear short sleeves or shave. For women the punishment if you're caught is a fine of 200,000 rials, a day shackled in prison and forty lashes of the whip. They let you off the whip if you're pregnant.'

When I returned to London I remarked to the man in the Foreign Office that the only advice they had given me for travelling in Iran was to take dollars in cash, but they hadn't said anything about dress. 'You didn't warn me that for wearing a bit of lipstick or showing a strand of hair you get forty lashes of the whip.'

'We thought it was seventy-two' he said.

Qeshm

'Kesh, my island. Come tomorrow, I will take you to Kesh, my island. Come at six.'

In the half-light of dawn the sands glistened, mirroring the dark shapes of people pressing close to the sea's edge where hundreds of small launches bobbed. In the silver space of sea and strand the people looked tiny, like puppets from a Lowry painting. They clustered around high wheeled trolleys that were just small railed wooden platforms balanced a metre or so above the sand on spindly legs. The beach thronged with these rickety trolleys and with surging figures that appeared only more ghost-like as we walked towards them. 'Smugglers' said Hussein.

Qeshm Island was a centre for smuggling. Set in the Strait of Hormuz just opposite Dubai it was a paradise for contraband. Not dope or alcohol but mundane things like shoes, Japanese fabrics and television sets, deodorants, cigarettes. The authorities knew about it but could do nothing and people came huge distances to go over to the island before sunrise and catch the traders' night pickings.

Hussein – one of Atefeh's relatives – had left his shop for the day. 'Who's looking after it?' I asked.

'Anyone. Only me. Brother in Sweden scientist in practical tropics. Any human work here is only man, no woman.' He had brought two dictionaries, one Persian/English, the other English/Persian and a large bag of apples. He was a neat man with a bristly black moustache and white socks that made him look like a pedantic French schoolmaster.

We were hoisted up on to one of the trolleys by several strong bare arms and then trundled into the sea to the waiting launches. These were simple grey moulded fibreglass hulls, sunk at the stern by an outboard motor, bows riding high. Half a dozen of us clambered in and sat in rows. The skipper took the helm at the back while the navigator, an oilskin bonnet tied under his chin, perched in the front, moving from side to side to balance the boat as we kept changing tack in the choppy seas. Sitting behind us three traders from Azerbaijan clutched large plastic bags. In the next boat several red-masked women stared our way.

A low line of trading stalls, their metal doors rolled up, edged the beach at Dargehon on Qeshm Island. As we arrived some people were already leaving with their loot – a turbaned man bent low passed us pushing a trolley back out to sea. On it a very fat businessman sat regally, his shrouded wife and piles of television sets around him. Hussein and I were bustled on to a trolley and wheeled to the beach by a young boy with shorn black hair, clear blue eyes and immensely strong arms. He was fourteen years old and had come from a village north of Zahedan, near the Afghan border, to do this job. 'Men of Kesh my island never do this work. No for gentlemen.' Though we were a considerably lighter load than the businessman Mohammed's bare feet splayed deep into the wet grey sand as he pushed with all his strength. He cleared us over steel cables and around anchors. His toes squelched through a muddy jetsam of rusty tins, broken bottles, bits of old tyres. 'Give him a hundred toman' said Hussein. I gave him much more and said I hoped he would be able to return soon to his village.

Hussein's cousin had recently married. We found her sitting on the carpet bedecked in gold. A bonnet of gold plate embroidery – like the Azute work of Egypt in which small strips of gold are inserted into net and then cut to make patterns of trees, mosques and geometric shapes – was held by gold ornaments under a gauze shawl embroidered with gold. Trousers embroidered with flowers in gold tamboured chain stitch up to the knees were visible below her gold embroidered shift. And it was only nine in the morning. She offered us cardamom-flavoured hot milk and cakes. She was about sixteen. Her husband, Abdullah, had made good in trading in Dubai and drove a new Toyota Cressida, its seats still protected by polythene, a keyring of pink and yellow swansdown dangling from the ignition. He was to drive us round the island. Offers I made of payment were rejected out of hand. We took with us a four-year-old with a snotty nose, Fatima, whose mother had died in childbirth – of high blood pressure, they said – who attached herself to anyone, leaned against them and fell asleep.

The island was a desert, just a few stunted trees in the shape of

mushrooms breaking the monotony. Donkeys were the only sign
of life. Beehive structures marked the site of sweet water wells.
Many people, they told me, suffered from the water-borne
disease that erupts on the skin, breaking the surface so that
worms about a metre long can make their way out. Signposts
indicated not what was there but what it was hoped might be
there one day: Hope General Hospital. International Airport. The
usual daub 'Down with the USA' had faded over the years and
there was no one fervent enough to bother to repaint it. Most of
the people were engaged in smuggling, some in shrimp fishing,
some in shipbuilding. The same handmade clinker wooden boats
were fashioned on the beach at Loft as at Gwadar and Chah
Bahar.

Every remark I made to Hussein met with the response
'What?' as he stiffened like a startled rabbit and rolled the whites
of his eyes. Before he spoke, his mind churned slowly and visibly,
his sensitive hands describing small circles by his forehead. The
English that came out was either simple 'now go we' or complex:
a girl he described as an 'eighteen daughter' as in 'Woman wear
mask. Eighteen daughter no.' And sand he persistently and engag-
ingly referred to as 'seasand dust'. He had had four lessons in
photography and bossed me around, insisting on lining up his
female relatives and his sisters for me to photograph. 'Green
screen. Necessary green screen' he said, trooping them all from
the verandah of their home to a group of scraggy palms nearby.

We drove the full length of the island to Buseidu, a desolate,
windswept place forsaken by God. It had been an outpost of the
Portuguese and then the British Empire. The locals still used
English words like 'tomato', 'glass', 'towel'. Ruined barracks
('Building to sleeping soldier. English soldier' said Hussein), a
mess and captain's house ('Captain Clark. You must know him'
said Hussein), a superimposed Muslim shrine, all lay crumbling
on the bleak tip of the island. A few black stones jutting into the
sea marked the precarious shelter used by the British as a
harbour. British graves, piles of crumbling stone decorated with
green rags chewed by mice, had been desecrated long ago and
the memorial tablet was missing from the cenotaph ('Gone
Tehran Museum' said Hussein.) At the very tip of the island,
where the beaches met in a point, was the metal post of the old
British telegraph line, bent crazily sideways. It was here that the

overhead lines ended and the underwater cable of the Persian Gulf began.

This underwater cable had caused untold trouble. When Sir William O'Shaughnessy had suggested it in 1855 there was considerable debate that it would incur danger from troublesome Arabs and coral reefs and would prove no safer than the land route. By 1858 construction had gone ahead and the telegraph line had reached Malta from Whitehall. From there thirteen hundred kilometres were needed to Alexandria and then sixty-four hundred from Suez to Karachi. By 1867 the stretch from Gwadar to Karachi had been completed and two years later the lines were extended from Gwadar to Jask, eastward along the coast from Qeshm, but they worked badly as the insulators got coated with salt and fine dust. By Derby Day 1872 some British officers, watching for news in the Calcutta telegraph office, had received Reuters' telegram with the name of the winning horse just a few minutes after it had passed the post. After this spectacular event the underwater cable through the Gulf was attacked and pierced by swordfish. Then a whale got its tail caught in it and tangled it up. Now it lay completely forgotten and no one knew what the bent post at the grassy tip of the island was.

Back at Dargehon Hussein insisted I meet the old lady of the family. 'Old Mummy' he said 'meet.'

She was lying on blankets on the floor, frail, blind, ninety years old. She grasped my hand. 'English? England near Sweden. You have been?'

'Yes.'

'Did you see my boy?'

'I'm sorry, I'm sure not. Where is he?'

'At Linköping.'

'That's Saab. Yes, I went there.'

She raised herself on her thin elbow and looked with glazed eyes in the direction of my voice. 'My boy, did you see my boy? Have you seen my boy?' She relaxed her grip on my hand. 'God bless you. Come back to me.' How could she have a son young enough to work in Sweden, I wondered, but he wasn't her son, they said. He was her daughter's son. She had brought him up. There had been problems at the birth and as there was no medical care in Qeshm they had put her daughter on one of the old wooden boats to Bandar Abbas. She died in rough seas.

It was essential, Hussein said, to have coffee at his father's house with his second mother, his sisters and cousins. We drank from tiny cups and ate halwa, sticky sesame and date juice. Darkness was falling rapidly and when we reached the beach it was almost deserted. A few plover, a couple of trollies, some boxes waiting to be loaded remained, otherwise the sands were empty. In the sea only three boats waited to leave. We were wheeled out in a trolley but Hussein moved from one boat to the next ('Too heavy. Old motor.') until he seemed satisfied by the third. 'New motor. No heavy.' There was also no captain and as we sat waiting darkness drew in completely until we could see almost nothing and hear only the lap of the water. The captain – a black-skinned Baluch with a white turban wrapped across his nose – was finally wheeled out with dozens of boxes marked 'Glass. Fragile. Made in Indonesia.', which were hurled with clinking noises into the bottom of the boat. We set off into the pitch black with no light, not even a torch, and no lifejackets. The lookout crouched up in the bows peering into the darkness and raising his hand to indicate left or right if he spotted some obstacle. Lit boats passed close by, dark moored ones were skirted, harbour lights flickered a long way off on the horizon. Hussein waved towards them. 'This port. Full of sheep.'

Isfahan

'Your amulet' said Majeed, as the plane was about to take off seven hours late and the passengers were being shooed through a narrow gap between blank walls where friendly uniformed staff should have stood, 'the women here hang them on cradles to keep away the evil eye. An old woman told me.'

'Which women do? Which tribe? Embroidered or what?' I shouted, pushed along with the crowds.

'All women' Majeed smilingly called, waving his last goodbyes. It was a tantalizing farewell. The amulet belonged to isolated regions where pagan beliefs still lingered, to forgotten islands where men still waded ashore barefoot and to desert oases where women masked their faces in stiff red cloth: it would never be found in Isfahan, a civilized city of exquisite turquoise dedicated to the praise of Islam.

The flagstoned floors of the royal mosque were dusted with snow and discarded builders' rags lay scrumpled on them in dirty white heaps, like sleeping people in an Indian railway station. There was no one there. No one walked under the turquoise domes, starred with gold and azure flowers and trailing Chinese clouds. Only one woman in black bent to pray, her shoes on the ground beside her. Huge alabaster bowls glowed translucent in the evening sun. A soft murmur was all that remained of the cacophony of the nearby bazaar where cavernous grey arcades reverberated to the noise of the coppersmiths sitting crouched on low stools around brazier fires, beating and pounding vast copper bowls with mallets and hammers.

The tomato ketchup was housed in red plastic teddy bears with white hats, one on each table of the coffee shop of the Shah Abbas Hotel, once a caravanserai, then converted to a fabulously ornate hotel encrusted with gold where flunkeys in old Persian costume now greeted unstylish customers in anoraks and trainers. Next to the ketchup was a dirty green napkin and on this the liveried waiter placed my coffee: a spoonful of Nescafé in the bottom of a cup, a silver jug of not terribly hot water and another silver jug of milk. Two other Europeans were there, the only ones – bar my colleagues in Makran and a young German engineer at Bandar Abbas airport who had been servicing some machinery – that I was to see between Quetta and Istanbul. They were two Dutchmen cycling round the world: 'We just want to get home'.

A portrait of the Ayatollah scowled down at us and a huge banner across the front of the hotel announced the 'International Conference on Physical Planning (National and Regional)'. Its days as a caravanserai would have been very different. These lodgings for itinerant traders, each one day's camel ride apart, offered security in a world of plundered wealth. Travellers had lodgings for themselves and their animals free of charge if they stayed for three days and their goods reimbursed if they were stolen. Accommodation was within a fortified enclosure which sheltered a mosque, baths, even a library and in some cases wandering musicians. The walls surrounding the courtyard were galleried with small individual domed rooms, usually with a fireplace, where the traveller rested while his camels and donkeys were safeguarded in the courtyard below or in stabling outside. Such rooms around a courtyard of course lend themselves splendidly to hotel use by the modern traveller and many of those Seljuk constructions of the twelfth and thirteenth centuries that have not fallen into ruin, together with later examples, have been so converted. The Shah Abbas Hotel, named after the man who ruled Isfahan at the end of the sixteenth and beginning of the seventeenth centuries and was responsible for most of its magnificent buildings, is one.

The arched stone bridge that Shah Abbas had built across the river was beautiful. It linked the celestially tiled city to the Armenian quarter, where an old woman held bunches of clanking keys to Byzantine churches. Small, dark, domed and alcoved, they were rich with gold and colour, with tile and paint in a dense jigsaw of European and Safavid Persian patterns: cypress trees, animals, birds, flowers, and stories from the Bible.

But mostly Isfahan was a city of nougat. Packets of it were everywhere. The boxes were highly coloured and depicted scenes from *The Thousand and One Nights*: fair maidens with long silken locks sitting by lucent pools; rose arbours and orange groves;

wild white stallions whose eddying manes whirled like Turkish marbling into swoops of wailing women in flowing black raiment ('One of our legends of death' the nougat salesman said). But the best was one brand whose nougat was marketed in a plain white box decorated only with the face of a particularly surly, scowling religious fanatic surrounded by excited revolutionary Arabic calligraphy.

At the bus station a video of *The Wizard of Oz* in English intrigued a few uncomprehending potential passengers, but most sat around gloomily ignoring it. The bus for Tabriz was very late. ('Only twelve hours on a night bus' the Dutchmen had said. 'Will be fine for you.') When the bus finally left, my travelling companion was not a woman, nor an old man, nor a boy, nor an empty seat, but a good-looking young man with red hair and freckles.

Tabriz

Bahram was a computer student who spoke no English but carried with him a manual, *Telecommunications Techniques*, in which he had scribbled Farsi translations in the margin against the American text, as directed by his tutor. Though he was, in fact, Iranian, his red hair, fair skin and freckles had misled the bus booking clerk into thinking he was a foreigner and thus presented a solution to the perennial problem of who to seat next to me.

It was night when the bus set off, so it was by the dim red light over the aisle that Bahram flicked through his marginal notes in order to make conversation. My travelling bag, left on the floor because it was wet, though it was small enough to put up on the rack, clearly preoccupied him for a while. He thumbed through his manual, then, triumphant, indicated the bag and the luggage rack. 'Superimpose?' he asked. As he warmed to this new concept of communication and scrabbled endlessly through his digital jargon I waited patiently, smile fixed, hoping his remarks would be clear. 'Single entry?' he enquired, addressing the usual puzzle of my lack of a man.

After a brief stop for supper – yet again rice, kebabs and tea – the bus resumed, heading for open country. It was customary on such occasions, and also on plane flights, to say a prayer to Allah, everyone chanting it out loud. This done, Bahram fished out his manual again, then turned to me. 'Good exit' he explained.

The bus was stationary in a snow-covered landscape when I woke. We seemed to have stopped near a wood, the first I had seen. Two hours later I woke again and the view was the same. A further few hours and dawn had broken to reveal that what I thought were trees were only the usual fissures in the rock face and that the bus was still in the same place. Seeing that I had woken, Bahram addressed me with some agitation. 'Bus connect, contact, more bus entry, lorry entry, all lorries, buses connect contact, you sleeping' – his voice rose to a crescendo with excitement – 'buses, lorries all connect contact. You just sleeping.' We were at the tag end of a multiple pile-up.

Once we were moving again the bus continued along the dreary endless plateau fringed by low mountain ranges which occasionally closed in on the edge of the road with low cliffs of sharp rock. The bus juddered to a halt at nine for breakfast in some roadside café. Bread and tea. Whereas in Makran tea was served as a thick milky sugary mass, in Iran it was black and lumps of sugar were handed round separately. These were held between the teeth and the tea siphoned through them. I had persistently put the lumps of sugar into the tea and stirred them with a pen, having left my teaspoon on the train in the dim light of dawn when getting off at Zahedan. Two women watched me intently. 'We are from Turkmenchay' they said. 'British used to be in our country fifty years ago. Also stirred tea with pen.'

'Where's Turkmenchay?' I asked.

'Satellite' said Bahram, checking in his manual.

We trundled on past the old British telegraph line. Curious because of its link to the West, I observed it carefully. I noted whether the posts were to the right or the left of the road and therefore accorded with the old maps or not. I asked Bahram about them, but it was like talking to a Hare Krishna convert and I got only dogma. 'Telecommunications conversion. Unisphere.'

After twenty-two hours on the bus, the passengers, famished and thirsty, were offloaded in Tabriz into slush and snow at five in the evening instead of seven in the morning. No one complained, no one even seemed to comment. It had been much the same when the flight to Isfahan from Bandar Abbas had arrived eighteen hours late, having been diverted to Tehran. Here we spent the night sleeping on wooden seats, babies and toddlers without milk or food. No one said anything. 'Stoic' I commented to an Iranian newly arrived from London.

'Just apathetic idiots' he said. 'No wonder they were easily led astray by revolutionaries.'

Tabriz was Bahram's home town. But instead of joining his family, he first installed me in a cheap hotel on a noisy street corner, where the men at the reception desk counted on abacuses, and then placed me in a restaurant serving kebabs, rice and tea.

The town was deep in snow, the ditch between pavement and road that is normal in Iranian towns now presenting a worse hazard than in Kerman to those immersed in chadors. I fell down to my waist in one on the way to the bazaar. Here too the men counted on abacuses. As the nearest bazaar town to the Kurdish territory of Iran, Tabriz might have examples of their textiles and perhaps amuletic embroideries of the kind the Kurds in Iran make. I searched among the stalls. But there were only canvas-work kits of black swans on a moonlit lake and the Quorn in Full Cry. And knitted socks.

'How can I improve?' the English teacher asked, approaching me in the street. 'What can I need? Here *Time* and *Newsweek* are forbidden. No foreign newspapers or reviews. No films. Only BBC World Service. There must be more.'

The bus for the Turkish border left Tabriz at midday. The tramped snow at the bus station had turned to filthy black slush. People milled around though few were journeying north. 'Are you Turkish?' an Indian man asked.

Suddenly in the crowd I saw a head of red hair. There was Bahram clutching a box of nougat in one hand and an old-fashioned English phrasebook in the other. 'Take care of her' he said in Farsi to the Indian. 'More than your wife.' As the bus pulled away he rubbed GOOD DAY! on the grime-encrusted window.

The Indian surgeon was a large, ungainly man and lay sprawled across two seats, as the bus staff had insisted his wife sit next to me. 'This is where we live' she said, as the bus stopped at a small town a few hours north of Tabriz. 'We had to go back south into Tabriz yesterday and stay the night to catch the bus. We've got to go to Istanbul to take some exams. It's because we're foreigners working here – I'm a paediatrician. They've given us an exit visa for seven days and we've had to leave all our stuff behind.

'Bushan thought it would be interesting to work here, but we had no idea it would be like this. We've got a contract for two years so we can't escape. My mother's looking after my little boy in Delhi and I miss him. He's only two. I hate it here. The Islamic Guards tried to arrest me because of my *bindi*, you know that red spot we have on our forehead. I made a fuss and explained it was a custom of our country. They let me go in the end.

'And nobody works. They come into the hospital late in the morning and start by having breakfast. They make themselves tea and bread. Then they stop at lunchtime and do the same, more tea, only rice this time, and again in the afternoon, more tea and bread. Then they go home early. Nobody can do anything about it. I never have enough help, nurses and so on. And they've got no equipment or medicines. Just think too how stupid to have to go to Istanbul to take an exam. It's only a day but we have to allow three days to get there because of the buses, and then three days back. What a waste of our time, especially my husband's. Think what operations he could be doing.'

It was dark by the time we reached the small frontier town which was the end of the line for the bus. In the café, where we inevitably stopped for tea, a Pakistani doctor was waiting to cross into Turkey. 'Can I tag on? I didn't want to go over alone at night and thought I'd try to stop here. Got to go to Istanbul to take an exam.' He chatted guardedly to Bushan. 'I've been here a year and can't wait to get out. I shall have forgotten what a woman looks like.'

The border consisted of a few scattered half-finished buildings with dim lights slung between them. Scraped snow packed into banks, icy crevasses, shallow frozen ditches had to be negotiated in the dark to walk to them. The passport officer's face appeared at a small window two metres up on the building – a rickety stool to stand on had thoughtfully been provided for those passing through. There were five of us and our passports were held for an hour or so: the doctors' special permits required the most careful attention, my visa expired at midnight and pumpkin hour had almost arrived.

The fifth person was a Turk who had been on the bus. A Mister Fixit, such as one finds all over the world, who knew everybody and everything and would see us across safely and find us cheap rooms at his cousin's hotel in Dogubayazit. All he had done so far was to hold us up while he did some wheeler-dealing with the local populace, fetching wads of notes out of his inside coat pocket, shuffling them, counting them, adding to them, giving change. He was selling jeans. His passport was glanced at and returned immediately.

We walked on to the gate which led into Turkey. It was unattended and padlocked. 'The country's locked' said Bushan.

The Kurds

The Turkish officers sat around a wood stove in their cosy guard room, smoking and reading newspapers that they then poked on the fire. They spoke in German. 'The doctors' permits are OK but you have no visa. You can buy one. Ten dollars.'

The Indian woman's first gesture had been to throw off her headshawl, mine to wrap my chador round my shoulders and free my hair. I couldn't part with the garment entirely for the temperature was − 10°C and my self-imposed luggage limit of five kilos was beginning to tell. I was wearing everything I had, seven layers of clothes: underwear, woolly tights and a silk vest, shalwar kameez, cardigan, mohair coat knitted with sleeves too long so they served as gloves, shawl and chador.

We hung around for ages but nothing happened. 'Someone's gone to change your ten dollars' the officers said. The doctors grew impatient. After another long wait the officers admitted: 'He's gone for dinner.' The doctors departed with Mister Fixit in a taxi; Bushan taking care of his wife, I reflected. I waited for another hour or so.

A Turkish fellow hovered around. 'He's my cousin' he said of Mister Fixit 'his father my father's brother. You come with me to cousin's hotel. Thirteen dollars for taxi.' There was little choice.

We sped off down an icy road. 'I love you, you need friend, you spend night. Eat, drink whisky, you need friend, me thirty-two.' He leant towards me, swerving the car. 'You no need friend?' He immediately speeded up to eighty on the icy road. 'Slowly? More slowly? ... You need friend I tell you. You eat, drink whisky, you sleep friend, Turkey friend. I love you ... You say no, so is it. So you not need friend.' His foot hovered over the accelerator. 'You sleep Turkey friend.' We skidded dangerously towards the edge of the road. He slowed down as he turned and observed my frostily scowling face, then finally delivered me to the Hotel Nuh, a desolate place of threadbare red carpeting and hot radiators. It was too late to get a meal so I sat in my small room chewing Bahram's nougat and pondering on true love and charity.

148

It was most fortunate for the citizens of Dogubayazit that Noah's ark had landed nearby. As it was, they shuffled round the streets wearing patched shabby overcoats, hems hanging and pockets darned, and down-at-heel shoes. Their horse blankets were cobbled together out of bits of felt, poor cloth and plastic shopping bags. But it was apparent that in the summer months the small town supported a modest tourist industry. Simple hotels comprised most of the solid buildings of the town, and their glass doors, though not those of the Nuh, were covered with the stickers of European overland adventure companies. Coach operators in cramped little offices advertised trips up to Mount Ararat, where Noah's ark supposedly came to rest.

In midwinter, however, the town was utterly silent and still. There was no traffic, only the muffled pad of horses pulling flat wooden carts. Their breath hung cobwebbed in the frozen air. The roads were corrugated with the compounded frozen slush of half a winter, on which the horses hoofs constantly slipped. The buildings were small shacks with unstable wooden balconies and tin roofs, striped with snow and glazed by the low winter sun.

There was no sign of the amulet; the horses were protected by blue beads and red pompoms. 'It wouldn't have come to us with the Turks' the Bulgarian ethnographer had said. 'It's much too old a pattern for that.' I bought a bus ticket to Trabzon.

It was mid-afternoon when the two women flounced past the Hotel Nuh. Their wide bright skirts skittered along the frozen road, their shawls and jewels swung as they walked. 'Kurds' said the hotel manager. I rushed out, leaving my purse and all my belongings unattended, overtook the women and then turned to scrutinize their clothing. It was bold and flowery, but it wasn't embroidered. I dawdled back.

'My village Kurd' said Ömer, the hotel manager. 'I see you like Kurd. Come to my village. We called it Barbara, but the Turks call it Alentepi. Come with me to see my milk mother. Tomorrow come. Forget bus.'

The countryside was bleak. The empty expanse of a vast icy plain rolled to a white ridge of mountains that merged on the horizon into the snow-laden clouds of a winter sky. The van bounced along a ridged scrunchy track, past a flat frozen surface that might have been a lake, submerged under blown snow. In the distance, closer to the mountains, the low clustered buildings of an isolated village stained the white plain with a narrow blur of brown.

'Fifteen million Kurds in Turkey' said Ömer. 'Eight in Iran, six in Iraq, four in Syria, maybe five million in Soviet. We want our own Kurdistan.

'You help' he added. 'Kurds love Europeans. When Saddam gassed us Danielle Mitterrand came, took three thousand to live in France. Governments of Holland, England, Denmark, France, Italy, Germany sent money. That's why we love European peoples.'

The village on approach was a small huddle of ugly concrete and breezeblock houses, no doubt rebuilt on the site of a destroyed Kurdish settlement. The buildings were set in old enclosures of dry-stone walling where sheep, cows and hayricks were penned for the winter. Husky dogs prowled and snarled as we entered one of the houses. Inside a bright felt rug decorated with solar patterns lay on the earth floor. The ceiling was of wood and twig as in southern Iran and Makran. It was bitterly cold and the family rushed around gathering bits of rubbish to light the stove in the middle of the room. 'They wish to kill a chicken for your lunch' said Ömer.

'No, no, please not.' Bread, butter, cheese, yoghurt, halwa were served instead.

'Is my milk mother made.' Ömer handed her a parcel of biscuits and sweets and gave her a hug. His own mother had died in childbirth, he explained, 'so my uncle's wife gave me milk'.

Haiba was a tiny woman dressed, disappointingly, in European clothes: black boots, red woolly skirt, black jumpers and a sleeveless handwoven waistcoat. Only a huge white scarf draped all round her face, head, neck and shoulders was reminiscent of more exotic ancient dress. Not only did she rise early each morning to find fuel and make the family bread, said Ömer, but she cared for the animals, milked them and made all the food the family normally had, the butter, the cheese, the yoghurt. Halwa she made when there was money and then there would be tea and sugar from the town. In winter she made felts and carpets, she knitted and crocheted.

The amulet I was looking for was everywhere. It was the pattern knitted into their winter stockings and their woolly slippers; it hung as crocheted pendants on cupboard doors. 'Ameri' we call it, said Haiba. It could be triangular with tassels or it could be square.. Some words from the Koran were written on paper by the Muslim teacher in Arabic, she explained. Then it was covered in wool or embroidery for people, and in cloth for animals. Babies wore it from two months to three years to protect them from illness. Yes, Haiba's babies had all worn it. She had nine living and nine dead. She was forty-five.

It was also the pattern cut into their handmade agricultural tools: the kergit, a jagged-edged digging tool, and the peesh, a small fork. Haiba demonstrated how they were used. Her husband had no idea even what they were for. 'Men do no work here,' said Ömer 'only women. Money? No money here. But now for six years we have electricity and school.'

Haiba pressed on me a pair of woolly socks she had knitted and a piece of paper with the words of the mullah that she had been intending to make into an amulet. It was folded into a triangle, ready to cover with fabric and embroider. I hugged it with huge excitement. It was one step nearer to Bulgaria, one more step where the amulet had surfaced. But while in Makran and southern Iran the examples had been only isolated, here they were everywhere. This was real amulet territory.

Ömer knocked on the door of my hotel room. It was now −20°C outside, he said, and I should not go out. 'Here is supper.' It was the same meal that I had had for breakfast, lunch and supper each day: bread, cheese, honey, tea. He refused payment and clasped my hand. 'Please,' he urged 'your countrymen are my brothers. I do not want money.' He raised my hand to his lips and kissed it. 'I love you. You are my mother.' Then he knelt: 'I am your son.' My toes curled.

It was hard to come to terms with the sexual twilight in which I found myself. Though physically OK I am none the less indisputably old. I considered myself neither in the category of my contemporaries in the countries through which I journeyed – comfortably padded, aproned and slippered – nor in that of the wandering foreign female viewed as fair game. I was consequently often caught foolishly off guard when the approach was sexual and abrasively defensive when all I was attracting was respect for my age.

'What present can I send for your milk mother?'
'Aspirin, only aspirin. Her legs are bad.'

When, in 1870, Beheram Agha, having been named director of the government salt monopoly at Van, asked if he and his harem might go along with Major Frederick Millingen into Kurdistan, this army officer, wandering among 'rough and half savage people', was startled. It threw a kind of gloom over his prospects, for 'whatever may be my predilection for, and devotion to, the fair sex, I have always been of opinion that, invaluable in the domestic recess, women are not quite the sort of companions which one would like to have while en route.'

The 'domestic recess' of Haiba was common to all Kurdish women. Nothing had changed, no doubt for thousands of years and certainly not since Millingen observed them over a hundred years ago or Thomas Bois thirty years ago. They were on their feet from five in the morning till eleven at night, said Bois, milking, making butter and cheese, making bread, fetching water – often half an hour's walk from the village. Then finding fuel, either looking for wood or drying pats of manure on the house walls, and cooking. Food was rice for the rich or cracked wheat for the poor. The only vegetable was tomato when it was in season; the fruits were grapes and melon. For guests chicken or strong-smelling mutton kebabs were prepared. Otherwise it was only water, very sweet tea and yoghurt. Washing was done at the communal fountain with soap and beater on a piece of board. In the winter the women made felts and wove. They spun while busy at other tasks. 'In Koordistan' Millingen had said 'men do literally nothing.' Bois had found the same and today it was still so.

Djinn haunt the threshold of the house, said Bois. The evil eye watches for women in childbirth and for young children. The townspeople don't believe all this but in the country women and children are protected with amulets, with cloves, agates, onyx and coral, with blue beads and shells, bits of wood and stone, with bells, red bonnets edged in zigzags and triangles. Or with sachets holding verses from the Koran, or bits of paper on which little squares are drawn in red ink where a 'magician' inscribes numbers and words, a magician 'who outside this activity would hardly inspire confidence.' These pieces of paper are folded into the shape of a triangle – often a needle is broken in two and inserted – and then wrapped in a little bag. In spite of all these precautions fifty per cent of infants die. Of malnutrition. Today for Haiba it was still so.

The Kurds decorate the tombs of their men with daggers, guns and tools, and those of their women with flowers, combs and bracelets. All are carved with solar circles. Just like the tombs in Sind.

They worship the sun and fire. Just like the Zoroastrians.

They believe in the magic of a circle which, drawn around them, will protect them. Just like the snake charmer in Makran.

They believe in horns. Just like in Kohistan.

They believe, said Bois, in the forces of nature, sacred trees from where they hang rags, sacred wells and springs and fish. Were these not always attributes of the earth goddess, the mother goddess, the goddess of fertility?

The Kurds invited further investigation but their villages were cut off by snow – Barbara was isolated the next day – their safe havens were closed to outsiders, the borders of Iraq and Syria were impenetrable, the military presence was heavy and blizzards obliterated every road. It would be better to return in fairer weather. And there was still Afghanistan.

Afghanistan

❖ ❖ ❖

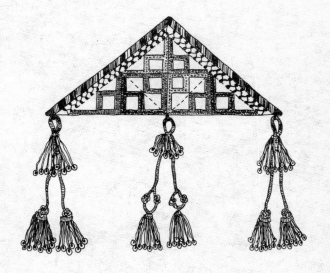

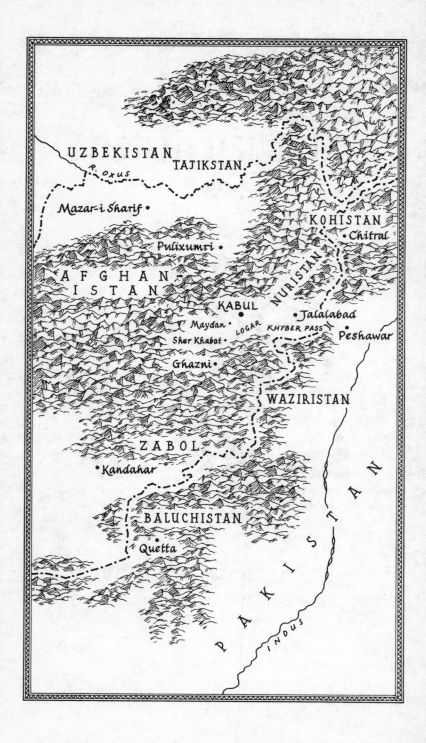

Quetta Again

The two men faced each other across the huge, almost snooker-dimensioned mahogany table of the London publishing house. The publisher, a slight, thoughtful man in a smart suit and round horn-rimmed glasses too big for him, shuffled the colour prints, his delicate spatula-nailed fingers flinching gently. They were not good. They had the flat, smudged quality of thousands of pictures in Soviet tourist brochures vaunting Uzbek steel plants and Georgian folk dancers. It was as if the negatives had been slid between two wet glass plates in some old-fashioned colour separation process long superseded in the West. Pierre of the United Nations in Quetta was the man for whom I had translated the book of Afghan embroidery on my way to Makran earlier in the year while Sheila, Ugo and I were waiting for our permits to come through. He now leaned back on his executive chair and peered at the photographs through thyroidal eyes and small thick bottle glasses. As the *grand séducteur* I had observed him to be, his eyesight must have been a curse to him always.

'These are not of the right quality for us' was the expected verdict of the publisher, who fetched the technical director, equipped with magnifying glass, to confirm his opinion, 'but if we can make our own edition from the original transparencies, with not only a translation but also a preface from Sheila, we would agree.' I said nothing: the book was on the traditional embroidery of Afghanistan and the preface would clearly have to update it. Would the women still be embroidering after fourteen years of war? And how could anyone know without going there? And by going there would it be possible to get as far north as Mazar-i Sharif, amulet country?

'Would you be interested in doing the same sort of book for Baluchi embroidery?' asked Pierre. 'It's much finer than Afghan, superb.'

'Yes' said the publisher. Pierre swung his chair round towards me. 'In exchange for writing the Baluchi text and the Afghan preface I'll guarantee you safe passage from Quetta to Kandahar. Then you're on your own.'

'Done' I said. 'Next week.'

A few days later, on his way back to Pakistan, he phoned. 'Total curfew in Quetta, huge problems. United Nations are pulling me out so the Baluchi book is off. But you still have to do the Afghan one and I'll get you through.'

And so it was that a week or so later I found myself again in the care of the nuns of St Joseph's. Sister Virginia was flustering around in readiness for her return home. She needed an all-clear from the authorities, a No Objection Certificate, to prove she had paid all her taxes and hadn't any debts, before they would let her go. She was very chirrupy. The swings and slides in the playground had been painted and rang with the delighted shrieks of little brown-faced girls in blue check pinafores. My room had a different poster: a blond toddler in yellow T-shirt bent double in a meadow kissing a white rabbit. 'Be Ye Kind' it preached. The curfew and the wheeljam strikes confining the vehicles to one part of the city had ended a few days before and all was quiet, though I went to bed assailed by weird chanting and woke to the muezzin calling the faithful.

I skulked around the city, fervently hoping that Dr Kholiq would be buried in the dusty files of his office and that I would not bump into him. The nuns certainly would not think to tell him of my arrival and I trusted he would not hear of it from anyone else. He did not.

'Take one hundred dollars' said Pierre. 'That's all you'll need. A hundred dollars will buy the whole of Afghanistan. Or half at least. They have nothing.' Even the Sudan had sent food. The harvest there had been good and they had donated tons of grain to their fellow Muslims. 'A hundred trucks of wheat a day are going illegally across the border. But no one can buy it. There's no money in Kandahar. No one can pay any wages. No one can buy anything. There's no electricity. No water. No food. We don't know what happens to the grain.' The orchards had been destroyed. Afghanaid had launched an appeal: 'plant a fruit tree, replenish the Afghan orchards'. Where the land had been cleared of mines it had been tilled, irrigated, ready for crops. 'Farmers of Kandahar using their irrigated fields for poppy planting. Afghanistan to become the largest world producer of opium' said the UN report.

Abdul Ahad, Mujahedin Commander, had been briefed by Pierre. Tall and heavy-jowled, with a bushy black beard and the odd curl escaping from under his neatly swathed turban, he cut a dashing figure, but his proposition for getting me into Afghanistan was decidedly shaky. I would be concealed under a burqa – that tentlike garment that shrouds a woman from head to toe, leaving only a mesh visor to see through – and we would catch a bus or hail a pick-up truck to the border and then walk across. Under my burqa no one would notice me, he said, and once across he could find us another truck. Satisfied with this arrangement, he leaned back in his chair and expounded his views on Afghanistan. 'Election now and it will be one Kalashnikov, one vote. Refugees must return first, then we must have rights. Every human has three rights: democracy, education, job and food. You will see we have none of this. Even just the men have nothing.'

Still his proposition seemed risky. Pierre didn't like it. 'Go the day after tomorrow with Gailani's convoy.' This Sufi 'saint', leader of the National Islamic Front for Afghanistan, was returning with a convoy of followers to his home town of Kandahar after an absence of fourteen years. Anyone would just suppose I was a woman belonging to one of the men. It was agreed.

We all hung around the Serena Hotel, a swish complex of tasteful low adobe-type buildings, that was one of four established by the Aga Khan in what should have been tourist centres in Pakistan: Gilgit, Faisalabad, Swat and Quetta. But there were no tourists. The manager, Mosin, whom I had met on my last visit, ran the place as a club with a mixture of diplomacy, smooth administration and streetwise savvy of the local scene, its con tricks, ruffians, market opportunities and loopholes. ('Nice face, your cousin' said Pierre. 'Yes' said Mosin. 'Just come out of prison after nine years. Shrewd fellow. Built a bank within a bank.') No one who entered escaped the scrutiny of the door-keeper, Shahbuddin, a smiling bearded Pathan. His Persil-white turban stood out in starched wisped edges like a cock's tail, and his waistcoat was dense with three hundred badges: 'Bring Our Troops Home'; 'No Blood for Oil'.

'You were right not to take the Mand to Pishin road,' said

Mosin 'it's the smugglers' track. Not big stuff, not heroin I think. Little stuff – liquor, apples. And bottles. They come from the Far East. There's a bottling plant at Mand. The whisky comes there from the Far East too and they bottle it. Then they've got camels and they load up the crates of whisky and send the camels off by themselves in a caravan of ten. They know exactly where to go. They come to a house on the outskirts of Quetta. And if the police caught them what could they do? What can you do with a camel?'

'Do they wait to take the empties back?' asked Pierre.

'You can't be going to Afghanistan' said Marco of the International Committee for the Red Cross. 'We lost one of our people there three weeks back. Icelandic nurse. We were on the road south of Kabul transferring patients from one lot of ambulances to another and a crowd of fifty to a hundred people gathered round to watch. Then one of them suddenly stepped forward with a Kalashnikov and fired at the nurse. Kept on firing at her. "All the unfaithful should be killed" he shouted.'

Most of the time I spent in Atar's shop, one of half a dozen in the bazaar of the Serena. He once had a hotel in Kandahar but had come to Quetta as a refugee as soon as the Russians moved in and had set up as a textile dealer. He was a thin brown man, rather small and sad, his curly hair hidden by an embroidered cap. 'Why do you want to go to Kandahar? There's nothing there.'

'For the embroidery. Those wonderful whitework shirts women used to make for their bridegroom. And their shawls.'

'Nothing there. Nothing left. No bazaar. Nothing to buy.'

'I don't want to buy. I want to talk to the women. See what they're doing now.'

Pierre bought me a blue burqa from Atar's stock in preparation for the journey.

Pier Sayed Ahmad Gailani – a small man who gave gentle gestures of benediction to the waiting crowd – and his party of followers arrived the next day. Not a tribe, they said, but men of aristocracy. Descendants of a prophet who came to Afghanistan from Iraq at the end of the last century. The importance of the embroidery situation in Afghanistan today seemed to escape them but one old man knew the amulet. 'I remember it from my childhood' he said. 'It's Koochi from Kandahar, Helmand, Zabol. There's a charm inside. Sometimes the skin of an animal to take the look of djinn away from a healthy child, or it's hung on the head for a headache or on the arm. Sometimes the mullah says put in green colour and hang for months on a tree, then the djinn will disappear. They even dug holes in the ground and put the charm in there against the enemy, so it wouldn't be stolen.'

They agreed to take me with them, in the care of Abdul Kahlid Gailani. We were to meet at the Serena at five in the morning. The night was fitful. Flashing lights betrayed a distant storm or illicit torches in the grounds of St Joseph's. Mynah birds shrieked. My small bag was ready; my moneybelt was stuffed with low denomination dollar notes while the hundreds were secreted in pockets sewn into my bra and fifties were stitched into my socks. I crept out before dawn, past a poster which read:

> Let nothing disturb You.
> Nothing affright You:
> *GOD* alone is changeless.
> ST TERESA OF AVILA

The chowkidar, roused from his bed, let me out.

Nine o'clock breakfast at the Serena coffee shop, I noted, was attended by a few Pakistani businessmen, an aid worker reading the *International Herald Tribune* of the day before and an elderly homosexual in khaki fatigues gasping on his first cigarette of the day and talking to two manly Afghans. Finally a message came: 'Programme changed.'

Kandahar

The road was terrible; the driving was terrible. Twenty vehicles or so, black flags flying, snaked at breakneck speed up the pass, then jammed on the brakes at the top. The men all piled out laughing and gazed at the hazy plain that lay before us across the hills. 'I love Afghanistan' one of them shouted. 'Afghanistan' they shouted, breathing the air of home. Muffled and airless, I peered through my visor at the road ahead.

They drove straight through the flags at the border and sped on. Dark tribesmen in torn clothing and embroidered shawls, guns at the ready, stopped the convoy trucks and demanded money to allow them to pass. Abandoned military vehicles lay everywhere and lengths of roadside were marked out with small white cairns where sniffer dogs had cleared the fields of mines. Tanks clanked past, driven like Ferraris down the fast lane.

At the approach to Kandahar I was dropped from the truck to allow the convoy to make its triumphant entry into the town unencumbered. The driver's brother-in-law led me away in my burqa to his home where I was to stay for several days.

It was an adobe house, built much in the same style as Arg, of dried mud strengthened with straw and embedded stone. It lay among a group of similar simple adobe buildings at a short distance from the town, across a dusty track and near a river. The family had fled from this home fourteen years before when the Russians had come and the mujahedin had occupied it. The walls were pocked with bullet holes and a new concrete domed ceiling had replaced the one sent crashing down by a bomb. Sheets of cardboard from Chinese packing cases filled the gaping windows.

The family had returned a few months before and life was hard. They had no land and, though the father went off on his bicycle every day, he had no job. The poor man had his wife, seven children, various sisters and hosts of old relatives to support.

The house was built around a courtyard of earth and dust.

The main reception rooms ran along one side of it and were raised to a higher level. A terrace in front of them overlooked the activity of the courtyard, which was divided into areas: a tip for waste at one end, a water supply in the centre and a muddy plot for the kitchen. In the waste section the rubbish was thrown – old paper, kitchen ordure, leaves and firewood – which served as fuel for the family. This large sunken, chaotic and dirty yard was as important to the household as the neatly stacked log store of a Swiss chalet. In the centre of the courtyard a water pipe feeding into a pit supplied the household. A blue lined concrete bath by it perhaps once served as the family washtub, but now was full of rubbish. A few rose trees and shrubs grew in the mud around the standpipe. Among them a ginger cat lurked and a crippled, featherless chicken staggered around. Along the side of the courtyard was the area that might be called the kitchen. A shallow dip in the ground, into which rubbish and twigs were slipped, was the bread oven. A large drum of water, a tap at the bottom, took the place of a sink where dishes were washed and pots filled. There were flies everywhere.

The courtyard was the centre of activity of the family. All day long the girls and women, especially Sarah the daughter-in-law (was the biblical Sarah ever so busy?), filled the water drum with small plastic jugs taken from the standpipe. They made hot sweet tea and washed tea glasses continually. At mealtimes they boiled rice at ground level on little stoves fired with motor oil. Sarah would fetch out a small folded red quilt and lay it on the ground by the dip that formed the oven and in which she lit a small fire of rubbish. Inside the quilt was a ball of dough from the previous day's baking, leavening for today's batch of bread, and a sprinkling of flour. Mixing the doughs together in a basin beside her, she would deftly form the paste into balls and roll them from hand to hand. Then with a twist of the wrist she would stretch and toss and flip and pull with her fingers until she had a large disc that she would slap over the metal dome warming above the fire. This in turn would be flipped three or four times until it was cooked. These huge discs of bread were the mainstay of the family diet and, when the plastic cloth was laid on the floor for meals, they would be set, folded in half, like massive place mats, one in front of each man.

I never saw where the women ate but the men's food was

served to them in the reception room where I slept. After they
had eaten I was fed: very spicy cold vegetables, okra in oil, naan
and a cottage cheese that tasted of udders. It was the best food I
was to have in Afghanistan but I ate little, knowing they could ill
afford to feed me. Men and women were brought to stare at me.
Gailani's men came and went. At night I would roll my sleeping
bag out on the floor and men, women and children of the family
would lie on cushions around me. I was never alone and there
was no chance to undress, nor even to comb my hair, an
intensely provocative act in front of a man.

In the mornings when I stepped out on to the terrace overlooking the courtyard a young girl would be sitting embroidering. To
my indescribable joy she was working the traditional stitches of
Kandahar, as fine and disciplined as ever they were. Her baby
played around her. She was the wife of a mujahed, the commander
of the group that had requisitioned the house and, a few months
ago, had handed it back to the family.

He was never to be seen, until one evening he suddenly
appeared and strode across the terrace, diving into his room and
slamming the door. He was an impressive figure. He had frizzy
black matted hair under a twisted dark striped turban that flew
out behind him, wild brown eyes under bushy eyebrows, a thick
curly moustache and beard. He wore a dark shalwar kameez and
khaki jerkin, the pockets stuffed with bullets, and wrapped around
him a large shawl bordered by his wife's embroidery – delicate
little squares of finely patterned silk stitching in a white floss silk
that shimmered with each turn of the thread. His Kalashnikov he
threw to his young brother-in-law.

It was pleasant in the evenings to sit on the terrace and watch the
red lights of tracer bullets flare into the sky as intermittent
gunshots rang out or rockets were launched and a pause ensued
– exactly like the doodlebugs I remember from the Second
World War – before they crashed. At this time of day our
mujahed was always absent, presumably in the thick of things.

'Who are they fighting now that an agreement has been
signed?'

'It is toys. They have nothing else to do.'

On such evenings the family would gather in the light of
paraffin lamps around a crackly old-fashioned battery radio

covered in quilted gold paper. Squatting on the ground they would bend to listen to BBC News, the World Service, though they didn't understand a word. The President's plane had been shot down at Kabul airport. Things didn't look good.

As the intensity of the heat and light of the day faded, the old lady of the household, who was nearly blind, threw my burqa on the floor, wrapped me in her shawl and led me by the hand to the river behind the house. Here goats were feeding, women washing, girls collecting water, men paddling. Gunshots rang out from the town behind us. The view on the other side of the river was of a dappled plain with an adobe village and low mountain ranges in the distance. 'It's beautiful' I said.

'Beautikot. Beautikot' she repeated, clasping my hands and gazing ahead through cataracted eyes at an image held for fourteen years.

On the first day in Kandahar I was led to the bazaar shrouded in my burqa. Its weight clung heavily to my shoulders; it flapped all around my body and legs, crowding me on all sides and hobbling my progress. It encircled my head entirely, leaving just the small meshed visor over my eyes that gave me vision only straight ahead, so that I lost any awareness of approach from the side and felt strangely vulnerable. The sights of the bazaar were a true kaleidoscope, fractured as they were by the grid through which I saw them. The middle distance dissolved into a Rouault painting of vivid colours outlined in black. Figures further away, I discovered, could be centred in one of the holes as if pinpointed in the sights of a gun, but it was the images close to my eyes that were terrifying. They assaulted the mesh enclosing me like flies splatting on an electric flyscreen: shrilling green birds in domed wooden cages, baskets of chickpeas, bloody goats' heads covered in flies, hanks of brilliant silks, shelves of grinning false teeth, pompommed donkeys munching lucerne (no amuletic triangles there), the muzzles of Kalashnikovs, the gold and flashing colours of the men's embroidered caps.

I was at least able to walk unobserved, only the ridge of my Boots' glasses giving any clue to the alert, for no women in any rural tribal area of any country I had ever been to wore glasses. Afghanistan was no exception.

On my second visit to the bazaar, as the guest by then of a

different group of mujahedin – moderates rather than fundamentalists – I was allowed to go without my burqa but was accompanied instead by a bodyguard. He was a youth with the first fuzz of a moustache, carrying a Kalashnikov and wearing a kameez decorated with a triangular amulet of white shirt buttons. Two other bodyguards later joined him. It seemed, considering they stared at me all the time and didn't look around them once, that they might be useful for later retaliation rather than immediate protection.

Abdul Ahad had come from Quetta and had made it his business to find where I was. He strode into the house, throwing his revolver and bullets on the floor for the children to pick up, then stroking his black beard began to talk. 'I hate Afghanistan' he said. 'I want to see the world. What have we here? No dance. No whisky. Only Kalashnikov. I want to find my own girl. Not one my father chose. Her I leave in Quetta. If the fundamentalists win it is the end of Afghanistan.'

In those early days of fragile peace following the signing of a compromise agreement between Masood and Hekmatyar, seven parties were fighting for the future of Afghanistan, ranged into two confronting groups: moderates and fundamentalists. But that was simplistic. There were also a myriad tribal factions as well as large divisions, such as the Pathan against the Tajik, to whom Masood belonged. And the religious factions. The fundamentalists had already declared that women would not be allowed to sing, or listen to the radio, or go out to the bazaar. They were for rearing children, nothing else. 'But does not an educated woman bring up better children?' said some, by education meaning primary school.

No planes or runways identified the airport. Instead groups of huts and crumbling blocks of flats, too many storeys high, were scattered in a landscape of waste ground and cracked concrete roads. People had stayed there throughout the war, protected by the mujahedin who had based themselves in an old administrative building. 'You must tell the world, the US, Japan, Germany, what is happening here.' Hati Ahmad, Mujahedin Commander of Kandahar Province, insisted on an interview. The flippant 'I'm only here for the embroidery' I pushed out of my mind, brought out pen and notepad and, assuming the role of war correspondent, listened earnestly to what he had to say.

It was all rather confusing. 'Kabul is not normal' he explained. 'The government is not in control. We work only for this province Kandahar. Hekmatyar and Masood want two Afghanistans, one fundamentalist, one moderate. We want one. We want control from here. Kandahar is different. Here we are many tribes – Populzai, Halakozai, Achakzai, Nurzai, Ishaczai, Khagwani and other small ones.'

It seemed pertinent to ask what all the evening shooting was for, was it perhaps these tribes and small groups fighting each other? 'No, no. Shooting and rockets are just my mujahedin. Not for any purpose. Just doing' he replied 'while waiting.'

'Waiting for what?'

'We are waiting for seven leaders to get together with a programme for the future. In between I control my poor people. I give you thanks for coming to see my poor people. Now you must give message to US and Japan, we lost everything, lost government, no money, no salary.'

What did they need? I wondered. 'Quick help. Not for mujahedin but for government. Yes, money. And stores. There is no food.'

'What food should be sent and where?'

'Wheat, ghee, sugar, tea, medicine. Send to me, Mujahedin Commander of Kandahar Province at airport. I will make sure lorries get through. But food is not for us, you understand. There are two thousand mujahedin in the airport area, but we are strong. It is for the families. Two thousand five hundred families in airport. We need food for our sons and our women.'

As darkness fell the paraffin lamps glazed the white embroidery of the men's shirts, as we sat in the courtyard of one of the airport homes, eating rice and goat stew. The women who had prepared it all waited for the leftovers, squatting on the ground below the raised wooden platform on which the men and boys were tucking in. It seemed unlikely that any aid food would reach them rather than the men. As usual I was treated as an honorary man, in the way South Africans treated Japanese businessmen as honorary whites, not knowing where to slot them. 'Eating bread?' said one, as he leant over to take mine. '*Pajalista.*' At the end of the meal the newest son of the family, stiffly swaddled, was handed to its father. The baby was wrapped in three large cloths tightly bound by a long tape covered with amulets: pieces of turquoise, ceramic, coral-coloured agate and metal discs, but not what I was looking for. At the centre, where a safety pin might be, there were two triangles, one of leather and one of cloth, but without tassels. To protect him, his thirty-year-old mother Sernahgwula explained; she had lost five children in a bomb attack on the house and now had only five left.

Her home, shared with all her husband's relatives, was another series of rooms around a dirt courtyard that had at one end a reception room full of quilts and with a domed ceiling like houses in Iran and at the other a small privy with a piece of sacking for a door. By the gateway a herd of goats was penned for the night and led out at six in the morning by a little girl with a stick. I sat on the ground on a wooden wheel inscribed in Russian to wash under a garden tap. There were bits of Russian rubbish and equipment everywhere and the people readily said *niet* and *da*.

The men all proudly wore beautiful embroidered shirts and shawls. 'Who made that for you?'

'My darling' said Naposgwul's husband.

Asked how many children she had, this wonderful embroideress hesitated and counted on her fingers. It was six. Young mothers in their twenties, girls of nine, girls of fifteen, brought me their embroideries to see, embroideries that would get the girls a husband, and Abdul Ahad took me to homes around the airport to look at others. 'I see you like it here, but it is not safe. We move you again to town. Another place.'

'Children girls. *Jungly* girls' said Mir Ahmad, the friend Abdul Ahad had chosen to lodge me with. Indeed, the three of them tumbled around the flat like tiger cubs, cuffing each other and rolling around giggling in the cushions. They spent their days so, cooped up in this dark flat, its drawn curtains billowing slightly around the intrusive sounds of the street: gunshot, rumbling armoured cars and the peppered thud of tanks on the rutted roadway. They never thought to clean the place but just cooked bread and rice and goat stew, made tea and rollicked around. 'Children girls. *Jungly* girls' Mir Ahmad repeated as he watched them indulgently.

The skinny boyish one with a shock of black hair was his wife. 'Very angry. I am very angry' he said. 'No baby yet.' The thirteen-year-old was his sister – the parents and the rest of the family were in Karachi – and the quieter girl was his brother's wife. After a day or so she brought a swaddled baby who never cried or uttered a sound to show me. Seven months old. The last one had died at eight months. Of the sickness, her husband said.

Though the flat was on the first floor of a building in the centre of town – one of the very few not totally destroyed by bombing – the kitchen was floored in dirt and what looked like earth. Rusty tins were used as cooking pots and lay lined up against the walls. There was no furniture, only a place for a fire on the earth, where the girls crouched to cook. Next to the kitchen was the lavatory, a hole in the ground with firewood and rubbish piled up beside it, where a rat foraged.

The flat was approached by a staircase from the street, a mujahed standing guard at top and bottom. The young couple with the baby had a room of their own with a television set; I shared the room belonging to Mir Ahmad and his wife and sister, all of us sleeping on cushions on the floor. The front rooms of the flat were the meeting place of the mujahedin group that Abdul Ahad supported. Large thermoses of tea and dishes piled high with mulberries – soft white and purple raspberry-like fruits – were continually on tap as men came and went. With each new visitor I was hauled out from my room to talk and to listen to them.

Thirteen sat around discussing the situation in Iran, grasping the mulberries in handfuls. 'Just our king must come back, then with peace all will be well. Our girls will go to school, our women will be free, they will work in offices, all will be good. Just our king we need.'

'He is King Mohammed Zai Shah. Now he is in Rome. And your amulet? What it is? It is not before Islam. It came with the Arabs fifteen hundred years ago.'

'Why triangle? Because inside folded paper written by mullah, name of God and piece from Koran or saying. It protects from all evils. It is Turkmen. Also for horse or car.'

'Why tassels? Mean nothing. Only beautiful.'

'Where from? All Afghan country and villages. No towns.'

Wandering away from the overpowering presence of males I

discovered a group of mujahedin in a room beyond the staircase guarded by an extra sentry, among them a ten-year-old whose father proudly boasted he had killed two Russians. They had hung their Kalashnikovs on the wall and were playing bridge.

The jungly girls were also bridge addicts and though they seemed to be ignorant of bidding, let alone of systems such as Culbertson and Crane or indeed even of trumps, and though I hate playing games in case I don't win, it proved an unexpected diversion in what was virtual imprisonment. If I tried to move on to the balcony to observe the life below – the armoured vehicles, the men and boys sitting on the grass verge throwing paper kites in the air, the bicycles, the carts, the donkeys, the blue trucks of 'Afghanistan First Aid' speeding past full of trigger-happy youths, embroidered scarves flying – I was dragged back into the flat. Dangerous, they said. Five people killed in Kandahar today.

Abdul Kahlid Gailani called to take me with him back to Quetta. When I pointed out that I was going on to Kabul, even had a bus ticket for the next day, he made me write a letter to Pierre saying he disapproved completely of my continuing to Kabul and would accept no responsibility for me. His instructions, he had understood, were to take me to Kandahar and then deliver me safely back to Quetta. I exonerated him from all responsibility and prepared to leave for Kabul at the crack of dawn.

The evening was spent watching an Indian video from Dubai in which paunchy males in woolly pullovers darted suggestive pelvic thrusts at coy women whose outfits changed with each frame of the film. The two young husbands were enraptured. TV supper was a bowl of gravy made from goat bones into which stale bread had been broken. It lay heavily on my stomach and by dawn I felt queasy. The lavatory was occupied by a squatting mujahed. I stayed close to a window but a few minutes later was pleased to find the place free and to be able to throw up everything. Though I then felt much better there was no question of embarking on a two-day bus journey to Kabul and I lay on the cushions all day drinking sweet tea and eating nothing. It was the only time I was ill in all my journeyings. My jungly hostesses were as sweet as could be. They picked up the dead mouse that lay by my ear and dealt more cards.

Bus to Kabul

The simple fragile mud dwellings of village after village had been blasted and bombed into stalagmites when just a huff and a puff could surely have blown them all down. The most mutilated hedged the roadway, others lay as huddled groups in the crook of distant hills. Scarred clumps of fruit trees, apricots, mulberries, stood in tufted grass where orchards once had been. Nomads, their women ablaze in brilliant dresses and silver amulets, led herds of goats and camels past the abandoned and rusting military equipment that littered the wheatfields and the road.

The buses had left in convoy at five in the morning. They were all old German stock: 'Rheingraf Reisen.' 'Schul Bus.' 'Elsweiler Burken.' They pitched and tossed, lurched from side to side as if on the high seas, and were overtaken by donkeys. The road was impossible. It was pitted by potholes, bomb craters and pock-marks, scarred by bullet strafing and explosions. 'Road is bad' said one of the men. 'Russians farting on it for fourteen years.' Where bridges had been blown away the men got out and walked while the bus toppled down the river bank and up the other side, encumbered by the huge weight of furniture strapped to its roof. It was full of refugees returning home from the south or from Pakistan: anxious men, a few women in burqas and a handful of babies and small children, one with blond hair, blue eyes and a square Russian face.

All had brought their own supplies of food and drank water from streams where we stopped and from the drum on the bus, sharing the same tin mug. We should reach Kabul tomorrow, they said. 'Ghazni tonight. If not Ghazni we sleep on the earth.'

The bus kept stopping. It broke down continually and each time the driver would shake a tin of old screws out on to the road and look for something to mend it with. It stopped for men to go to the loo. It stopped for men to say their prayers. By nightfall it was still a long way from Ghazni so it teetered on, until a puncture forced it to stop and turn back to a desolate wayside pull-up, a sort of Afghan 'Baghdad Café'. It was a low building of mud with a roof of jutting ribs of twigs half covered with peeling thatch. 'Hotel not safe' said one of the men. 'Thieves steal. You will stay on bus.' Hard sacks of grain were piled in the back of the bus – the United Nations High Commission for Refugees in Pakistan gives each returning refugee three hundred kilos. I rolled out my sleeping bag on them and the men, taking their women, locked me in the bus.

The bicycles leaning on mud walls had saddle covers embroidered with gold thread and blue beads, the women carrying firewood flashed a cuff of orange and puce stitchery, the men wore turbans that twisted and flared around their faces like Medusa's snakes, almost concealing the embroidered caps below. We had stopped at yet another village where the bus had found a small workshop with welding equipment. Traders sat in stalls that were simply American shipping containers, boys and more boys followed me everywhere, an old man knelt his camel down and tethered it while his aged wife slid off its back on her bottom. In the teahouse, an empty room where men kicked their shoes off and lolled on the floor, a man from the bus invited me to stay with him in Ghazni. A stranger, listening to our conversation, looked at him, then at me and shook his head gently. I declined the invitation.

Ghazni was in any case still a long way off. We had left Kandahar at four in the morning. The woman behind me had been terribly sick under her burqa, the babies had been crying, the children fretful, the axle had broken by seven. I had now been in Afghanistan for more than a week. I had not been able to wash or clean my teeth properly or change my clothes. I had managed to slip my knickers off inside my sleeping bag, but not to wash them. I had not been able to comb my hair as I was always in the presence of men and it hung around my face matted with sweat and sand and tangled by burqa and shawl. In all that time I had spent only eleven dollars: ten on the bus fare and one on cups of tea. I had given away in Kandahar almost all my stock of presents – pens, children's toothbrushes, cigarettes, face creams and lipsticks – and on the bus had shared out all my biscuits and dried fruit. And after thirty-six hours on the road we were still less than halfway to Kabul.

South of Ghazni fields gave way to desert. There were few

settlements, the odd irrigated field was protected by a high enclosing wall, mujahedin manned road-blocks and demanded money to allow the bus to continue. A lorryload of Uzbeks passed going south, the triangular amulet hanging on their windscreen. The horizon still swung up and down as if we were on a boat. When we finally reached Ghazni the bus stopped only to offload some people and we were able to buy watermelon. It was a small scattered town of single-storey mud buildings, less damaged than Kandahar and spilling from the slopes of the hillsides and mountains ahead on to the plain we had traversed.

As darkness fell we lumbered on up into the mountains until another puncture forced us to stop. We lurched into another 'hotel'. The kitchen where the men gathered was a small smoky room lit by wan lamplight. The floor was of beaten earth, the ceiling of treetrunks and twigs covered with leaves. A dirty wooden cupboard, its door off the hinges, was piled high with naan. By it a rough wooden plank nailed to the wall as a cock-eyed shelf held rows of tin teapots. Water for tea boiled in a huge metal urn, over a fire of sticks, its fractured flue leading out through the roof. A boy squatted on the floor washing tin bowls for our supper in a bigger bowl of dirty water.

One corner of the room was separated off by a low mud wall and filled with wood fires over which tin pans bubbled. The men from the bus took away dishes of food for themselves and their families, leaving me alone to eat in the kitchen. A rug was placed on the floor for me and a cushion put against the wall for my back. Green and black tea were shown to me and my preference was asked. It was served in the way I had now become accustomed to: with two tablespoons of sugar in the bottom of a small glass, which was then constantly refilled so that the tea got less and less sweet. A naan was handed to me and a tin bowl with a small piece of tough meat, a potato in oil and two large lumps of fat. I wondered whether they were part of the fatty pendulous tails of the local sheep. Payment was waved away.

Dawn revealed another broken-down bus – '*Fern Schnell Gut*' – and the accommodation. It was an L-shaped construction of mud and wood with a flat roof of twigs, surrounded by a verandah where a cow's leg and the scraped bones of another hung in the low morning light. Small chinked plank doors, chained to their

ill-fitting frames, led into the men's rooms and the tiny room that
the women and children had shared – there had just been room
for me to roll out my sleeping bag on the cold earth floor.
Outside stood the usual 'sign' that indicated a hotel or teahouse:
a small metal trough mounted on split twigs and above it a metal
cylinder of water with three taps.

The bus continued painfully northwards, past skeletal villages
and small walled irrigated fields where men already worked in
the first light of dawn. At eightish we stopped just for tea at a
group of shacks.

We were to remain there for three days and nights.

It was a small settlement, a dusty road lined with huts, separated
from the surrounding fields by a shallow stream. The place was
crowded with lorries and buses. The old *Rheingraf Reisen*, *Elsweiler
Burken* and others of our convoy were there and had been for
some time, it transpired. Hundreds of men hung about shiftlessly.
One came over to our bus. Moheb. He had been living in Quetta
and spoke perfect English. My fellow passengers gathered round,
realizing that here was an interpreter. The bus driver was the
first to pounce. Could he please treat the lady to a cup of tea and
did she have any money because if not he could give her some.
'Is she a journalist?' others asked. 'Why does she keep saying
embroidery *gul dozi*? Why is she here? Where is her man? Isn't
she afraid? Where are her sons? How did she get to Kandahar?
How old is she?'

Heavy fighting had broken out early that day just north of
where we were and south of Kabul. The lorries and buses were
waiting for news before setting off in convoy. The radios had
gone dead and no one could get the BBC World Service, so the
only news would be from someone coming south. 'We may wait
all day' Moheb said. 'It's bad, very bad here. Afghanistan has
nothing. Eighty per cent of the men are armed, everyone thinks
it's brave to kill, there are no doctors, no real government. No
one's educated, there are no schools, even though the Koran says
everyone should be educated, women too. It says you should
even go from Saudi to China to get education. But here ninety-
eight per cent are uneducated. It's easier like that for the rulers
to get power over them. We want democracy but the future
looks bleak. There are twenty-eight mujahedin commanders and

they'll block any attempt to install a strong interim government before democracy is introduced. The king's no good, most people don't want him back. Then there's all the rebuilding to do. Kandahar is the most badly damaged of all the cities, but Kabul is hideously overcrowded. There used to be ninety thousand people there, now it's three-quarters of a million, with many of the buildings gone.

'Your amulet? It's from Mazar-i Sharif. It's safer up there and the road's better. You should be able to get through. There's another route to Kabul from here' Moheb continued 'but it's controlled by fundamentalists and someone may have told them about you, so you mustn't go. Then there's a way over the mountains that brings you to the outskirts. You have to walk for an hour into the city. Some of us men will go today. We have to, there are all these people here and no food. We'll wait for news till about two then we'll go. It's too dangerous for you. Even here you must keep your burqa on.'

Two buses later came in from Kabul. It was OK an old man said. 'No' said the drivers. 'There was a ceasefire at eight but the fighting's started again. Fighting, fighting' they said, pulling imaginary triggers. '*Jungly, jungly.*' So that was the meaning of the jungly girls. It was rather disappointing.

'There's a Red Cross building outside the settlement' a man said. 'You must come with me. Come with me. It's half an hour's walk. They will want to see you.' I refused to go. Gunshot blared around. The Hazara had killed three and injured two, very close by. Three hundred years ago the Afghan ruler said the Hazara Shi'ites were to be killed, now they've revived the idea. Hazara against Pathan, Shia against Sunni. Another man came to me. 'Come now to mujahedin.' He butted me in the back with his gun and marched me to a small dark hut. The walls were lined with men squatting on the ground, a mujahedin commander at the head of them. They all stared. Words I recognized – journalist, *gul dozi*, Inglistan – kept cropping up as they stared and fidgeted with their guns. I smiled but felt uneasy. Eventually they pushed me out into the sunlight again.

A father and child had just arrived from Kabul. Bad news. Fighting had broken out again and they were taking hostages. The bus drivers met to discuss plans. The buses would stay here for now and they would come to a final decision the next day.

'If it's still bad we'll go back to Kandahar.'

'There's fighting now in Kandahar too' one man said.
We seemed to be trapped.

The settlement – its name was Sher Khabat I learned – had a few roadside stalls and I wandered over to look for food. Hundreds of menacing armed men and boys stared. The stalls were again old shipping containers and they sold only eggs, cigarettes, garden forks, fabrics – mainly pink and red satin – batteries and potatoes. 'Don't walk in bazaar' a man said. 'It's dangerous. Bad men there.'

Throughout the day tension built up with one small incident after another, some benign, some threatening. At the slightest provocation men grabbed each other by the throat, shouted, argued. A few buses moved. Where for? Where from? A police truck with a blue lamp sped through, the men's faces concealed in black scarves and their guns pointing at the people. 'They're not police. No police here' said Moheb. 'I don't understand you: aren't you scared?' The atmosphere of menace and danger in fact just heightened the senses: the stream beside our bus sparkled with intense clarity, the wild mint I crushed with my fingers was dense with perfume.

'Sayid Farid Ahmad is my name' said the man who sat beside me in the teahouse as a storm broke and lightning flashed outside the cracked windows. 'I shall tell you what Afghanistan needs, in this order. Mine clearance. Hospitals and medicines. Housing for returning refugees. Highways, transport, communications. Education, but with girls in separate rooms. Higher education for girls? That must be only as doctors or teachers. If they become engineers their brothers will never let them work on the roads.'

At dusk – that 'time of the cows' dust' – small girls calmly brought the cows home from the countryside, sporadic gunfire bursting around them. As darkness fell the few women from the buses, hidden under their burqas, searched for discreet corners of the nearby field. There were no facilities for us otherwise and only darkness shielded us from the eyes of the men.

Dinner was served in the teahouse, only for the men, of course, about eighty of them squatting beside rolled-out strips of plastic cloth, each man's place marked with a naan. It was a spoonful of rice, half a potato, a small piece of meat, and tea. I was not allowed to pay for mine. Conversation halted when a man walked in. From Kabul. Fighting much worse, spreading.

While the atmosphere of the first day had been timorous, suspect, few had moved, men and boys had hung indolently and menacingly about; by the second day a kind of *fête champêtre* had begun to take place. People had gravitated to the banks of the stream. Old men scrubbed their feet in it with stones. Others had prised their wives out of obscure huts and were picnicking *en famille*, someone had hung cages of canaries from the trees. An air of expectation, of movement, had pervaded what by now had become an encampment. Mongoloid faces, Uzbek girls in dresses of ikat had suddenly appeared standing by the stream, harbingers from the north. Trucks and buses were clearly coming through. Southwards. But what of northwards? 'Today go Kabul. *Jungly, jungly, niet.*'

Three huge lorries loaded with furniture and refugees set off, a bus arrived from Kandahar. Drivers began tinkering with their engines, revolving the notched rubber belts, but then gave up. One stuck a rose in one of the cogs and they all sat down to eat, using empty Duckham's motor oil cans as tables.

Animals lay about in the heat: scabby dogs and puppies, bearded goats with long silky coats like the best bred Afghan hounds, panting sheep with gross dirty pink udders, fat swab tails and matted wool.

A man wandered up to the stream and offered me a lift to Kabul later in the day on a Hilex 2000 by the Logar valley route. 'Dangerous' said the men from my bus.

Life by the stream continued. Men spat in it, young girls washed the family clothes in it, a fellow in dirty grey side-buttoning pyjamas, two large tin cans carried on a yoke of wood across his rounded shoulders, appeared from the teahouse to fetch water. To wash the glasses or make the tea? It seemed prudent not to enquire. The sugar-free chewing gum which of necessity I used to clean my teeth proved difficult to dispose of, sitting as I was under the intense scrutiny of hundreds of men and boys. I shifted it from one side of my mouth to the other and then threw it in the stream too. My hair was still densely matted and my person was, in general, malodorous.

Men came up and invited me to join their wives for tea. Makeshift shelters had been made to hide the women by slinging towels and dirty blankets from bushes and I skulked behind these with them. 'Inglistan' the men proudly introduced me and the wives asked about husband and sons.

'Excuse me, Miss' a voice said in perfect English. 'I'm on a bus that's about to leave for Kabul. You can come with us.' The man, dressed in clean clothes with a spectacle case and pen tucked in his pocket, led me to it. He would look after me and help me find somewhere to stay, he said. The driver, hands taut around the wheel, looked anxiously at me and refused to wait, though I rushed off quickly to collect my bag. Gradually the place seemed to be emptying but our convoy went nowhere.

'We go not to Kabul' said the men on my bus, listening to a portable radio, '*jungly* again' – the word was always accompanied by the pulling of imaginary triggers. 'We go Maydan.' I found it on the map, somewhat to the south of Kabul. But we went nowhere.

Babies started being sick and were brought to the stream. A man washing dishes in it threw water at me and when I moved away followed me and threw more. Boys came and pushed bundles of mint in my face that they had gathered for that purpose. Others went and fetched their baby sisters to stare along with them. Two youths grabbed my handbag and ran off with it but were pursued by the men from my bus: my travel bag, locked inside the bus, had already been ripped open, to their distress. I felt vulnerably rich with my old sunglasses, my torch and my clothes of European cloth.

Still we went nowhere.

By mid-afternoon the bus that had refused to wait for me had returned. They had gone about thirty kilometres and encountered intense fighting so the driver, scared, had turned back. My bus men looked satisfied.

'Come, come quick' said a young boy suddenly and took me to a jeep full of men, including the fellow with the spectacle case. 'We're going the Logar valley route. If it isn't safe to get into Kabul we'll stay in the valley tonight and go on in the morning. It's safe in the valley. We have relatives there. You can come. We'll wait while you get your bag.' As I tried to do so the men from my bus surrounded me and carefully, without touching me, prevented my leaving. 'You our woman' said one. 'You go not without our care.'

In the teahouse Sayid Farid Ahmad was listening to the radio. 'BBC World News says two hundred killed in Kabul today. Serious fighting between Shia and Sunni groups.'

By twilight the cows were coming home again, the sound of sub-machine guns was petering out against the croaking of frogs. Many buses and trucks had left and with them all the men who had offered me lifts and help.

'Why do you always say you're English?' said a man who walked up to me in the dusk. 'Why not say you come from America or Germany. People would respect you then. No one has ever heard of England.'

'But surely they know we do things to help Afghanistan?'

'Never heard. But USA, Germany, even France we know.'

'That's nonsense. What about the BBC? People are always listening to the World News.'

'They don't know it's from England.'

'But it says "London calling" doesn't it?'

'How do they know where London is? If you won't say you're from America or Germany it is better you say you are the lady Sheila from the BBC. Not from England. Also you should not be in the teahouse with the men. You will eat with my women.'

Striding ahead, he led me to a small hut, full of chattering, vividly dressed women, and brought me a large plate of rice and meat. 'One thousand eight hundred afghanis' he said.

'It can't be. A meal is usually two hundred and fifty.'

'It's special.' He looked threatening and fingered his gun. I paid, ate a small mouthful and, somewhat scared, got up to leave. The women pounced on the food immediately and I wondered what they had been getting to eat for the last few days.

Kabul

The approach to Kabul was inauspicious, though it had taken five days and nights to cover the three hundred and fifty kilometres there from Kandahar and expectations were high. Wide streets, potholed by bombs, were festooned with cut telegraph and electricity wires and flanked by dreary buildings like old army drill halls, burnt out or shelled. There were broken bottles everywhere. After the departure of the Russians the interim government had destroyed sixty thousand bottles of vodka in Kabul alone. A dull misery enveloped me.

The bus dumped us at the roadside leaving the returning refugee families sitting disconsolately among the sacks and quilts that comprised their total belongings. The men gathered together and put me in a taxi to the only hotel whose name they remembered.

It was boarded up and padlocked. I set off in search of another, only to find every one of them taken over as their command headquarters by a different group of mujahedin. They sat at the top of the steps, the plate glass doors behind them clustered with sun-blued photographs of their various leaders. Their Kalashnikovs were leaning at the ready against the rickety plastic chairs they had lined up as a barrier, and their kettles of tea steamed at their feet. All waved me away. In one I was taken to see the manager, a prosperous-looking fellow in a pale grey patterned silk jacket of the type affected by Sicilians, and a Kandahar embroidered shirt. It was not clear whether he was in charge or a hostage, but he also waved me away. I resisted ingratiating myself with him by complimenting him on his shirt as it was a machine-made version, but trudged on to the last remaining hotel. The reception was the same. A row of bearded mujahedin, guns glinting, gestured me on.

There was nowhere to go. It was one of those moments in travelling when momentum is lost, when scuttling off to somewhere else will not retrieve that momentum and when it is best just to hang about till something happens. Like a dog panting to a standstill after chasing rabbits, I flopped down in the heat at the top of the hotel steps and requested tea. Old courtesies surfaced and tea was brought. I engaged the men in halting conversation, though we had no mutual language, until one asked tentatively: '*Sprechen Sie Deutsch?*' In earlier days these men had been boys together in the school up the road, sharing the same German master. I had had the luck to fall on what must be the only German-speaking group of mujahedin in Afghanistan. They too had taken over the hotel as their headquarters. One offered me his own room and took me there.

He shifted from one foot to another. 'Are you going to wash?' he asked. 'Change your clothes? Swim?'

'Swim?' I hesitated, took off my shoes and put them back on again, while he tried to convince me there had once been a pool at the hotel. Finally he left and I locked the door but opened it again later in response to a knock. He pushed in, locked the door behind him, grabbed me in his arms and kissed me with some passion and obvious experience. I struggled wildly, trapped in a tangled creeper of strong young arms and whiskers. His grip softened as I pummelled him and he drew back. '*Entschuldigung.*' I nodded breathlessly. 'I'm sorry' – he looked contrite and I observed was rather beautiful – 'but I'll only leave when you say it doesn't matter.'

'*Macht nichts*' I muttered and he quietly left. The next knock on the door was his room-mate calling to collect his gun from under the bed and his football from the cupboard.

They were Shia fundamentalists, members of the Arakati Islami Afghanistan. They had walked into the hotel with their Kalashnikovs, pasting a picture of their leader Mohammed Asif Mosini on the cracked glass entrance door, and had taken it over but having taken it over they were unsure what to do with it other than use it as their base. They had not expected any visitors actually to turn up. The coffee shop they had padlocked, the manager they had confined to his office. The restaurant, manned by a fat veiled woman and an old grandfather with a thermos flask, opened occasionally to serve tea and rice. There was, of course, no glimmer of a swimming pool. They were unsure whether to charge four thousand afghanis for the room or two or nothing.

'Any chance of getting some clothes washed?'

'Yusaf will do it.'

I combed gently through my matted hair – it took half an hour
– and undressed for the first time for over ten days. Yusaf was a
little stooped old man who grasped the bundle of clothes with
alacrity. I never saw them again.

Kabul can never have been much of a place ('There are not four
substantial houses in the town' wrote Sir Alexander Burnes in
1841, before he was hacked to pieces by the inhabitants), even
before its nights crackled to intermittent gunfire, spitting red and
white fireworks in tracer lines across a watchful sky, and its days
thudded to bombs and mortar fire. Its lacerated buildings had
never been much more than a few dismal concrete offices and
hundreds of simple shacks. Some huddled stone-coloured up the
hillsides, their walls confounded into the stony ground in which
they were embedded so that only a jumble of square windows,
framed and crisscrossed in blue and green, betrayed their presence. Others were aligned into tin-shuttered locked bazaar stalls
or piled into flat-roofed blocks as the city converged to a vague
centre where footbridges crossed the river conduit and one tower
block pierced the skyline.

It was a small town crumbling inexorably and no rich city
destroyed by war. There were none of the buildings of a capital
city, no avenues of airline offices and fine residences, no government premises, just one functioning bank and a central post
office. Gap-toothed façades of old embassies and schools skulked
behind padlocked gates and no one could tell me what had
happened to the zoo. 'The Afghan Chambers of Commerce and
Industry. Central Office of Trade Association of Afghanistan' was
just a rusty sign over a grimy shut-up entrance, flyposted with
photographs of mujahedin leaders, the building itself a disintegrating apartment block painted apple green. A scarred French lycée,
set amid grassy banks and rose bushes festooned with barbed
wire, lurked unattended behind locked grilles. Here and there a
small blue stuccoed mosque, a flaked turquoise dome, a peach
office building, its windows and colonnades tricked out in white,
suggested warmer moments in the town's past.

At the intersections of its dusty potholed avenues tanks,
manned by mujahedin aligning their guns to pedestrian level,
stood guard. They vanished mysteriously during the hot lull of

midday or at night, but always returned to be repositioned at crossroads by the red and white traffic police booths. These were always empty. None of the traffic lights worked and the barriers around the pavements to filter pedestrians to safe crossings had been breached. There was, in any case, virtually no traffic, just the dawdle of a few buses and cycles and the plying of yellow and white taxi cabs, shattered every so often by the deafening metallic roll of tanks on the move and by the mujahedin root-a-tooting past in heavy armoured vehicles.

Crowds surged down the roads and through the breaches in the barriers, motley crowds in bizarre clothing, many, too many, on crutches, swinging their one good leg and the mine-blown stump of the one they had used to step forward in their wheatfield or goat pasture. They thronged along the pavements and the edge of the road where a ditch slurping with ordure tugged the women's shawls tighter across their faces. All the way along the pavement and roadside was a market display. High wooden carts held racks of cigarettes, trolleys shaded with rags and plastic awnings offered mangoes, bananas, radishes and tomatoes. People squeezed the produce, revolved it in their hands and rejected or bought, but mostly they just gawped at the goods laid out on the ground and hanging from the traffic barriers. Goods smuggled from Pakistan, a plethora of shoddy merchandise – plastic shoes, glitzy earrings, tin aeroplanes – smugly fussed over by cleanly dressed, digital-watched merchants.

Every building had been taken over by the mujahedin, their green or white flags flying. The Ministry of Information and Culture gave no information (though smuggled in visaless I felt it best to make no enquiry) but from its roof flags flew and a strongly beamed searchlight shone day and night at passers-by. Nothing worked except anarchy. There were no police, the letter-boxes were sealed, the phones were dead, the clocks were all wrong, the electricity sputtered into darkness.

There was one part of the town to which I constantly returned. The river tumbled between stone walls flanked on both sides by a wide road and a terrace of yellow stucco buildings. They were not quite symmetrical on each side of the river, nor indeed within each terrace. Some gables rose in semi-circular lunettes, some in flat pediments, some in pointed architraves, while others bulged into bow windows encircled with carved balconies of

wood that had peeled and flaked to the texture of potato skin.
Clerestory windows pierced the old tin roof while the windows
of the façade, originally framed in dark green paint, had faded to
speckled duck egg which here and there had been replaced by
bright turquoise, buff or a discordant dreary brown. They were
paned in tiny squares and squatted in by pigeons.

The ground floor stalls were shuttered with sunpeeled green
wood and signs above them of rusted metal, stuck skew-whiff on
the building's walls, noted their trade in Arabic and Latin script.
In no case did the seedy premises live up to the promise of the
sign. Some claimed to be health clubs: 'Arash Club Body Building.' Some, selling plastic hairslides and German shampoo, chem-
ists: 'J.A. Smeet & Co. Importers of Pharmaceutical Chemicals.'
Others, 'Asia Optic.' 'Ophthalmologist.', claimed to be opticians,
but were permanently locked and crumbling into desuetude.
'How should we have eye doctors when we have no doctors at
all?'

But most of the stalls belonged to tailors, who beavered away
at old-fashioned machines, and especially to makers of fur hats.
Hats of karakul, Persian lamb, astrakhan, to be precise. These
tiny dark shops glimpsed through grimy windows bore pretentious fasciae: 'Tailoring Industry of Karakul. M. Ali.' or 'Cottage
Industry of Karakul' illustrated by drawings of fat curly sheep
and bare-headed women wearing the fur coats they used to make
for tourists. The international trade that prompted one to describe
itself '*Magasin et Ateliers de Fourrures parlant français*. Conversation
to English. *Deutschsprecher*' had long since vanished and customers
were now just the local men.

'Not good trade now' the plump furrier smiled wanly. 'Better
in winter when snow.' Tiny pelts in black and all shades of beige
and grey from the warm gold of butter to the dry dust of dead
twigs festooned the walls of his cupboard-like shop. On the
counter and the window shelf stood rows of tall domed wooden
lasts that looked at least a hundred years old, each capped by fur
in various stages of modelling. He gently stretched a skin around
one of the lasts. Fourteen years he said he'd been making fur
hats, and his father before him. His family watched. 'This is my
son' he said of a five-year-old. 'This my sister', a pretty little girl
of about the same age, with swinging hair, 'and this my woman',
pointing to a burqa crouched in the corner, 'with new son. My

new son sick, but no doctor in Kabul.' He scurried out to fetch tea for me, then a saucer of toffees and, when I ate nothing, a packet of biscuits and finally a paper twist of sultanas. I bought one of his best hats for my son, certain that he would not like it at all, and stepped outside, feeling that it should have been on to a snow-covered pavement of St Petersburg, fur-hatted citizens and the icy floes of the Neva hurrying past.

There were another three guests, I discovered, who had breached the defences of the mujahedin and were staying in the hotel: the only Westerners I had seen in Afghanistan. The consulate at Peshawar, in defiance of Islamabad and all other Afghan consulates, was issuing a few visas. The news had whipped round the backpacker contingent there and one or two had decided to risk a trip to Kabul. One was a young American taking photographs of the detritus of war, hoping to sell them to magazines. His companion I never saw. He was too sick ever to leave his room and soon made his way back to Peshawar. And the other was Luc.

Luc was a French hippie who had strayed over from Goa. He remembered the hashish, he said, from when he last came through Kabul fourteen years ago and had come back to enjoy it again. He wore a flowery shirt he had bought on that occasion, with baggy red Indian trousers and a bum bag of money. A necklace of coral and turquoise amulets hung round his neck and his hair was tied back in a ponytail with dirty ribbon. He carried his belongings in a mauve and pink striped haversack with silver bells and a large embroidered bag of the wandering Banjara tribe of India, though he only knew it came from the bazaar and had no idea of its origin.

He described himself as an advertising designer but said he would be '*con*' to go back to France and that job so that 'they' could screw him for everything. Instead now and then he did something artistic when he was there – a sculpture, a drawing, some prostitution – and with the money went back to Goa. He talked – with a nervous eye twitch and dramatic gestures of the arms – for hours on end about his life and fortunate escape from the fate of the rest of his compatriots, those '*cons*' who sit in front of the television all day while 'they' kill them with taxes and ruin their minds. He felt deeply the injustices 'they' cause. He talked of ecstasy and acid and said 'they've' killed all the people who really meant anything: Hendrix, Lennon, Marley. Now songs are just stupid rhythms and people eat drugs like sweets. He grew irate. 'They have poisoned even these people. Here they think they fight for Afghanistan but they fight only for America and France.'

He drew breath. I had caught him at a bad moment, he explained, frustrated by his hour or so spent at the bank trying to change money. As an artist and sensitive person, he pointed out, he was swinging low because of this but soon I would be privileged to see him in one of his highs. (Spotted unawares in the street the next day he was a slightly bent little man, shuffling nervously along and peering through small thick-lensed glasses at the dealers trailing him.) He denounced capitalism, communism, Christianity, racism, greed, women. Only for Islam did he find a good word. 'Though they've made a mockery of the Koran, the women are treated well, so they're very content with their lives. And protected. Some of these mujahedin have never seen a woman, never. They know men marry and have children but they don't know how or what it means. They fuck each other.'

The second mujahed to pounce on me sidled into my room with the manager some days later, as I got ready to leave Kabul at four in the morning, and quickly locked the door as the manager left. This time in the struggle I felt a hand clasp over my mouth and a hard loaded Kalashnikov press into my body. But he was smaller than the other mujahed and not so strong. Nor had he expected resistance. Finally admitting defeat, he rearranged my shawl in a seemly manner and insisted on putting my burqa on me before letting me go.

I walked away in the dark to the bus stand, guns blazing around me, keeping plumb in the middle of the road, past the searchlight on the ministry building and the tank at the crossroads, its gun pointed vigilantly towards me.

Mazar-i Sharif

'Fresh Eggs from the farm' 'Holiday Land: Lübeck Bay' 'Daily Trips to Augsburg' proclaimed the old German buses and vans that had pulled to a halt on the blocked highway as I journeyed north to Turkmen amulet country around Mazar-i Sharif. Camouflaged tanks and Pakistani lorries dolled up like tarts in evening dress pulled up alongside. The river had come down in spate, gorged with the melting snows of the mountains, and had washed away the fragile temporary bridge and the war-weakened road. Vehicles had jammed up on both sides while a single line forded the raging waters. Impatient drivers headed into the river straight into the file of traffic coming the other way, bringing everything to a standstill. Fisticuffs were exchanged, more vehicles piled up, more waited, until finally some were forced to reverse and things got moving again.

Passengers scrambled down the banks to an eddying sidestream while they waited for the jam to be sorted out and sat drinking the water. 'Ten per cent of babies die of gastroenteritis and diarrhoea in their first year' said the doctor. 'What can you do? I'm a physician and there are hardly any of us left. The others all went to America and Europe. They won't come back. And we have no medicine. And no clean drinking water.'

It took about four hours for our bus to get through the jam; it then snaked up the mountain pass that followed the course of the precipitous river. Abandoned army equipment lay everywhere. The pass must have been fiercely fought over: perhaps it had been the first real resistance the Russians had met as they invaded from the north, taking the Afghans by surprise and passing unopposed through Tajik territory. Mujahedin barriers again blocked the road. Armed men – sometimes it seemed only to be a small boy and his grandfather – demanded money to let the bus pass without shooting the passengers. One thousand afghanis each time, which they busily counted. The driver's assistant always had a wodge of notes at the ready.

Beyond the pass and the mountains the landscape opened out

into wheatfields, golden in the evening light and scattered with villages here and there. The one where the bus stopped was nondescript. A thicket of windowless mud walls that the setting sun imbued with the translucency of amber, it lay on the east side of the road, while to the west a fast shallow river separated the people from the fields they presumably worked. Men scrambled on to the top of the bus, others opened the side stowage. They unloaded everything and piled it up on the pavement: wooden benches, quilts, cupboards, tin buckets, men's bikes. Almost all the passengers got off, one boy clutching a spanking new electric fan, though the village undoubtedly had no electricity. They were one large family of refugees – uncles, brothers, cousins, grandfathers and their womenfolk – returning home with all their possessions, on the public bus. The shrouded women walked straight into houses that must once have been their homes, with undimmed familiarity. Boys kicked around the stones in the street; a girl was sent immediately to fetch water from the river. No one came out to meet them.

There was clearly no hope of reaching Mazar-i Sharif that night as the bus was supposed to do. It stopped instead at the small town of Pulixumri, to a night free of gunfire and a sordid room I rented for a packet of cigarettes. There were subtle changes. Many more faces had Mongol features, the bread was no longer an oval naan but a thick circular disc, the countryside the bus passed through at dawn the next morning glistened with rice paddies, men tilled the soil with oxen and wooden ploughs. Soon the land undulated into rolling green hillocks, sprinkled with yellow and mauve daisies like hundreds and thousands. Tiny thistles, minute poppies and bonsai hollyhocks edged the road. Where the hillocks levelled out trucks of refugees careered past, laden with hessian sacks, petrol drums and beautifully painted lac cradles. Vast plains to the north announced the proximity of the great steppelands of Asia.

It was still early in the morning when the bus ran the gauntlet of a tank waiting in its path and reached the outskirts of Mazar-i Sharif. Here groups of domed mud houses thinned out and the bus passed small wheatfields and waste lots dumped with oil drums, tractors and stacks of wood. Abandoned petrol pumps leaned crazily and tanks both manned and rusting defended strategic spots.

Mazar-i Sharif itself was an unprepossessing town approached through a triumphal arch of blue concrete. It was set in a dusty grid around what looked like a huge turquoise mosque in Brighton Pavilion style, but turned out to be a shrine to Ali, a son-in-law of the Prophet. 'He already had a shrine somewhere else but then someone thought it would be a good idea to find some of his bones here and build another one. Bring pilgrims and trade.' The town was full of white pigeons.

Parychehr was unlike other women in Afghanistan. Their hair hung down untrimmed under layers of shawls; hers stood out from her face almost horizontally, cut in a short curly bob. They wore baggy trousers that hung in folds over ankle cuffs; she wore tight white jeans. They covered their trousers with a full-skirted, flouncy dress; she wore an oversized turquoise T-shirt. It was meant as a nightshirt, she explained, but she had been sent to Mazar-i Sharif in March for just a couple of weeks and had no summer clothes with her. And no Tampax, no Kotex. Her boss had said he would get what she needed from her flat and send it. 'But how can I ask him to get the Tampax from the second shelf down in my bedroom cupboard?'

She was Iranian and had fled at the revolution to work as a human rights agitator in New York. Now she had come as a volunteer to help in Afghanistan and ran the UNHCR office where the mujahedin had brought me. After her initial shock her welcome was very friendly and she plied me with ice-cold mango juice and questions about Iran. It was OK for me to stay in their guest house, she added — she herself stayed at her man friend's place — and it would be twenty-five afghanis.

'Twenty-five for a room? That can't be right, that's nothing. Thousand? Twenty-five thousand? That's impossible. Fifty dollars for a room?' Parychehr smiled patiently. 'It's Western standard. Satellite television. Hot water.' I began to brighten: it would be the first I had come across in Afghanistan. 'A bar.' At this I must have looked visibly cheered as she immediately added 'No alcohol yet, of course. It's ready in case we get international people here in the future.'

Empty shelves lined the wall behind the bar and a row of unoccupied stools stood in front of it. The TV showed American football. I brooded moodily on a refund. Still, there was no choice. The first hotel I had found was part of a terrace of pale green concrete buildings, its name entirely obliterated. The windows had all been blown out and grass was growing on its flat roof. The narrow entrance doorway disclosed a flight of steps that led to a landing where white pigeons flew around. A man lay asleep on a pile of quilts. '*Niet, niet. Niet* hotel' he said, waving me away and pointing in another direction 'Mazar Hotel.'

The Mazar Hotel was a very large pink affair that must have once been quite fine, but armed mujahedin had barred the way. 'Hotel' I said, inclining my head on my hands and snoring. This seemed to amuse them and they had led me to the UNHCR office. I was somewhat piqued that Pierre had not told me of its existence and my original excitement at finding in such a remote spot the protection of the people I was supposedly working for was considerably tempered by the outlay of fifty dollars.

It was to be one third of my total expenditure over nearly four weeks in Afghanistan, just for one night.

'Amulet? Is from Bokhara.' (Yet again, over the hill.) 'Triangle? Is centuries people like this shape. Others follow. Three tassels? Look beautiful and the people is habit it be.' The dealer was very knowledgeable and described the amulet as a kind of Muslim version of the chastity belt. 'Is girl wear on arm. If one person want to marry, other man want to marry to her, he try to get her away, girl wears so. Means that other man cannot interrupt, cannot touch her. Our religion not one girl to marry two men.'

That it contained something written by the mullah he confirmed unreservedly, but with a new slant. 'Girl keep it from wedding till she find a baby, one baby, then not necessary. Also is small one for baby being sick.'

The amulet was everywhere, embroidered, with tassels, exactly what I was looking for. It hung over doorways and was worked as a motif on the men's and boys' caps. It came from the villages round about, everyone said. There was, however, absolutely no possibility of getting to any of them. There were mines all over the place; public transport didn't exist; enquiries about lifts with the UN came to nothing. Parychehr was dogmatic. I was to leave. It was Eid, she said. 'Not the Eid that celebrates the end of Ramadan but another one. Traditionally we slaughter animals

and everyone eats, but not now. Not in Afghanistan. Still everything closes down for four days, no buses run. Except first thing
tomorrow morning for Kabul. You can't get anywhere else and it
would be terrible for you to be stuck here so I've bought you a
ticket. It's two dollars. Our driver will take you to the bus stand.
He'll call for you at three in the morning.'

Back to Kabul

Should Mazar-i Sharif not have been the end of the rainbow? Should I not have found there a tribe who remembered why their ancestors had thought an embroidered triangle with dangling tassels could protect them from evil, guard their women for themselves and shield their babies from sickness? And if the rainbow now seemed to extend further north, locating the crock of gold at Bokhara, why was I not going there? Why had I not resolutely, even with no transport and nowhere to sleep, just continued? And why, oh why, because of fifty dollars and a bossy woman was I heading in the wrong direction?

With the same resentment that makes us drive faster when we realize we've taken the wrong turning I scowled at the passing scene. Pulixumri, an innocuous town on the previous visit, now revealed itself as a tumble of buildings, their doors and windows replaced by wonky bits of wood and iron, chewed cardboard, (Why not Bokhara?) bales of straw, frayed cloth, rags, torn gauze, (Why, now that the Soviet Union is disintegrating, am I not there? Isn't this just the moment to go?) bricks, stones, corrugated iron, polythene sheeting and dirty paper (What made me choose the southerly route?).

As the bus trundled southwards and stopped at teahouses all I noted was that the roofs were made of sagging mud and twigs, of old car bonnets and tyres, and of ripped sheets of palm matting held down by stones and twists of string.

Disenchanted I watched women making bread by the roadside, girls fetching water. Boys brought tin bowls of mulberries to the bus, others sold rhubarb which the passengers ate raw. We passed what looked like vineyards. 'Angur' they said.

'No room' said the manager at the Spinzar, my old hotel in Kabul. 'Problems. You can't stay here.' Then in a *volte-face*: 'You can stay. Must be two nights or three. Tomorrow clothes Yusaf will bring. All days holiday.'

'*Noch ein Küss*' added my mujahed. They gave me a different room with one clean starched pink and blue striped sheet but even so I piled all the furniture behind the door.

It was the first Eid celebrated in peace for fourteen years. Though tracer fire sketched the sky it was now a firework display; though gunshots rang out through the night they were now celebratory; though there was no food and everywhere had closed it was only to mark Eid. It could end tomorrow or the next day or the next. There was no hurry. And Yusaf never came.

Jalalabad

The road to Jalalabad streamed with refugees heading in the other direction towards Kabul, most crowded into lorries and trucks with all their possessions piled on top and slung on the back, others driving camels, goats and sheep. Rusting armaments littered every pass, every orchard had been burnt and every village only cobbled back to life. The road itself wound down like a helter-skelter through dizzying passes and then levelled alongside a dam, grassy banks on either side.

The pick-up suddenly braked; all the men leapt out and scrambled up a bank, gathering stuff in the grass. They returned clutching handfuls of tiny baby birds. 'Good to eat' they said, cradling the frightened creatures in their dirty handkerchiefs or watching them struggle, cupped in their hands.

The hotel lay on the outskirts of Jalalabad, set in a quiet garden of trees on a wide avenue where small ragamuffin girls scooped up into frayed sacks anything they could find – leaves, fag ends, nails, tin cans – that might be used for something. The avenue was just like many others in old cantonments of the British Raj except that all the mansions had been blasted instead of left to fall into ruins. The hotel itself had survived and must once have been rather grand. Now its paint was peeling, its windows were cracked, the electricity was sporadic and nothing had been cleaned. A contingent of mujahedin was in charge as usual. Dinner was a scoop of plain rice, three plums and a cup of black tea. The next day it was a scoop of plain rice, some okra and a cup of black tea. The next day a scoop of plain rice, some spring onions and a cup of black tea. When I finally left Afghanistan I weighed seven and a half stone.

The group of men sitting under the vines of the hotel porch looked very important and were eating watermelon. 'I'm looking for the manager' I said, clutching a large bundle of Afghan notes worth three dollars that I owed for my board and lodging and was reluctant to hand to any old mujahed.

'I'm the manager' said one, looking directly at me with

intelligent amber eyes and a distinct twinkle. He handed the money straight back. He was Commander Abdul Haq, Chief of Police for Kabul and one of Afghanistan's major leaders.

'Since the so-called revolution six weeks ago,' he explained 'the fundamentalists have taken over all the public buildings. They're mostly stupid boys of fourteen or seventeen. How old are you?' he called to the callow youth pointing a gun at us all from the hotel entrance.

'Seventeen.'

'Better than fourteen' said Haq.

'Our problem is not Pathan/Tajik or Sunni/Shia, it is getting our refugees back and rebuilding the country. First we must get rid of the mines — four to five million of them. We must have a strong government, an interim one before we can have an election. That will take two years. We need democracy, we want to live like human beings, that is what we fought for. Now some mujahedin want a radical Islamic state but "mujahed" means volunteer resistance fighter, defending his homeland — it's only later they became political. We don't want to be told what to eat, what to wear, hit with a stick every day. My friend here, they think he isn't Muslim just because he prefers to shave. We don't want to have to put our women in purdah — if they want it themselves, so be it — we want freedom, that is what we were fighting for.

'America has a lot to answer for. The Soviets too, of course, they invaded us and destroyed us. But the Americans, with the Arabs — Saudis and so on — armed the radicals, so now what have we got? A hotbed of fundamentalist Islam, a haven for terrorists, a threat to the world. You will all suffer but we will suffer first. We could be prosperous, we have gas, we have oil, minerals, everything. In fifteen years we could be like the West [a vision of the jungly girls' kitchen in Kandahar flashed across my mind]. We could pay back any money we borrowed.

'You're here to look at the embroidery? An amulet? It doesn't mean anything to me. You came from Kandahar? Alone? I don't believe it. I would not have done it. Who helped you across from Quetta to Kandahar?'

'The UNHCR. I'm writing about embroidery for them.' He nodded wisely and I knew I didn't need to mention Gailani.

*

The indiscriminate cast of the dice of travel had thrown them together, two backpackers 'lucky' enough to get a visa for Afghanistan. Stephan from Antwerp, tall and fair, not just in colouring but fair with a clarity and honesty of mind that seemed formed by the windblown air of the North Sea and the sharp light of Flemish Masters. And his travelling companion, Paul from Colorado, who was short, dark-haired and tanned, and couldn't spell.

I had bumped into them on my return to Kabul, the only other Europeans there, and we had shared the pick-up truck towards Jalalabad for a kilometre or so. Then they wanted to walk, to experience the desert landscape, the mountains, the scorched orchards, the shattered villages, the glinting Kabul river and share the road with the nomads driving their camels and goats. Two days from Kabul to Jalalabad they said. I continued in the truck without them but half an hour after I took possession of my room in the hotel in Jalalabad they were brought in. 'Far too dangerous' they had been told by some well-wisher ten minutes after leaving the truck and setting out on their long hike. 'Your cameras, your rucksacks, everything, will be taken from you at gunpoint.' So they had been bundled on to another truck and brought safely into Jalalabad.

We had shared the dinners of plain rice, the three of us sitting alone in a dining room built for two hundred, at the head of a long table set with a white tablecloth covered with black marks as if a dirty dog had padded across it; halfway down, an ashtray crammed with cigarette stubs, lining the sides, dozens of empty red plastic chairs. The ordeal had been worse for them, they needed real food.

Hunger had kept us all awake on the last night. While theirs was more intense at least they were not racked by bones battered and bruised from being shaken around on the truck. Tossing from one skin-taut joint to another, assailed by sporadic gunfire at each attempt to doze, I was suddenly alerted at two in the morning by the most beautiful music. It lasted for an hour. It was like the chanting of monks in a medieval abbey, but with the shrill edge of Islamic harmonies. When it suddenly stopped I fell asleep, only to be woken by a mouse running across my feet.

We hired a pick-up truck together, the three of us, to take us to the Afghan border. We passed stunted, charred fruit trees, burnt-out military vehicles and tribesmen wielding sticks to guide camels and goats. We passed from arid plains to gaunt bare rocks, the sky clear, the sun relentless. Then the mountains gradually closed in again and the road climbed. More refugees passed in the other direction, their lorries piled with wooden beams they had taken from the refugee camps to use to rebuild their homes. Furniture and quilts wobbled on top, the father's bicycle hung on the back, as they trundled westwards to start life again.

The road at the border led straight through an open farm gate into a large space surrounded by commercial agencies, where a few taxis waited. Stephan had all the right papers: Afghan visa, double-entry Pakistani visa. Paul had an Afghan visa but not a Pakistani one. I had a valid Pakistani visa but no Afghan one. We walked through purposefully, Paul bent under the weight of a rolled-up carpet he had bought in Kabul that gave him the air of a wandering Bokharan dealer. Stephan and I were hauled back, Paul went through unchallenged.

A few official scribbles and stamps and we were released. The boys were desperate for food and we headed for the bazaar a few hundred metres away where they had bought chapattis and kebabs on their way through a few days before. It was empty, completely empty. The stalls, now just small patches of litter-strewn dry mud separated from each other by flimsy partitions, were inhabited only by flies. It was like coming across the bare skeleton of a flamboyant oriental dancer. The chattering vendors, the vivid displays, the animation, the smell of cooking, the sweat of bodies, the shuffle of hot dust had vanished. It wasn't Friday, it wasn't Ramadan, there seemed no explanation for this terrible desolation. With stomachs empty against sharp ribs, there was nothing for it. We caught a bus across the Khyber Pass.

It was one-way. The two roads that shimmied up and down through narrow clefts, up steep flanks and over bleached plateaux each carried traffic in one direction only. The road that used to be 'for the camel caravans, the strings of asses, mules, bullocks and shaggy ponies, and the scraggly medley of travellers passing this way twice each week, the hook-nosed tribesmen with bulging turbans and loop-the-loop shoes' and the other one intended for heavy motor lorries and troops had been bureaucratically tidied up. Forts far below in deep gorges and above on high peaks could occasionally be glimpsed through the dirty bus windows above the clustered turbans of the passengers. Gears groaned and ground until the level desert plain – where 'Heat Stroke Huts' once stood to revive British Tommies – was reached, and then the suburban ribbon roads leading into Peshawar.

Out of Afghanistan

The Khyber Hotel in Peshawar was one much favoured by backpackers. It was situated on a noisy main street and an old bearded woman was always asleep on the pavement just outside the door, lying on a pile of newspapers and accompanied by two tethered black hens and a large black cockerel sitting on a sack.

The hotel accommodation was in the form of dormitories and spartan rooms that had no windows but masses of holes, like dovecotes. These could be covered and uncovered by a system of small bolted wooden panels so that air and light could be let in together, but never one without the other. The doors opened in a similar manner on to a central landing that had no roof but stood exposed to the elements.

The backpackers were American, German, Swiss, Belgian and French. There didn't seem to be any English. One ('Name's Joe') was reading Martin Amis's *London Fields*. ('Just want to absorb other cultures.')

They wore, almost to a man, the same uniform: one earring, long hair in a ponytail, a light flowered shirt, baggy cotton trousers, open sandals and a small rucksack that they never took off. 'Going to Kabul, man' was a favourite phrase and they exchanged small boasts, jealousies and snippets of travel information. They were young and large and their health was of major concern. They bothered that their bodies needed salt and lamented the lack of protein in their diet. They explained how they ate fruit on its own and on an empty stomach so as to derive the maximum nutrition from it. They discussed endlessly their problems with diarrhoea. In the evenings they shrivelled down to lone diners or uncommunicating pairs in the next-door hotel they could not afford to sleep in but which offered fish and chips.

'I am wanting to see the emerald mines in Afghanistan. I am wishing to buy' the hugely fat Pakistani surrounded by an array of metal dishes in the same next-door hotel restaurant explained. 'I am having mines myself.' Despite the brown colour of the rotund arms that poked out from concealing swathes of shalwar kameez he resembled nothing so much as a Frankfurt business-man contemplating the potential of Erfurt. 'I am wishing to know from you how much bread? How many rupees? How many rupees dinner?' He beamed until a graphic description of the size of Afghan kebabs and the definition of dinner as a spoonful of plain rice and three plums caused his facial features to sag. They registered indeed a gentle withdrawal from the vaguely entrepre-neurial vision he had been entertaining of a virgin territory within his grasp. 'How road? How much bus? How much hotel? What hotels Kabul? What Mazar-i Sharif? How much?' He noted everything meticulously but missed the essential. He burped. It seemed doubtful he would actually go or survive the first pothole if he did.

The road to the bazaar was lined with dead animals, newly slaughtered, sacrificial. So the Eid of penitence and slaughter was celebrated here as it should be.

'For Eidul Azha' said Rashid. 'Your amulet is called Taweezak. Three things. One: is put on on advice of mullah. Two: is put on each shoulder, also with advice of mullah. Placed always on top of clothes against sickness. Three: before wedding started, father and mother of both man and woman go to mullah, take advice, then mullah told to them hang it or sew it in front of skirt. They believe in magic but they are laughing, keeps them in love. Till to one month. Can also keep it for long time. When wedding finished love is finished. First, second, third night very interesting, both of them have power. If don't take advice of mullah it is end of love of wedding. Woman who wear till child? Is only being romantic. Triangle? Because from before time of nation of Afghani-stan. So old. Also can be diamond-shaped with silver and cowrie shells and thimbles. Hang it on necklace. Also Turkmen. Sequin and mirror? Because light is Allah. Tassels? Only for fashion.'

The landing of the Kyber Hotel, open to the sky, was the meeting place of the backpackers. Here they chatted – 'any news of Kabul, man?' – while they crisscrossed between dorms, rooms, showers and the hotel office. They were observed, I noted, by a

tall rather stooping fellow wearing only baggy black trousers tied
with a pyjama cord and a waistcoat open to the waist over his
naked torso. He had a pale face, soft hair, gentle brown eyes and
some sort of a claw on a string hanging round his neck. Every day
he watered a pergola of rampant plants that formed an arbour
before the doorway of his room, like the cool entrance bower of a
chic restaurant in Italy. He was clearly a permanent fixture in
the hotel. 'Twelve years,' he said in an American accent 'refugee
from Afghanistan.'

His room was small and windowless, warm, dark and cosy,
piled with textiles, like a nomad's tent. The bed, low dark
polished wood cupboards and a black hi-fi system filled most of
the space. Kalter's *Arts and Crafts of the Swat Valley* and *Arts and
Crafts of Turkestan* lay around. The walls were covered with
posters of Afghanistan, with photos of Afghan boys and with
textiles: amulets, an Uzbek embroidered coat, a Tekke Turkmen
cloak. He brewed some milky tea in a small burner on the floor.
He was a textile dealer, he said. 'Look at these embroideries.' He
picked up a basket. 'Museum pieces. The best I've got.' I unfolded
a fine piece of work from Swat. It was crawling with maggots.
'Shit' he said.

He had left the States and hitchhiked to Afghanistan from
Germany in '73, he said. Loved Kabul and stayed. Wasn't anything much in the way of architecture but the people were sweet.
When he couldn't pay for his hotel any more they just told him
to stay on and pay when he could. Same with the chicken and
bread man up the road. That's when he set up as a carpet and
textile dealer. But the bottom's fallen out of the market now and
he couldn't think the world economy was ever going to recover.
'Still, I'm going back there as soon as I can. I'm horrified at the
vacuous youngsters who stay in this place and are trying to get to
Kabul just to say they've been there. When I tell them they
shouldn't they just say "Why? Is there a problem?"

'There was terrible shooting there on the fourth and fifth of
June – that's when your bus waited – lots killed. It was mainly
Sunni against Shia. The Hazara. But except for the fanatics the
Hazara are good people. They have problems because they're
Shia and also because they're supposed to be descendants of
Genghis Khan. As he killed two million and laid the country to
waste you can understand they're not liked.

'Your amulet? Yes, it's Turkmen but I should think much earlier than Islam. And the dress and shawl? They're from Kohistan.'

'Yes, but where in Kohistan?'

'Palas. The Palas valley.'

Kurdistan

❖ ❖ ❖

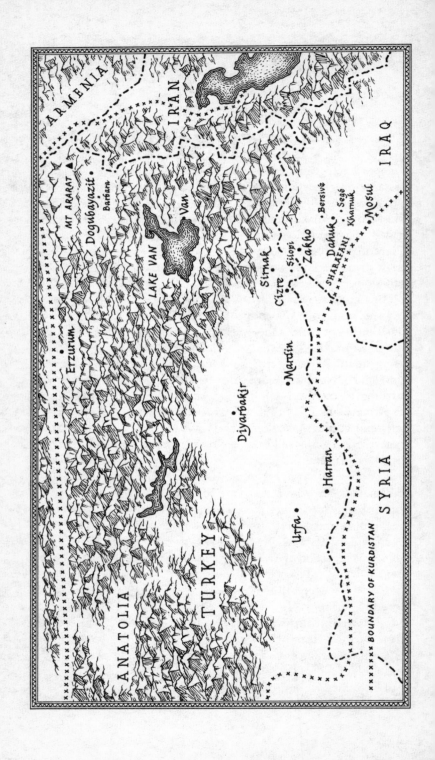

Back to the Kurds

Before I left England for Kurdistan three months later the message was clear (how could I have to gone to Dogubayazit and Barbara so heedlessly?): this was a war zone. 'Turkish State Massacre in Sirnak' proclaimed the Kurdish Workers' pamphlets, striped in national colours. 'Eighth Anniversary of the National Liberation Struggle.' The Gulf War had begun and ended nearly two years previously, hardly denting the Kurds' fight for autonomy.

The two centres of Kurdish resistance in north London lay not far away from each other in the vicinity of Archway tube station and Finsbury Park. One was in a large smoky hall full of lounging men drinking tea, with a few odd women in headscarves sitting apart. These were the Turkish Kurds, who called their homeland 'Northern Kurdistan' and claimed the Turks were pursuing a course of genocide against them as they had against the Armenians. The other was in a local leisure centre with pine walls and ceilings, snooker tables, and notices of the neighbourhood lesbian groups. These were the Iraqi Kurds, who called their homeland 'Southern Kurdistan' or sometimes simply 'Kurdistan'.

A couple of earnest young women with cocker spaniel hair and smart boots, whom marriage had passed by, gave the impression of being in charge, the energy they would have devoted to the childbearing years slipping out of their grasp, channelled into revolutionary fervour. News bulletins were issued daily, full of rabid invective involving names liberally larded with 'Ks' that stood always for Kurd: ARGK, KDP, PUK, PAK, PKK, ERNK. They were all fighting each other and Harold Pinter had signed his support.

In Northern Kurdistan bodies were everywhere it was claimed: burnt corpses, dozens of wounded unable to receive treatment, dead animals. Police were shooting at random any woman, child, youth, elder – in fact, anything that moved that wasn't a strong, armed, trained young man – killing and wounding them by the hundred. Telephone lines were cut, houses set on fire, the

pamphlets shrieked, until 'break in fax communication' silenced
them. A German human rights delegation to Kurdistan had been
arrested at the bus station in Diyarbakir (I had myself some years
previously been apprehended for vagrancy at Diyarbakir bus
station, I recalled). They were waiting for the five o'clock bus to
Ankara, the press release said. A seventy-four-year-old journalist
had been gunned down in the streets of the same town, the ninth
to be killed there in eight months. It was Turk against Kurd,
Kurd against Kurd.

For those visitors somewhat vague as to the precise location of
Kurdistan – beyond Dogubayazit – helpful maps lined the walls.
They delineated a territory that seemingly embraced the whole
of eastern Turkey, its boundary in the north the range of
mountains that separated it from the Black Sea, and in the south
clipped the north-eastern corner of Syria, cut a swathe through
northern Iraq and sliced into western Iran.

It was the swathe in northern Iraq that I wished to enter:
leftover region of the safe havens of the Gulf War, under the
control of the Kurds with the weaponry of the West hovering
across the border in Turkey ready to pounce if Saddam made a
false move. Though most Kurds are Sunni Muslims, in this
region traces of old Zoroastrian beliefs remained – worship of
fire and so the sanctity of wood – especially among the Yezidis,
heretics who had broken from Islam and taken refuge in isolated
groups. They hung cloths on branches of trees – maybe embroidered like those of the heartland of Russia – and tied them
around piles of stones placed under the trees where the sick
would come and sit, waiting to be cured. But the border was
dangerous territory both on the Turkish and the Iraqi sides. I had
come for help to get across.

'You walk across the bridge' said the Freedom Fighters, evok-
ing memories of the vulnerable figure of Sakharov as he trod
those few steps to freedom over a snow-covered Berlin bridge.
'Only for God's sake don't get into a taxi. Never get into a taxi
alone. They drive you down to Mosul. That's Saddam territory.
They can sell you there for a lot of money and you disappear or
get seven, maybe ten, years in prison.'

'This letter' they said 'for the border guards when you walk
across the bridge. This for the English teacher in Zakho. Don't
mix them up.'

Though I was not intending voluntarily to step across from protected Kurdish Iraq into Saddam's lair, I had felt a certain unease at this last lap of the journey. I had chosen to wear my clothing for true travelling: the bra with hidden pocket for hundred dollar notes, the socks with pockets for fifties, layers of concealing garments and my mother's wedding ring that the nursing home had thought to remove and hand me. I had packed, unpacked and repacked my sleeping bag. I had spoken to all my children, or at least to their answerphones. I had set the burglar alarm, thrown out the neighbour's cat and checked the Istanbul address of my Turkish colleague at our annual Arts Festival.

Istanbul

The huge tents go up every year in July in a field in Oxfordshire.
'Where d'yer want the chicken 'eads, Guv?'

'Chicken heads?'

'Yeah, Guv, fer the foxes. Dinner like.'

'Foxes? But this is an Arts Festival.'

'Works from life 'e sez, this bloke. Sculpture or summat.'

'I see. Well I'm the beachmaster. You may leave them here
with me.'

The tents are labelled 'Sculpture', 'Printmaking', 'Middle Eastern Arts', 'Traditional Crafts'. When the crowds arrive the women
tend to be dressed in long skirts and floppy hats decorated with
cherries and cornflowers, or in the kind of chiffon Indian dresses
with handkerchief skirts fashionable in the seventies. Some carry
trugs of flowers or posies and all wear sensible shoes for the mud.
Strolling musicians play medieval harmonies on lutes or trill
'April is in my mistresse's breast', dogs sniff around each other,
men in woolly socks and sandals and short-sleeved shirts organize
their families. There is a warm atmosphere of Love and bygone
serenity and a general whiff of pig slurry in the air.

Terribly polite announcements are made on the Tannoy: 'it
might interest you to know that the Japanese tea ceremony ...';
'unbeknownst to you the violin makers ...' The beauty of the
organizers' belief that 'in art perhaps there is a key as to how
society might turn from the misery of conflict to the happiness of
mutual consideration and respect' shines through the whole
event.

Tipping rain deters no one and wellies churn the grass into
creamed spinach inside the tents as the public watch intently – in
a way that only the English could – an Ethiopian calligrapher,
the sculptor carving foxes, an engraver etching glass, and the
Turkish marbler.

Hikmet always gets a round of applause. He stirs ox gall into
his paints so that the colours will spread but stay apart from each
other as he marbles paper and silk. As soon as he starts to work

the people watching my embroidery demonstrations of the waste canvas technique used in Syria move away across to Hikmet's stand opposite mine in the Middle Eastern Arts tent. The shallow dish of water in front of him is thickened with tragacanth. The shepherds gather the sap from the plants in the mountains in Turkey, then dry it into curly white flakes and sell it in the bazaar, he says, usually for making Turkish delight. Hikmet drops one colour on to the bath, then another, and draws them across the water, the ox gall holding the surface tension. A final flourish of paper across the marbled water, and the crowd applauds, then drifts away to watch Indian dancing, moving meditation that is said to still the mind and express inner serenity.

'If ever you come to Turkey,' calls Hikmet across the tent 'I have a B & B in Istanbul.'

It was instantly recognizable: even the plant containers on the steps outside were marbled. The curtains were marbled, the chair covers were marbled, the discs round the light switches were marbled. It lay close to the church of Aya Sophia, floodlit at night into piled copper jelly moulds. Hikmet's wife Füsun ran the establishment with a charming smile and extra cups of Nescafé. The carpets were threadbare.

'I'll find Mehmet,' said Füsun 'he used to work for us, but now he's waiting for a visa for America and he's just been back to Anatolia while he waits. He's a Kurd so he might be able to help you.' Mehmet was twenty-four and had a shy smile, rather like a girl's. The shoulders of his silky green suit were too broad for his slim frame and his watch was too big. He had grown up, he said, in a small village of apricot orchards in eastern Anatolia: 'If you have apricots you have money, if no, no.' Because of his recent trip home he knew something of the situation, what fighting there was between Turks and Kurds and the PKK. 'We must go upstairs to talk, it's much too dangerous down here with other people around.'

We went upstairs to the breakfast terrace and Mehmet switched on the light. We sat at a table with a map of eastern Anatolia. 'There's terrible fighting in the whole border area: Turks against Kurds, PKK against Peshmerga, Iran against Iraq.' At each mention of danger he thumped the map with the back of his delicate olive-skinned hand. 'And if you intend to go over the border into Iraq it's very dangerous. Saddam's agents are everywhere.' I showed him the letter I had been given for the border guards. 'This is in Arabic script. It's almost certainly PKK.'

'Yes, but who are they?'

'They call themselves Freedom Fighters, fighting for the independence of Kurdistan but they're terrorists. Showing your letter to the border guards is like trying to cross an international border with a letter of recommendation from the IRA.'

'When you get to Diyarbakir go to the Caravanserai Hotel. There you might find contacts. Foreigners working in the area. Aid people, journalists. It's the best advice I can give you. Be very careful.'

'Don't go,' said Füsun 'it's too dangerous.'

Diyarbakir

Gerd was dressed as any good traveller should be: crumpled but clean, casual but conventional. The only frivolities were the discreet logo on his T-shirt 'Andy Baum and the Trix. Extra Feathers' and a leather bracelet. For love, he explained, from his girlfriend. They can be in fabric or leather and when they break the relationship is over.

'Leather must be good then?'

He twinkled: 'It's only a game'.

He worked in Munich in a pathology lab and travelled two or three times a year. Just for a couple of weeks. His clear blue eyes, framed in steel-rimmed granny glasses, saw and understood everything. He felt deeply the shortcomings of mankind and tried personally to atone for them. The poverty around him, the history of his own German race, the insensitiveness of tourists to the places they tramped around, the deprivation of the kids: he made everything his own concern. Every pocket was stuffed with small notes which he distributed with largesse; he apologized to the Kurds that Germany had sold weapons to the Turks; he had taken on a young guide who styled himself 'Imperator' when he learned that two New Zealanders had used him for a day's sightseeing in Diyarbakir and had paid him nothing.

They were taking tea, Gerd and Imperator, in the courtyard of the old Caravanserai Hotel, an oasis of roses and fountains. Here, following Mehmet's instructions, I was looking for a contact who might take me into Iraq. Only two Dutchmen were checking in, the hotel said. I presumed Gerd was one and approached him. He wasn't but he devoted himself to the task of helping me and was even tempted to escort me himself had Germans not been so disliked in these regions. Imperator, he decided, was too young to take the risk involved, so he despatched him to find someone mature who knew the ropes.

Ahmet was the man, soft-spoken, calm, reflective, wearing a shabby leather jacket, his hands still dyed with fading henna from his sister's wedding. A man to be trusted, thought Gerd. A price

needed to be agreed for him to escort me on the bus to Silopi
where he would get my letter to the border guards translated to
make sure it would not add to the dangers of the journey, as I
now suspected it would, and then take me over the border. One
hundred dollars, said Gerd, US dollars, that would be fair. He
was not a man to let down so we all shook hands on it, though it
seemed a fortune to me.

Everything then happened very quickly. By the time we
trooped off to the Kurdish information office for up-to-date news
on the fighting and border situation all sorts of other men had
joined us. It wasn't quite clear who they were or how they were
involved, only that the cost of tea for everyone increased rapidly
at each stop. Gerd paid.

The information officer said there had been heavy fighting
around Zakho and the border but it was all right to go. Just be
very careful. People were scared. The police were turning everyone off the highway by the early curfew hour of four as terrorists
had blown up a bus, after robbing and kicking all the passengers
but at least leaving them alive. 'Better phone your embassy and
tell them where you're going' Gerd suggested.

'Zakho? Where's that?' said the girl at the other end of the line.

That evening on television Zakho was shown on a map with
explosions all round it, drawn like a children's comic: Wham!
Bam! Zoom! Pound! Maybe someone from the embassy was
watching.

Ahmet was to meet me at eight in the morning.

The sun rose early and the pavements of Diyarbakir had already
been laid out into small squares defining one man's pitch, each
having room enough for one low stool and a display of cigarettes
or nuts or olives. An old man sipped his morning lentil soup,
another blew his nose into his fingers and dribbled the snot to
the ground.

The eight o'clock bus to Silopi surprisingly was full, also the
nine o'clock, so it was ten before we set out, Ahmet looking
apprehensive and Gerd – accompanying us as far as Mardin –
giving money to all the children around, saddened by the lack of
medical care, of social security, of schooling, of family planning
advice. The bus company prevented him from buying tea for
their waiting passengers and offered it themselves.

The scenery was, as ever, biblical: men tilled tiny fields with wooden ploughs, women beat washing in streams with stones. A dam glistening on the horizon promised a future of electricity and irrigation.

At Mardin – a hilltop town overlooking the Syrian plain and capped by three huge radar domes – Gerd got off the bus and was immediately surrounded by police for questioning. Carved in the hillside above the town were the words 'I am happy I am Turkish'. 'Ask for Kurdish music' Ahmet added 'and they sell you Turkish.'

Beyond Mardin the road skirted the scorched earth and watchtowers of the Syrian border. A flat expanse of immense cottonfields followed as the border became that of Iraq. Nomads from the mountains had come for the work of picking, setting up huts of matting and plastic for their homes. The men sat around talking while the women and children, spaced in lines along the fields, bent in the broiling sun. Bunches of tanks manned by armed men hung close to the road. At a village before Silopi an old man and a sheep and most of the passengers got off the bus. Ahmet and I stayed on. At Silopi he set off to find the contact given him by the information officer in Diyarbakir. I followed him carrying my bag. A cock crowed.

The contact was supposed to be found in a small shop selling lavatory pans. He wasn't there but his brother sent Ahmet on to another. The second contact turned out to be a rather elderly man sitting in a dusty shop full of unwanted packets of biscuits and sugar and large padlocks. He had fly-away hair that seemed to resist all combing, a brush moustache and several days' stubble, and was wearing a grey suit, a grubby open-necked white shirt and dark sunglasses. The shop was rather dim.

He looked doubtful. There had been heavy fighting at the border, Turkish helicopters and tanks attacking the Kurds, but a little to the south-east. The PKK were involved. The road to Zakho might be OK but transport was difficult. There were taxis but the drivers were afraid of being seized by the PKK and taken to the mountains to be turned into terrorists. Still the English-Kurdish relationship was good. He would see what he could do. Did I think Barzani or Talabani should be leader?

The taxi arrived with two drivers, a one-eyed old man and a dark gypsy. Ahmet looked at them. 'The Iraqi border guards charge Turkish Kurds one hundred dollars to cross, you only twenty-five. I will take you to the border then find a taxi there to take you to Zakho.' We climbed in and there was hardly time to wonder how he suddenly got this information. 'These men will try to take us to the border' said Ahmet. 'They may not want any money.'

The gypsy drove and the one-eyed man kept his good eye on us. We passed an Iraqi refugee camp, high concrete walls topped by wire mesh and floodlights. There were mountains in the distance over the other side of the Tigris.

At the border Ahmet handed my passport to the Turkish officer. ('Why are you Kurds bothering me with this?') Ahmet then found a friendly-looking taxi driver and negotiated a price with him to take me to Zakho and find the English teacher to whom my letter of introduction was addressed. It was generally agreed to forget about the letter to the border guards as its effect was only likely to be adverse. All things arranged, I fished surreptitiously in my bra and gave Ahmet a hundred-dollar note.

The taxi man drove me across the bridge to the first check-point. A dead ringer for Saddam Hussein stood there, bristly moustache, khaki uniform, dark beret. He stared and said nothing. A thin gentle-looking man greeted me warmly: 'Welcome to Kurdistan. You're most welcome. You will need no visa here.' He slid a piece of paper into my passport. 'Peshmerga' said the driver.

We continued to the next checkpoint over a second bridge. The welcome was the same. 'But you must now go to our Public Relations Office.' They bundled me and my bag into a taxi with an Iraqi woman. 'I live in Sweden now. Have for seven years. Hate it.' As I looked round I saw my taxi had turned tail and was speeding back into Turkey.

The men who greeted me at the Public Relations Office were educated, sophisticated, articulate, of a type I hadn't seen for some time. 'My goodness,' said the one who checked my passport 'you've been to some interesting places. Your project sounds fascinating. I know that embroidery pattern. If I weren't so busy here I'd love to come along with you.'

The second man was even more friendly. 'You must stay at our rest house. It will be a pleasure to look after you. We will supply you with an interpreter and with whatever transport you need. I'll arrange for a taxi to take you there now. No Iraqi dinars? Never mind, I can see to that for you right away. You will need to change a hundred dollars for your stay with us.' I fumbled discreetly. 'You are most welcome. We are always delighted to welcome Europeans. The Europeans have done so much for the Kurds. We owe our lives to you.'

He shortchanged me by twenty-five dollars.

Zakho

The Zakho Public Relations Office was a small building opposite the sandbagged military headquarters. It seemed to be staffed
mainly by English teachers. 'Six hundred teachers in Zakho'
they said 'for two thousand five hundred people. Most of us teach
English. Education is our future.'

I left my second letter tucked in my bag and set off for the rest
house with one of them. 'You must go nowhere unescorted' the
teacher said as he led me down the road. A small child came
running up, a three-year-old. He smiled, put his hand in mine
and walked along with me.

'We have no doctors and no medicines' the teacher continued.
'Food is short and there is no fuel because the PKK won't let
anything through. The winter will be hard. And aid is stopping,
we don't know why.'

The political situation was complicated and grew ever more
complicated with each question I asked, the answer depending
on the views of the person to whom it was addressed. 'What's the
PKK?' It was a terrorist, Marxist, guerrilla group, determined to
undermine any attempt to keep Northern Iraq as a Kurdish-
controlled entity. Or it was the group who bravely resisted
Turkey's massacre of innocent people and who by its military
efforts had managed to open the border to a certain amount of
trade. It was also thanks to the PKK that it was no longer a
crime to speak Kurdish on Turkish soil.

'Who's Barzani?' Massoud Barzani. He was the young, intelligent, moderate, freely elected leader of the KDP, who was the
best hope for a democratic future. Or he was a weak conciliator.
'And Talabani?' Jalal Talabani, PUK. He was older, would
achieve more for the Kurds. Or he was aggressive, flirted with
Turkey and would wreck the democratic machine.

'And Peshmerga?' They were a moderate democratic group
who didn't kill people and who had managed to keep Northern
Iraq out of Saddam's hands. Or they were the Kurds who had
sold the idea of an autonomous Kurdish homeland down the

216

river; they were Iraqi rebels, traitors who were helping the Turks flush the PKK from its mountain hideouts.

These mountains were visible from the roof of the rest house and every evening fighting would begin. About eight.

Zakho was an undistinguished little town with an air of having been rebuilt many times. The population included numbers of Christians but none the less salaam aleikums were exchanged all the time and some women wore the chador, though they might flash a shapely leg as they walked past. It was not the chador of Iran, at least not in spirit. Otherwise they appeared to be either in evening dress – gold brocade, pink chiffon over pale blue – or in nighties, ankle length and gathered on a round embroidered yoke. The men declared their allegiance to the cause by wearing the national Kurdish dress of baggy trousers, shirt, crocheted cap with keffiyeh draped around, cummerbund and gun.

The men wandered around the market area and squatted in booths exchanging dollars, though this activity soon stopped as no one else came over the border and they couldn't sell them again. Apart from a few fish laid out on a doorstep and stalls piled with grapes and cucumbers there was not a lot of food to buy. The bazaar itself was the kind which, eviscerated of its traditional handwork, was filling its empty shelves with the tawdry and flash of alien commerce.

At the rest house there were a group of Turkish journalists, tired and unshaven, one Greek TV reporter and a Brit, an aid worker, Angus. 'Don't go anywhere unescorted' he said. 'Don't get into any taxi or private car alone. There are Iraqi agents everywhere and you can't tell them from the Kurds. They'll either kill you or hand you over. You're worth fifty thousand. A lifetime's money for them.' It hardly seemed worth asking fifty thousand what.

The day before my arrival a parliamentary committee had stayed at the rest house and chickens had been killed. The men running the place – as in all such establishments everywhere there was never a woman to be seen – did no cleaning but organized rooms and prepared food, much of which they ate themselves. They presented for dinner a large dish of plain rice, topped with the chicken remains from the politicians' plates: 'I saw them scrape them up' said Angus. And the little frilly edges of the chicken wings. The Turks had brought their own supplies.

Ascertaining on the first night that there was no more fighting to be seen, we went to bed. The men in charge put me in Angus's room, presuming that was the way things were done in the West.

The Aid Project

Angus was a Jeremiah. He bemoaned the continual menace of
corruption and fraud and in the face of it clung tenaciously to
the funds donated to his Aid for Disaster charity and dispensed
them warily. Uneducated but for the wisdom acquired in a
lifetime of the army and then the freedom to do his own thing,
freedom, he stressed, to do just what he felt like doing: dabbling
in property, farming in Wales, horse eventing. Then, retiring to
Scotland, he had seen on television, as everyone had, the Kurds
tramping through mud up to the knees as they escaped from
Saddam to the mountains, and had decided that this was the next
thing he felt free to do.

His aid scheme was simple. He didn't go round with begging
bowls but approached those charities that had money to spare
with a project he would implement. In this case he would supply
Kurdish villagers with seed wheat. Half a ton for each farmer.
One sack of seed now as opposed to three sacks of flour next
year. And with half a ton of seed wheat it was up to them to
grow it, to work, harvest, pull themselves up and get going again.

It had been hard to interest the charities but in the end
Christian Aid and the Catholic CAFOD had backed him. 'I'm
not religious, but it makes you think.' He despised Save the
Children and UNICEF; he had seen their stupid road schemes.
'What use was that for a child?' He had seen them all leave.
'Oxfam even took their tents with them.' From more than a
hundred and fifty aid organizations active in Northern Iraq six
months ago, fewer than twenty were now left. One reason was
the fighting. Then the bounty that Saddam had put on the head of
any European killed or captured. And the sanctions. Not just the
United Nations ones that were a farce and meant Turkey hung
on to things saying they were for military purposes – 'Sewing
machines, for example. We've got ten of those stuck in Mersin, and
school desks. We need them to reopen the school.' – but mostly
the PKK ones in support of the struggle for independence
of the Turkish Kurds. As Baghdad had imposed a total embargo

on food and fuel going into Iraqi Kurdistan, supplies had to
come from Turkey, so the PKK had taken it on themselves to stop
all food crossing the border and set the lorries on fire if the
drivers refused to turn back.

'Then there's the corruption. The tribal chief of the Sharafani
we're helping – a young man educated at Glasgow and Dundee –
wanted a twenty thousand pound pay-off from me out of the
project money so he could buy himself a smart four-wheel drive.
I told him to get lost.' Later, on a trip to collect a load of seed
wheat, Angus was taken over to the supply lorry and then
pounced on by five armed men ('Walked into it, didn't I?') and
held to ransom for the twenty thousand. 'Haven't got it on me.
And anyway I don't hand over a penny of other people's money.'

'It's the villagers we love, so we can't leave. It's for them we
stay. But then if their own rulers, their own tribal chiefs, they
steal from them, their own people, what hope is there? The day
after we've gone the rulers take everything. They pull down our
signs, so the next charity that comes along thinks nothing is
being done here so they try to move in. It's the spider's web
catching the fly, it's the old trick of keeping a sick child. One sick
child,' said Angus lugubriously 'one food token. Two sick children, two tokens.'

He worked in a remote area a few miles from Saddam's troops,
together with an assistant, an overeducated, immature young
man who regarded all women, Kurdish or otherwise, as 'babes'.
Angus had recruited him by phone: 'One earring?' 'No.' 'Ponytail?'
'No.' 'You're on.' Together in public they strutted, but in private
they quietly brought hope to a myriad tiny neglected communities
and had not lost in megabucks the concept of what humanitarian
aid was all about. They took no expenses for themselves, only
'enough for the odd bacon sandwich', which they tried to cover
simply by fluctuations in rates of exchange. They were both of
necessity armed.

The drive down to the Sharafani tribal territory at the southern
boundary of the 'safe haven' area where they worked was
through an empty landscape of tufted hillocks. The scene was
broken only occasionally by the odd small town and ruined
village of stone and mud houses, its replica built in concrete a
few metres away. Road checks by armed Peshmerga were frequent. Angus was always recognized 'Hello, Mister!' and we were

waved through. Trucks passed, high open vehicles with huge metal tanks strapped to their sides. 'An oil fiddle' said Angus ruefully. 'They bring medicines in and then get oil illegally from Saddam and take it out to Turkey. The Kurds make money out of it. The rulers, of course.' The tanks looked makeshift and leaked badly so that the roads were black with oil spillage. It splashed up on the windscreen so the driver could see nothing and hit every pothole square on and barely missed a flock of sheep.

'Then those mechanical shovels on top of the hill, they were sent to rebuild the country but they're just used to haul oil trucks up so they can make money' said Angus gloomily. 'The rulers again, of course. The people, they see them go by in a flash car and they admire them for being successful. They don't understand it's money given for them. At our meeting the young Sharafani ruler, he looked at the farmers and said "Didn't he say one ton of seed wheat each?" They nodded. Of course they would nod. "And now, what have you got? Only half a ton." They nodded. He didn't say that it had been given by our charities and our hard work and that he had taken the rest.'

As we passed small towns men by the roadside stood with drums of petrol, sucking it up in a tube to their mouth and then pinching the bottom of the tube and releasing the petrol into plastic containers, a spoonful at a time. 'To sell on the black market' said Angus glumly. 'Without the black market there'd be nothing. And think of their lungs.'

Lorries piled with wool passed us; women walked by bearing water. Some areas were marked 'Danger. Heavily mined'. 'Blood feuds here too' said Angus. 'Just by these steps on the hillside there was a man with a café once but men from another tribe they came and killed him. Just because someone from his tribe had killed one of theirs. They still go on, these blood feuds.'

Families squatting in tents by the roadside sold firewood. 'All they have to make a living' said Angus. Another family of nomads stood outside their matting huts. Angus stopped the driver and walked over to them. 'Here you are, some tools' he said, handing them a good hammer, pliers, a saw. The men just stared in disbelief.

Angus's project was run from a small building – a hole knocked in the ceiling to let smoke out now let rain in – in a village of wide streets and low simple houses in Sharafani territory not far from Saddam's border. His assistant, Peter, had been left behind to work alone, supported by flip-top packets of American cigarettes and a pistol he described as 'kosher'. One load of seed wheat had been paid for but not delivered. Sixteen thousand pounds' worth. 'Find out what's happened to it, then get out of here' said Angus.

'Oh no, just when I've got myself a babe.' He enjoyed working in Iraq he said. Went down well with the dolly birds back home.

Corruption and bureaucracy regularly delayed consignments so that deliveries were often made in the small hours of the morning to remote mountain villages, sometimes inaccessible in the darkness. Then the village's allocation of seed wheat would be dumped by the nearest roadside on a sheet of tarpaulin. All the men of the village would walk down the mountain to the road and guard the seed by lamplight, their women joining them with tea for the night's vigil. 'This is ours. This is new life for our village. No one shall steal it.'

The English Teacher

It was the second wife who had broken her hand, the interpreter explained. The young one. Slipped down the stone steps carrying the washing. We would have to sit in the garden and wait till she got back from the hospital.

'I understood there was no medical care here.'

'Oh, yes, there's a good hospital. Six or seven doctors. And an even better one in Dahuk. It's in the countryside that there's nothing.'

'This is a rich man' the interpreter went on. 'Two wives and eleven children and they're still working at it. Most of us can afford only one wife, but this man has a stall in the bazaar and a four-wheel-drive truck he hires out.' We waited in the warm morning sun. The washing that had caused the problem now hung on the line. Close scrutiny revealed among the worn clothing an embroidered cloth, tulips worked in cross-stitch. The interpreter explained how it was done. 'The woman can't count the threads in the fabric, it's too close a weave, so she puts some sort of gauze on top, étamine we call it – the French word. Then she embroiders, counting the threads on that. When the work is finished she cuts the gauze and pulls the threads away, leaving the pattern on the fabric.' This was the waste canvas technique that the women also use in Syria and that I had demonstrated at our Arts Festival. 'I'll bring you back this afternoon to see her doing it, when they're home from the hospital' the interpreter added. I waited for him in the afternoon with great excitement but he didn't turn up.

The second interpreter the Public Relations Office found for me was another English teacher. The first had worn Kurdish dress in a beautiful fine handwoven woollen fabric that I had rubbed with pleasure between my fingers. 'Made here' he said. 'I'll show you where', but of course he never did. The second wore cheap Western trousers and a freshly ironed open-necked shirt. He was clean-shaven and had fine laughter lines around his eyes and a soft voice.

'We'll begin with the Kurdish Union of Women' he said, buying me a pomegranate juice on the way. Here a blind woman showed me how they spun, holding the wool in a piece of tubing wound round her hand, and rolling the spindle on her thigh. Cupboards were emptied of terrible white lace flowers, sequinned trimmings of oya work for scarves ('The men in prison make these too'), and ghastly pink roses embroidered on green satin. I tried to look pleased and the English teacher beamed. 'These they sell for children of the martyrs.'

We set off for the street in Zakho the English teacher remembered as the street of the weavers, who would set up their warp threads along the pavements, as they still do in India. The posts were there but the weavers had all gone. Left some years ago, people said. 'You'll only find them in the villages now.'

'We'll go on the bus this afternoon' – the English teacher was warming still further to what he saw as my project, though weaving has always bored me – 'but now to lunch at my home.' We passed women sitting by the roadside making bread exactly as Sarah had in the courtyard in Kandahar, flat discs of a flour and water dough thrown over a metal dome above a wood fire. 'They have nothing. They make it to sell so they can live.'

'Bread was all we had, and the clothes we stood up in when we fled to the mountains in March '91. This child was only forty-eight days old.' The English teacher indicated the eighth and youngest of his children. 'We owe everything we have now, our lives too, to you Europeans.' Lunch was clearly festive, though without meat ('We can only afford meat once a month at the most'). Onions, aubergines, peppers, tomatoes, vine leaves, all stuffed with plain rice, were served in a large dish on the floor. I ate very little, just enough to do the family honour without disappointing the eight pairs of eyes watching my every mouthful. The English teacher tucked in; his wife served the children.

They proudly showed me the kitchen. A large freezer held their food supplies for the winter – bread, tomatoes, onions. Otherwise a small sink with a drainer and a few pots, a gas ring on the floor and beside it a cushion where the wife sat to cook were the only contents of the room. It was hard to see where she ironed her husband's shirts.

The days passed with the English teacher and I journeying

around villages looking for embroideries and in particular for the pattern of the amulet. The countryside was arid in the extreme, totally colourless. Even the clear sky was washed of blue and became just an intensity of light. Only a few tufts of dry grass, a few stones halted the monotony of the neutral earth that rolled on relentlessly to a distant line of mountains. Where there had been villages their bombed stones only littered more densely the barren soil and added no colour or life. Occasionally where a village still stood the emptiness of the landscape might be broken by a thicket fence, a stone wall, a thatch roof, a lone tree.

We travelled between villages – from old ones that had survived to new ones of concrete – mostly on buses. One bus stopped by fields of workers to pick up a party of mourning women dressed in blue frocks and black chadors, bringing boxes of tomatoes from the fields to take to the home of the deceased; another passed us by with a wedding party waving sparkly pink banners out of the windows.

When there was no suitable bus the English teacher would splash my money out on shared taxis. One he hailed already had four people in the front but appeared to be empty in the back. As he opened the door we saw a sick young woman lying across the back seats. 'We're taking her to hospital in Dahuk' the driver explained. The English teacher propped her upright and sat me next to her.

'She's very sick' I said.

The English teacher peered at her then confided in me: 'Schizophrenia or the mother-in-law.'

'Mother-in-law?'

'Yes, young women burn themselves because of their mother-in-law. I even know a girl who burnt herself to death only because her brother struck her. It was unwise behaviour but the mind of women is smaller than the mind of men.'

In the evenings I returned to the rest house in Zakho, where the dish of rice and chicken bits was served repeatedly; the rice was renewed each day as we ate it, but the chicken bits, including the frilly ends of the wings, were still those from the politicians' plates. This went on for four days until Angus protested and they were replaced by a kind of ratatouille. More reporters had joined us. 'Of course the Save the Children road project was stupid. Seventy-five thousand they paid and the contractor was never seen again. And, anyway, there isn't a kilo of Tarmac in the country, no fuel, no machines.' As Angus talked the reporters tapped away on their laptops.

The English teacher added to our quest for embroidery and weaving an interest in goathair tents and felts and made it his business to take me to any village within a bus or taxi ride of Dahuk where these might be found. The villages were all rather similar: houses of mud or stone – or, where these had been destroyed, of concrete – set alongside wide roads or spaced arbitrarily in the countryside. They had no character or beauty. Most had no electricity, unlike the towns whose supply was free, courtesy of Saddam. If they had a market it was a simple one, selling cigarettes, soap, eggs, sacks of salt.

There was no market visible in the Christian village of Bersivé and in any case it was Sunday. The silver-haired priest ('Father, they call him') stood in his dog-collar telling his rosary. The pit loom in the floor of one of the houses was idle, but the weaver worked it to show me. 'Only the men weave. The women prepare the wool, sometimes they spin it, sometimes they buy it in the market.' This was a village of felt. They made it from the special wool of small black sheep, they said, laying it on the ground and then banging it unceasingly, adding water and compressing it until it felted. With the felt they made small hats for the men, a circle placed over the fist and then pulled in and in at the edge until a flower pot shape was achieved. Though the hats were festive gear the men standing around the village were wearing them. 'It's Sunday' they explained.

The small hillside village of Segé had been destroyed by bombs and a few Christian graves with crosses stood apart from the Muslim ones. 'Saddam grilled the orphans alive' the shepherd said. 'If it weren't for the Europeans we wouldn't be here.' They had put up temporary matting huts near the ruins, guarded by snarling husky dogs, and it would be another month before the women would set up their goathair tents for the winter. The English teacher looked crestfallen. 'No other textiles? No embroidery? No felts?' ('I don't like to lose face with you' he whispered to me.) 'Ah yes.' The shepherd fetched out his winter kepenek, the wide-shouldered heavy felt cloak of Kurdish and Turkish shepherds, and put it on. The English teacher beamed. The shepherd said they also made long felt rugs, patterned with lozenges, circles and stars, which the English teacher insisted on seeing. 'The Yezidis make these too. They're Zoroastrians.'

The Yezidis

We sat on the earth before the house, the Yezidi men, the English teacher, the grandmother and I, while the women and children stood around us. The men fixed me with a penetrating stare. 'They want to know if you've got any other clothes' explained the English teacher.

'Other clothes? What's the matter with these?'

'They don't like blue, don't like it at all.' Blue eyes, blue glasses, lapis earrings, blue shirt, spinel ring, blue trousers, only my shoes weren't blue. They had formerly been white – an unsuitable colour for travelling but a bargain at the time – and now, after years of trekking around the squalor of Asia, they were the colour of a garage floor. I fished a large scarf out of my bag but that didn't please them either, being a mixture of colours that still included blue.

'What's the matter with blue?'

'I can't say now' whispered the English teacher. 'They like white.' I edged my feet slightly forward.

The women brought out the textiles they made and lay them on the ground in front of me: long beige felt rugs with brown stars, circles, crosses and the tree of life; bags to sling across the back and carry babies or produce to market, called parzin and made of a rectangle of handwoven goathair, embroidered in simple patterns and decorated with floss silk tassels; woven rugs used only when high-ranking religious leaders visited. They had cloaks too, they said, but they were made by men in Bashukah near Mosul.

The old grandmother looked at me and started weeping. 'I'm terribly sorry' I said to the English teacher. 'All this blue, I didn't know.' I had learned not to wear white at Indian weddings and that red was considered a most unseemly colour for a woman of my age almost everywhere, but I had never come across an embargo on blue before. The women around me were wearing white clothes and headscarves and had lovely rough handwoven shawls of red and black chequered wool joined at the loom widths by multi-coloured embroidery.

'No' said the English teacher. 'It isn't the blue. In ten days she has lost two grandsons.' I touched her gently and she tried to smile. 'One in a blood feud. Someone from this tribe killed a man. We don't know who. But that tribe must then kill a man from this tribe. Any man. Any man will do. A shepherd is usually easy but they chose her grandson.'

'And the other one?'

'A road accident. Overtaking on the highway.'

Tribal mourning had been taken care of by the elected head of their village of Kharnuk, a thin wiry alert old man. He had first seen fit to change the rules. Formerly the family of the deceased was obliged to kill a sheep and invite the rest of the tribe to eat. As this procedure was very expensive for these poor people, and what with the fighting and now the highway adding to the traditional blood feuds, he had ruled no sheep were to be killed but the deceased's family should offer a glass of tea and a cigarette and then everyone was to go home for lunch. After all, they were all related and lived in the same small village. For the purpose of this communal mourning he had bought a large open-sided tent which was erected when fatalities occurred but dismantled for the short periods in between in case rain or sun should damage it.

We were led to this tent, the English teacher and I, as soon as we had finished looking at the women's textiles. It was immense. Down each side men in loose Kurdish clothing, turbaned in red or black, sat crosslegged. All were smoking. At the head of the tent were the brothers of the deceased, smoking and drinking tea. We offered our condolences, the English teacher and I, took our shoes off and were given tea. A tray of open packets of cigarettes was presented. We sat for some considerable time, nodding at everyone. Nothing was said. No women were present. 'Now we can go' said the English teacher, somewhat suddenly. I bowed obeisances, picked up my shoes and suggested contributing to the cigarettes on offer from my supply of gifts. 'No' said the English teacher scathingly. 'These are rich people.'

For the others, the poorer ones, he said, when they lose someone an old man goes round the village and gathers money or sugar and rice and gives it to the dead man's family. His friends don't shave for seven days. If a young man dies or is killed his sisters cut off their hair to show their sorrow.

*

'Any chance of coming to live in England with my children?'
asked one of the men at another home in the village. 'I have
twelve living, four dead. My brother has ten. He wishes to come
too.' No mention was made of wives.

'Is it good to have girl children or do you like just boys?' I
asked.

'It is better to have boys but good to have girls. We love boys
more but we respect girls and don't hurt them. And then with us
the mother of two daughters is considered blessed and can cure
illness by stroking the sick person's back. Then we get money for
girls when they marry. The father of the young man must pay
the father of the bride. Of course he has to buy his daughter beds
and blankets and maybe a cupboard with the money but much he
can keep for himself. And it's the young man who must buy the
girl her jewellery.'

They offered us tea, bread, dry sharp cheese and a bowl of
curd. I tasted and complimented, the English teacher stuffed
himself and the men watched like hawks as their precious food
disappeared. They then spread out a strip of goathair that was to
make one of their tents, about fifteen metres long, spun and
woven by the women. It's the women too who weave the tents
and make the carpets, and spin and dye the wool, they said. 'We
men weave the cloth for our own suits.'

The men stared pointedly at me, then one spoke. 'He knows
your amulet' said the English teacher. 'The Turks call it *muska*
but these Yezidis they call it *neveshti*. Their religious man, no, not
a mullah, no, no, they're not Muslim, writes something, something
asking God to bless and help the person wearing it. Not from the
Koran, no, no, of course not, just a prayer. For someone who is
sick. They put it in any piece of cloth folded into a triangle,
sometimes embroidered, sometimes not. Then they hang it round
the neck or put under the clothes. Also they hang it on animals.
And on a newborn baby when sick. Then they also put round his
neck a string of wool with seven bits of his hair tied on.' Even so,
infant mortality was more than one in five.

Their religious men, I later learned, were usually just ordinary
villagers who had no specific holy qualities other than a knowledge of the Koran and the ability to read and write in Arabic.
These were the men who wrote out the amulet for simple

complaints. For anything serious, like psychological disorders, the amulet was written only by powerful, respected sheiks.

'Do they hang the amulet on trees or rags on trees?'

'No, they say no. Not on stones under trees either, but they put rags and stones in their fire temples.'

The fire temples on the hilltop were two small circular buildings close to each other with roofs of inverted ice-cream cones topped with rags. They belonged to the tribe spread among the surrounding villages, who seemed to look after them much better than their own houses of stone and adobe, flat-roofed in twigs and mud. The doorway of the smaller temple was guarded by a drawing of snakes and a circle of stones, a blue one in the centre. 'Gifts of charity' said the English teacher. 'Blue just by chance.' The larger stones which lay around it denoted the power of man, he added. 'Here on Wednesdays and Fridays when the sun sets the Yezidis make a fire of cotton rags soaked in natural oils.' There was a blackened niche on the inside wall and an oil can and bits of rag lay untidily on the floor. Poles draped with cloth – sparkly brocades and bits of red and green – leant against the corner. 'Wednesday is their holy day' said the English teacher 'and Friday blessed before sunset. If a boy or man dies on a Friday before twelve o'clock this is good. If it's in the evening or the Saturday morning they bury an egg with him to tell God they don't want to lose another man before next Friday.'

Out of Iraq

The Kurds of Northern Iraq lived only under the protection of the Poised Hammer of international concern: their fragile freedom from Saddam's clutches was held by a watchdog of weaponry and men, both United Nations and Western, left over from the Gulf War and stationed in eastern Anatolia. It sent a few planes over Iraqi territory each day to growl at Saddam. It was the situation set up when the safe havens were established but after more than a year dissatisfaction was growing. The Turks no longer wanted the military presence of the Poised Hammer on their territory, the Kurds wanted more security. For the first time, all the Iraqi groups opposing Saddam – there were 'Kurds, Shi'ites, Sunnis, Syriac-Christians, democrats and Turkomans from Europe, North America and the Middle East' the newspaper said – were meeting to unite against Saddam and plan the future of a free Iraq. The meeting was to be on Friday, the place secret 'but we all know it'll be Erbil'. (It wasn't.) New reporters began to arrive, the rest house was buzzing. When an obese German cameraman was given my bed, relegating me to a flimsy campbed he would have grossly overlapped, I began to realize there would be problems at the rest house.

The English teacher had continued our quest with ardour. We had searched the market of Zakho from top to bottom for étamine, only to be told by a group of chadored women that because of the UN and PKK embargoes it was impossible to get hold of and they used old sacks instead. We bought suitable threads, on their advice, to embroider cross-stitch tulips and handed them to the English teacher's sister who, he said, would be happy to embroider something for us that day. When we called in the evening to collect it this young mother of six had understood exactly what was wanted and had embroidered tulips over a piece of old flour sack but had left the sack to show the technique. She refused payment so I gave money to her small paraplegic son. ('Did he have a wheelchair?' Angus anxiously later asked. 'Yes, he had been given one by an Englishwoman.'

Angus looked disappointed. 'Oh, because we would have given him one.')

We had also tried to track down hand-embroidered sheets in the market, which the English teacher knew were available, but which no stalls sold. Finally he took me up some rickety steps into a men's dosshouse where cell-like rooms led off a passageway equipped with a washbasin and a coolchest of cans of Coke. Indeed, there were sheets on the beds – a relic, for sure, of earlier times – which, though somewhat grimy, were hand-embroidered with daisies. The English teacher looked triumphant. But our days were numbered.

The *Toronto Star*, the *Boston Globe*, the *Chicago Tribune*, the *Guardian*, the BBC, the BBC World Service by now filled the rest house. In response to their curiosity I muttered about embroidery patterns and amulets and decided to get out from under their feet.

Taking an early morning stroll as I was ready to leave, I saw a figure in Western dress come running towards me waving. It was the English teacher in a clean shirt. 'I've come to tell you why the Yezidis don't like blue. I can tell you now. They are devil worshippers. They worship the devil as a prophet. His name is Shaitan, like your Satan. But they never like to mention him by name, Shaitan. And the word for blue is *shien* so as soon as they see blue and think of that sound "sh" the devil comes into their mind.' It occurred to me to be thankful they hadn't also politely asked my name when objecting to my clothes.

He wrote the words down carefully in my notebook and continued explaining. 'Here you see is blue *shien* and Satan Shaitan. So instead of calling him Satan they call him Malik Taws, King of the Birds.' He began to draw a bird. What would it be? A peacock perhaps, symbol of royal power, the power over Hades maybe. Or a cock, a bird believed to drive away the evil spirits of the night? He drew what looked like a lame gull.

'What bird is that?'

'I do not know. It is just a bird. He is king of all the birds.'

As it turned out the walk across the bridge was through scums of oil instead of through the snow of memory. The Kurds waved me on; the Turks wanted five pounds for a visa. With no difficulty I caught a taxi to Cizre from where buses left regularly for Diyarbakir.

I saw no good reason why I could not have done exactly the same in the opposite direction on the way in, thereby saving that one thin green note with which I could have bought Broadway and the Waterworks before Advancing to Go.

The Black Sea

❖ ❖ ❖

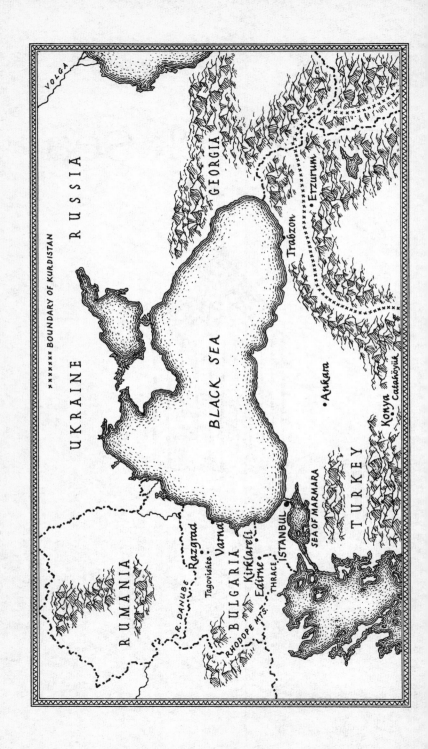

×××××× BOUNDARY OF KURDISTAN

VOLGA

RUSSIA

UKRAINE

GEORGIA

Trabzon

•Erzurum

BLACK SEA

•Ankara

Konya
Çatalhöyük

TURKEY

SEA OF MARMARA

ISTANBUL

THRACE

Kırklareli

Edirne

RHODOPE MTS.

BULGARIA

Varna

Tırgovişte•

Razgrad

R. DANUBE

RUMANIA

Turkey

Anatolia

'All Anatolia' the carpet man had said, looking at my photograph of the amulet as an embroidered pattern. 'This pattern we find in all Anatolia.' A trawl through the bazaars of Anatolia ('Buy carpet Miss, cheap, very cheap. Good carpet. Come in, just looking') was singularly uninviting. A tour of innumerable small towns of mazed streets spilling beyond their ancient walled precincts into stark clusters of blocks of flats, each cutting out the light of the next, held no appeal. To isolate one such town and let it serve as an example seemed reasonable enough. As the amulet was linked to fertility, to goddesses and rags, and maybe to Zoroastrianism and the sun, I chose Urfa and the nearby village of Harran.

The budgerigars were blue and green, maybe a hundred of them stifled in a wooden cage. It was left on the pavement at the bus station of Diyarbakir until the Urfa bus was ready to leave, when it was shoved with much twittering into the luggage hold and the side flaps were banged shut.

The bus trundled over a vast sun-baked empty plain, deceptively empty as it is one of the oldest inhabited regions on earth. Here dwelt Abraham, Elijah and Job, and before them palaeolithic man, the Hittites, the Assyrians, the Medes and Persians, Alexander who ruled the area on his eastern campaign in 332 BC, Byzantines, Romans, Mongols. Now there was only an immense expanse of dry yellow land stained by a few dark green cotton-fields and straddled by pylons of the hydroelectric scheme that was to bring it to life again. Along the road trotted donkey and horse carts; kilometre-long queues of tractors and trucks laden with hessian sacks of raw cotton waited to get into small roadside factories; overturned lorries and cars indicated some previous disturbance. There was a feeling of peace about Urfa. Sacred carp swam in pools where God had turned the fire consuming Abraham into water, cusped arches of mosques and madrashas were reflected on the calm surface, sparrows that, had they been

239

in Italy, hunters would have shot long ago, chattered in profusion in the trees. I wondered whether the budgerigars had survived.

The feltmakers in the bazaar laboured away in a urine-soaked courtyard and its adjacent unlit hovel. A huge beating machine pounded the layers of wet brown wool into long strips of felt. They laid them on the ground and decorated them with bands of black felt, straight or zigzag, which they arranged in a pattern of circles and lines. Here and there they put touches of bright pink and yellow, and pounded everything again. Yes, they knew the amulet pattern. It was one they used, though they had nothing at that moment with it on.

The horses that were all over town pulling flat sideless carts wore blue beads and red pompoms; the carpets hustled by traders in the bazaar were nasty red fluffy things with no patterns of any meaning; the decorations over doorways and water sources were solar – rosettes or the paired sun and moon. Museums displayed neolithic finds: pots incised with zigzags and diamonds, small goddess figurines and bead amulets. Only one kilim had the amulet as a border, each triangle topped by what seemed an anthropomorphic shape, arms akimbo. The goddess of fertility.

The road from Urfa runs south across the bleak, flat plain in a dead straight line to the Syrian border and, lying a few kilometres off it, is the village of Harran. Biblical it should have been – here dwelt Abraham in the kingdom of Nimrod 'the mighty hunter before the Lord' – but it was a tangle of telegraph poles, concrete shacks, souvenir shops, cafés selling Pepsi, old houses shaped like beehives and large lumps of carved stone littered around on the ground. 'Abram was seventy and five years old when he departed out of Haran ... and went forth to go into the land of Canaan.' Harran must have displeased him as a town for it was idolatrous, a centre of worship of the moon, sun and planets: the old Babylonian astral Trinity of Sin the moon god, Shemesh the sun god and Ishtar the god of the planet Venus. The temple to the moon god was destroyed long ago by the Byzantines and the mosque, the castle and the city walls now lay in various stages of ruin. There had been, too, schools of learning and gifted scholars: Albatanius, who correctly calculated the distance from the earth to the moon; Jabir bin Hayyan, who rejected Ionian philosophy that the atom was indivisible and claimed that it was not only divisible but also if divided it would release enough energy to destroy a city the size of Baghdad.

The beehive houses, made of stones from the ruins, were grouped like gathered tumuli, linked inside by low doorways so that one cool dome followed another, shielding all from the glaring sun. Each huddle was set in a courtyard and approached through a simple doorway, over which – the only colour on the bleached stones – was pinned the amulet. Not embroidered but made of corn, the corn of fertility, and hung not with three tassels but with eleven, made of ears of corn strung together and tied with bright rags.

Trabzon

'I was doing a large piece of embroidery from an ancient Irish pattern, arabesques on dark, apricot-coloured coarse silk in low-toned greens, pinks and blues, all outlined in gold. This work has been a real pleasure to me, and I relied on it for recreation for the rest of my journey. Gone, with all the silks and gold for finishing it ... Gone too my horse and saddle, my food, quinine and writing materials.'

For this last stretch of my journey in Anatolia I took as my companion Isabella Bird, who, diligently embroidering, had travelled the route on horseback a hundred years before. She had encountered the Kurds, who had been 'remorseless robbers for ages ... war and robbery are the business of Kurdish life' and knew the Yezidis 'usually called devil-worshippers. Probably there is not a wilder population on the face of the earth, or one of whose ideas, real beliefs, and ways Europeans are so ignorant.'

In Isabella Bird's day traffic on the caravan route between Tabriz and Trebizond was very heavy, chiefly in British goods. As she looked out of her windows in Erzurum in one day she counted as many as seven hundred laden camels passing through the Custom House, besides horse and mule caravans. These days Erzurum is mainly an unavoidable transfer point for travellers, and a journey that took her months on a horse now takes a few hours on a bus.

My journey from Urfa to Erzurum to Trabzon began once again on a night bus. In accordance with the usual logic of travel arrangements a hugely fat peasant woman with five large parcels and a small son blowing bubble gum were seated beside me. 'A Madam' the conductor explained as he showed her to her place. I dozed fitfully, pinioned like a broiler chicken, while her husband spent the night sleeping comfortably across two seats further back in the bus.

The deep snow and glacial temperatures of eastern Anatolia had kept me away from Trabzon on my journey through Turkey the previous winter. Now that I had returned to the Kurds and in the mild sunshine of autumn Trabzon had been easy to reach, it proved a great disappointment. Of Trapezus and Trebizond there remained only a few walls of the citadel atop a gaunt crag that overlooked the Black Sea and had once, no doubt, dominated a thousand petty rulers. It was a crag that appeared to me to rest on a *mille-feuille*, a sickly layered gâteau of history, an indigestible confusion of the trails that led to the city from the east and from it to the west.

The layers were Hittite, Greek, Persian, Roman, Byzantine, Mongol, Ottoman. They were certainly not Kurd. The Kurds bound the autonomous territory they hoped, or were fighting, for at the southern escarpment of the mountain range that separated them from Trabzon. It was not through the Kurds that the amulet reached the west. Through which of these peoples might it have been?

When the trails from Trabzon led clearly west they scarcely went east. The Greeks maybe, with their settlements around the Black Sea littoral and their conquests to India. But the amulet was nothing to do with the Greeks. The Achaemenid empire of Darius had extended from Persia through Anatolia and Thrace to Varna and its hinterland around Razgrad, but the amulet was not Persian. While both Varna and Trapezus were Roman settlements, the Anatolian hinterland was *ultra muri*; while both cities were Byzantine, and Justinian built similar fortifications and churches in each, the Anatolian hinterland was never part of the Byzantine empire either. And the amulet was neither Roman nor Byzantine.

Trade routes promised more. On the landward side, Trabzon was one of the tag ends of the Silk Road; the city prospered mightily from overland trade in the fourteenth century and the caravan route to it was still important a hundred years ago. On the seaward side, the Genoese and the Venetians traded, but was Varna not by then a small insignificant port with ruined Roman baths and buried Byzantine gold and Razgrad of no importance at all?

This was the point of rupture. It was the point of rupture between Zoroastrianism and Christianity, both since drowned in a sea of Islam. It was the point of rupture between the Western world and that of the Asian nomad, between the gods of Europe and the horned ibex of the hunter, the fertility goddess of the planter.

Trabzon seemed a mistake. Perhaps the trail led through earlier peoples from the neolithic Catahöyük site near Konya through the Mediterranean and thence to Thrace. As I reflected on this, Trabzon seemed more and more a mistake and I viewed the city with distaste. The Byzantine church of Aya Sofya, built on the site of a pagan temple, was now nothing but a closed museum, the other old churches were just closed mosques. Trabzon had become only a bustling modern city where silly men shouted 'hotel, hotel, sex, sex' and the boat service to Istanbul was suspended.

And so, yet again, it was from a bus that the wooded slopes, the cherry and hazelnut groves, the bleak black sands of the shoreline of the justly named Black Sea were tracked, without ever giving a lead as to how this region of Justinian's domains and of much more ancient riverine trade linked Mesopotamia and Asia with the western shores of the Black Sea. The scent was lost. The bus trundled on to Istanbul.

Tulips and Triangles

Well, yes, of course they were linked, the Anatolian hinterland, the ports of the Black Sea, the Balkans as far as the Danube – under Ottoman rule. By the mid-fifteenth century they were all united under Mehmet the Conqueror and under the tenets of Islam. But the amulet is pre-Ottoman, much, much earlier, the ethnographer from Sofia had said. 'It certainly didn't come to us with the Ottoman. It is pre-Islamic.'

'Becoming one with God, that is the aesthetic principle of Islamic art' Hikmet said. 'The Western temptation to depict human creation could lead to idolatry. Even Michelangelo had admitted as much when he stepped back from his completed "Moses" and declared "Speak, oh Moses!" So we choose instead floral motifs that remind us of the Garden of Eden. Tulips especially. For the Turkmen of Central Asia they're a symbol of fertility, for us the link is calligraphy. The *lale* of tulip in Arabic script reminds us of Allah.

'Why do I have stained glass tulips on the front door of my guest house? It is the symbol of Istanbul. Why do I paint tulips? We have always painted tulips' said Hikmet.

'And what of the triangle of the amulet. Why a triangle? When I had asked Ömer's milk mother she had merely said "We have always made it so."'

'But what of the significance of three, how close does that bring us to God?' we asked. 'What of all the religions of the world that worship a Trinity: God the Father, God the Son, God the Holy Ghost? What of Shi'ism: God, Mohammed, Ali? What of the Hindu Trimurti? The Buddhist Buddha, Dharma, Sangha. The moon, sun and Venus of Babylon? And what of the universe: earth, water, air? And of all that has a beginning, a middle and an end. And of the sun of morning, noon and even? And of the child, the third party between man and woman? Of plants with root, stem, blossom? Of fruit with peel, flesh, stone? And what of the primary colours red, blue, yellow from which all others are derived?'

245

'But the tassels, I still haven't understood the tassels' I said. 'When I ask "Why three tassels? Or five?" "Just for beauty. It has always been so." That's all anyone says. But then God is supposed to love odd numbers: He is, after all, One. The folklore even of Western Europe says so' I told Hikmet. 'The Germans, the Italians, the French offer flowers in odd-numbered bunches, five roses, never a dozen. Spells and oaths are repeated three times. And the Kyrie eleison. Three holds the strongest magical potency of all.'

'And five for us means the hand' said Hikmet 'the protective hand, the hand of Fatima.'

'And seven, the seven of the universe: Hippocrates claimed that seven ruled over illness and everything that might destroy the body; the Babylonians added to their astral Trinity four other planets to make the holy seven. Nine, the all-powerful three by three; nine, the sons of God in Mongolian mythology. Eleven, the earth, the moon, the sun and all the planets.

'Think, Hikmet, what I've come across: eleven tassels of wheatears and rags on the corn amulet at Harran. Nine twigs hanging from the tree of life drawn on a shaman's drum buried in a frozen tomb of Pazyryk in the Altai mountains in around the fifth century BC. Seven tassels on the amulet embroidered on the Razgrad cushion. Five on a triangle incised in a pot of *circa* 4000 BC found at Tordos on the Danube near sources of gold and copper. Three on a triangle painted on a Mamluk jug unearthed at Wadies-Sir in Jordan. Three and five stitched and knitted on the amulets of Kurdistan. Three on the embroidered amuletic pattern of Kohistan. But when I asked Ömer's milk mother "Why three tassels or five?" "We have always made it so" was all she had said.'

On the only carpet in the bazaar of Istanbul to have a triangular pattern it was woven with four.

Bulgaria

Bulgaristan

The old café owner turned up the row of cups he had left to drain the night before, one by one, hoping to find one that was clean and not chipped now that he had a customer, a lady customer to boot. The sign on the road outside said 'Bulgaristan' but there was no traffic in Kirklareli so early on a Sunday morning. The two budgies in the cage by the café door pecked and nipped each other, stirred by the slanting sunlight. Without being asked the old man brought tea, then cut a hunk of crisp new bread, a knob of butter, a wedge of hard cheese and filled a little bowl with warm honey.

This route through to Bulgaria was hardly used, he said. Very quiet. It was the other route through Edirne that was busy. A few years ago I had walked alone past fields of sunflowers out of Bulgaria into Turkey. Now that Communism had fallen and people were free to travel the road through Edirne was jampacked with lorries and cars from Eastern Europe. Queues even through the night. But nothing went this way. No buses, nothing. From Kirklareli you have to get a taxi, he explained. But it wouldn't cost much. The drivers had nothing to do, especially early on a Sunday morning. They'd be glad of the work.

The taxi drove through rolling wooded hills. The few villages were just like the villages of Western Europe except that instead of a church spire they clustered round the minaret of a mosque. 'Bulgaristan' said all the road signs. At the border the countryside was even more densely wooded. As I walked through, an armed Turkish soldier standing in the trees at the side of the road asked for a cigarette.

At the barrier that marked the frontier the script changed from Roman to Cyrillic, the guards from armed soldiers to one surly bureaucrat. No one else was crossing. He phoned through 'Anglichanka. Auto stop' and made me wait. No one returned the call and still he made me wait. When I was finally allowed through the barrier greetings on the other side, though inquisitive, were

warm and friendly. 'Why are you here? What are you doing?
Welcome. Why are you alone? Where have you come from? By
auto stop?'

'Bus.'

'Where are you going? By auto stop?'

'Bus again'

'There are no buses, nothing.'

So auto stop it would have to be. The only vehicle around was
a grimy red bus, so grimy its number plate was illegible. 'You
should pay them in dollars' said the border guards. 'Ten to
Varna. But get your money out now. Don't let them see
where you keep it. Don't trust them. They're Russian.'

The Ukrainians

Oleg was rather thin ('you eat with the head, not the eyes'), curly grey hair, a cheap grey zip-up sweatshirt, clear grey eyes. He spoke fluent French and his conversation roamed knowledgeably around the *joual* French of Quebec, Nessie the Loch Ness monster, the oracle at Delphi. He earned one dollar a day repairing machines in a factory in the Ukraine. 'I am a slave. Stalin made us all slaves. Our children and our grandchildren will be slaves. It is now in our soul.'

They were all from the Ukraine, the people on the red bus, he explained. Except for a few Russians. 'Look at the size of them. They eat with their eyes.' From two towns in the south of Ukraine. The men were all dressed in sixties style. The women had peroxided hair and wore shaggy nylon jumpers under which they hoped to conceal the fat of a food-today society. The older ones favoured short tight skirts – separated by a roll of very white flesh from knee-length stockings – and fluffy slippers; the younger ones long skirts or jeans and chipped purple nail polish. All, without exception, had gold teeth.

They ate compulsively – cold stew and mackerel out of tins, cucumber, fatty sausage, stale bread – and swigged vodka. They didn't offer me any. In between eating they snoozed and snored except when they squealed excitedly at the ripe grapes in the vineyards along the roadside beyond their reach or when high-pitched disputes broke out with the Russians or between the inhabitants of the Ukrainian towns, those from the larger one lording it over the others. 'I don't like women using these coarse Russian words' said Oleg.

It was a regular trip. Oleg did it twice a year; some of them made it maybe every month. They paid one hundred dollars to the tour operator for the thirteen days. That was for the bus and the interpreter and then they had to pay ten dollars a night for the hotel in Istanbul. The tour operator had a deal with the hotel so they had to stay there though it was really a place for rich Saudis and Westerners and the hotel next door was much cheaper but they weren't allowed to go there. They went to Istanbul to buy clothes. Trousers and jackets. No, not shirts. They're too expensive. 'Fifteen dollars for this jacket', he took off his denim blouson lined with fake sheepskin. 'That's three weeks' wages. All the wages, you understand. Nothing for food. But when I get back to Ukraine I can sell it for two months' wages. We sell on the streets. There is nothing in the shops. Then I take stuff to Istanbul to sell there. A good camera we can buy in Ukraine for eight or ten dollars and sell in Istanbul for fifteen. I have made the hundred dollars for the trip.'

Did he appreciate the freedom to travel? 'Yes, it was always a dream. But we have other dreams. Honey. Honey is for millionaires. A car, an apartment. Never will we have these. We live in a tiny apartment the company rents us. My second wife. It was my mother-in-law who finished my first marriage. Now there is no grandmother. It is a good thing. And my children like my new wife and my new little girl loves me and I love her. It is all good but a home we will never have. And to travel is too expensive. Very expensive. To China, to India. For us to go to India costs two hundred dollars.' No wonder I have never understood that currency.

'Of course' continued Oleg, peppering his remarks with yet more odd values of dollars, 'the women earn more than we do. Turkish men like Russian women. They buy their love.'

The busload of Ukrainian prostitutes and barrow boys lumbered slowly north through a beautiful rolling countryside of vineyards, oak woods and patches of grassland where fat goats grazed. At each dip and bend the waters of the Black Sea shimmered. In the dappled villages houses looked handmade: pitched red-tiled roofs, walls of wood or of small unmortared bricks (none of the flat-roofed cement found on the Turkish side of the border). As everywhere in Eastern Europe the houses were set sideways on to the road, flanked by a garden, a peasant's garden where almost no flowers grew but where cobs of corn lay drying for the winter and where the shawled wife tended a few pumpkins, a goose, a vine.

This was a region of solar worship, of fire dances, the ethnographer at Sofia had said. Relics of pagan belief had got mixed up with Christianity: at sunrise people would interrupt their work to make the sign of the cross, on Christmas day they left dinners at crossroads for the wolves. Christianity was a thin veneer. Theophylact, the Greek ecclesiastic who became archbishop of Ohrid in 1078 when it was still in Bulgaria, said the Bulgarians were wild Scythians who had still not abandoned the worship of the sun, moon and stars they had had before Christianity. Some jobs they reserved for sunrise, some were forbidden after sunset: no sweeping (always a mystical activity), no money lending, no water or rubbish to be thrown out, no young mothers allowed out of doors. And the sick hung pieces of clothing on trees to leave their sickness behind, usually on Wednesdays. Was Wednesday not the holy day of the Zoroastrians? All this stopped about fifty years ago. Only the older generation remembered.

The Ukrainians hurled out of the bus windows their litter of tins, cans, paper, bottles, but carefully folded their plastic bags. When the bus stopped for lunch – soup, kebabs, tomato salad, beer – they ate and paid and then rushed out to strip the neighbouring vineyard into their waiting plastic bags. They seemed to have no concern for their families and friends back home but ate all the grapes then and there.

'Come on to Ukraine with us. Stay on the bus' they said. 'Oleg can be your interpreter.' But I jumped off at the traffic lights in Varna, Black Sea site of world-renowned burials of gold – prehistoric gold, Hellenistic gold, early Byzantine gold – and waved goodbye to Ukraine and to the driver who could use my dollars to buy a camera to flog.

Varna

The tombs were littered with fertility goddesses, earth mother figurines in clay, marble or bone, fashioned in convex shape; anthropomorphic amulets of stone or even gold protected the bodies from evil; small clay altars to the cult of the sun and the moon were decorated in red with solar symbols – the swastika, the spiral, and the meander that linked their cult to that of the snake; tiny adobe houses, not unlike the simple mud dwellings of Makran but only about eight centimetres high, lodged the protective spirits of the tribe. And among this buried treasure lay the even greater treasure of the gold. Three thousand pieces of the purest carat, the earliest gold of mankind, predating the Pharaohs by a thousand years and the Indus valley civilization by two thousand.

Rings, bracelets, discs, ringed handles of sceptres, necklaces of round or spherical beads: almost everything was curved – circles, spheres, cylinders – a Chalcolithic continuation of the old Stone Age art forms. Among all the treasures of the necropolis of Varna there was not a single triangle, not in gold nor in stone nor in bone nor in mineral. There were gold amulets in the form of horned animals punched with holes through which they were probably attached to garments. There were discs clamped on to the clay and stone goddesses to form eyes and breasts, or marking the knee joints and eyes of skeletons or the features of clay masks, whose ears were hung with rings, five on the left ear, three on the right.

It was a society that had prospered in the fifth millennium BC around the port and lagoon of Varna. Few of its people lived beyond their late twenties, the women mostly dying much younger in childbirth. The distribution of gold in only four tombs out of nearly three hundred indicated an advanced society that already had a hierarchy and a system of exploitation of its workers. Its gold was local, its copper and beads were traded, its territory extended into the hinterland where other graves were found. The discovery in 1972 of so ancient and rich a civilization in Europe had caused a great stir in the archaeological world. Now no one in Varna knew where the necropolis lay. 'Closed' said the surly staff at the Archaeological Museum. 'We can tell you nothing.'

Varna had turned its back on its past and was grasping instead the dross of the world outside Communism. 'Night Club Splendid®', 'Hollywood Orgy' the neon lights proclaimed; 'Amigo Tourist Information' read the illuminated sign which led only to a small dark courtyard where an old car lay shrouded in tarpaulin. Along the traffic-free precinct, nailed to the façades of serious Baroque mansions and wavering between Roman and Cyrillic script, brazen fasciae advertised Fast Food, German Kitchen, Pizza Parlour, Money Exchange, Rock and Roll, their tinselly sparkle strung thinly along the street like small-town Christmas lights.

Tiny windows at pavement level displayed Western goods of displaced and dubious origin – Toblerone labelled in Arabic, orangeade from Huddersfield, mango juice from Germany, Swiss chocolate from Austria, Coke from everywhere. Curbside stands sold Amstel beer, digestive biscuits, Marlboro cigarettes and Milka bars. It was an eclectic mixture of goods hyped into prominence and street spectacle, goods that in the West would lurk unnoticed on supermarket shelves and would be bought only when required. Men sat all day with one box of bananas to sell, or packets of cigarettes split into ones. A small market had stalls of village produce, a few leeks, some chillis, tomatoes, white cabbages, amid other stalls of booze: Blue Curaçao from Greece, obscure Russian vodkas, dubious gin, real whisky. Schweppes tonic, which had been the only drink available in Bulgaria under Communism, every bus station, every shop full of it and nothing else, was now nowhere to be seen, jostled to the sidelines by Coke, J & B, Suncharm lemonade and an esoteric marketing system.

A little of the old Bulgaria I had known from Communist days still lay behind this façade. Supermarkets continued to display only row upon row of bottled gherkins, tinned peas and sauerkraut. Wedding cake buildings stuccoed in red, pink, pale green and blue, curlicues of white icing round their windows, doors and pediments, peeled, unattended, until the colours bleached and the stucco curled and they seemed covered in wood shavings. But it was a world fast disappearing. It was the young who manned the stalls and glitzy shops, the girls in tight minis and thigh-high boots, the men in jeans. They seemed a lost generation, tense, questioning, skeletal fingers curling around yet another cigarette, unsure where to go. The old, meanwhile, were in the church pattering among empty water bottles, dead flowers and half-burnt bent candlesticks, where aproned women cleaned with witches' broomsticks.

The shabby old restaurants serving bean soup and heavy bread were now hard to find. Microwaved fast food was all the rage and potatoes cooked in goose-fat had been discarded, and along with them the goose, the goosegirl, the niche for the village idiot, the tales recounted through the long dark evenings of winter, the superstitions of the fattening, the slaughter, the traditions of an impoverished world, impoverished in everything but spirit. 'A New Beginning' declared the Bulgarian Airlines calendar for 1992.

Varna seemed much more a resort than a mercantile port. A town of decaying elegance, whose modern hotels on sites more peripheral had failed to upstage its lovely turn-of-the-century theatre, it was a pleasure garden on the Black Sea, separated from it by parkland. The harbour was to the side of the town. From timetables pasted on the walls it was clear that boats plied up and down the coast in the holiday season, but not otherwise. Boats to and from Istanbul were 'problematic' said the female staff at the port terminal. 'There might be one tomorrow. We can't say. It could be two hundred dollars. We don't know. No one knows about any boats.'

I wandered through the port. Merchant ships pumped water alongside the quays. A three-masted barquentine, the *Kaliakra*, lay moored, recently returned from months sailing around Europe and America, an odyssey that would have been impossible under Communism. Heading westward, under full sail, she must have been a perfect symbol of the new freedom. Oleg would have felt so. I asked questions, but the women staff in the office of the port authority of Varna merely buffed their fingernails. 'Came from Poland, from a yard in Gdansk that was building fully-rigged sailing ships as late as the 1980s' the man on the quayside said.

Beyond the port the coast was beautifully wooded, the sands

by the deserted beach huts were golden and not black. Distant shipping rested still and palely grey on the horizon, a lone fisherman sat beside a cradle of spools and wires in the calm warmth of the autumn sun.

'Thirty dollars a room' snarled the receptionist at the cheapest hotel in town. I lodged instead with an old couple who had squashed themselves into the kitchen to live and sleep so as to free a room to rent out. They wanted my dollars in cash right away. The old house spy of Communist days was still there, the concierge who observed everything and reported to the Party. She suddenly appeared, busying herself with dustpan and brush outside the old couple's flat, while they quickly pushed me inside.

'Breakfast,' said the granddaughter imperiously 'on the street.' Only the old lady was concerned to show me extra blankets, plastic shoes for the bathroom, to give me soap powder for my washing and to offer me a sausage. 'Don't change money at the exchange office, only at the bank' she warned me. 'Gypsies wait there to steal.'

Gypsies. Perhaps gypsies were the link between Kohistan and Bulgaria. Dr Leitner, Barrister-at-law of the Middle Temple, in service in British India and sent in 1866 to the remote North-West Frontier on what he termed a 'Mission of Linguistic Discovery', had recorded the languages and customs of the tribes of Chitral and of Indus Kohistan. He noted that the lowest caste of the Dards of Kohistan were the musicians, called Dôms. These were the Rôms of gypsy lore, the Romany of Europe, he had claimed. And the Zigeuner and zingari of Germany and Italy, this was nothing but a corruption of the word Sinkari, the inhabitants of the borders of the river Sin, the Upper Indus. Gypsies, Leitner commented, were behind the mythology of the origin of bears. These animals were the offspring of a man driven to madness by the inability to pay his debts, who had taken to the hills to avoid his creditors. It was well known, he added, that gypsies were always scrupulous in paying debts when contracted with members of the same race.

These Rôms or gypsies, Major John Biddulph, Political Officer at Gilgit, had commented when writing on the tribes of the

Hindu Kush in 1880, belonged to the Shin caste of Gilgit, Chitral, Astor and thereabouts. They had large eyes like the gypsies of Europe and were thieves.

Gypsies I had seen in Iran, their brilliant flouncy skirts for sale in the bazaar of Shiraz. And in Eastern Europe they were endemic. But they didn't embroider. Did they wear amulets?

'Nothing here' snapped the custodians at the two ethnographic museums in Varna, both old wooden houses of the National Revival Period of the nineteenth century. One was only a schoolroom and a chapel full of icons; the other had embroidered costumes, the usual Bulgarian linen shifts with sober stitchery on hem, cuffs and neck that didn't match but with more exuberant work on the aprons. Only a cushion had the amuletic triangle. From Razgrad perhaps, though they couldn't say. 'There's a good ethnographic museum there.'

Razgrad would be the end of my journeys for it was from Razgrad that the Sofia ethnographer had claimed the Kohistani embroidery of the amulet came. When I reached that town I should find embroideries, cushions he had said, with precisely the same motif – the triangle with three pendants – as on the dress from Kohistan. Maybe I should also find the amulet itself: Bulgarians do hang talismanic trinkets of red and white around their houses and on their person on the first of March to bring good fortune and fertility of crops and couples. They even used to hang amulets on animals, on fruit trees and spinning wheels, adding the usual blue beads, coins and garlic for their magic powers. Perhaps some might turn out to be triangular, perhaps some still dangled from the reins of a few rural donkeys, though it seemed highly unlikely I would come across any woman with an amulet strung around her neck like the one I had worn throughout all my travels. The time had come to open it.

The work of the Turkmen, my amulet was finely embroidered in tent stitch in silks of pink, beige and black, one small part left blank in deference to the perfection of Allah. The pattern on it was vaguely anthropomorphic and resembled the fertility goddess. The edges were crudely overstitched with green wool, giving every possibility of there being something inside.

The green wool zigzagged to and fro, twisted up, in and around and over. Djinn, who like straight lines, would have been greatly discouraged from entering. The green woolly stitches went deeper and deeper, firmly holding the piece of paper now visible inside. A few more snips and it was possible to ease the paper out. It was a plain piece of ridged packing carton with no writing. No message from Allah or any other gods.

Razgrad

The old house lay at the foot of the escarpment, a homely building of rough stone set in a walled garden approached through high wooden gates. The gravel path to its door skirted round a well of the nursery rhyme type, a system of ropes and bucket hanging from its small tiled roof. Flowers now grew in straight lines at each side of the path, but the homestead appeared previously to have been a farm and no doubt geese and chickens once cackled and pecked among its vegetable patches. It had been quite a long ride out from town past horse and donkey carts and the odd lorry, and the custodian, an old woman in black apron and carpet slippers, greeted us with some surprise, jangling her heavy keys.

Old wooden agricultural tools – flails, scythes, harrows, pitch-forks, swaphooks – hung on the walls. In one room snippets cut from the embroidered fronts of linen shirts had been stuck on card, labelled and framed and were displayed on the wall. In the next room the matching snippets from the other side of the shirt neck had been treated in the same way. 'This is the ethnographic museum? This is all there is?' The old woman smiled proudly. It had been delightful for her to show someone round.

It was hard to say why I should have expected anything special of Razgrad, why I hoped to find at the end of my journey a kind of magical homecoming of Asia in Europe. Even the name had been a disappointment. The 'Raz' with sizzling 'z' had promised a derivation of some interest. '"Grad" means town so what did "Raz" mean?' I asked.

'Nothing' was the reply.

'Nothing? What do you mean, nothing?'

'Nothing. Zero. A no town.'

This last stage hadn't promised well. The journey from Varna had been easy enough through a fertile landscape gradually climbing to an undulating plateau. My travelling companion on the train had been a young man studying marketing and business economy at university. 'I hope you will use your skills to help rebuild Bulgaria's economy.' Even without ending my sentence with 'young man' it had a pompous ring.

'No way. I'm going into fast food. Already got a contact in Varna.' He got off at his home town where the cooking oil factory near the station spewed thick black smoke and acrid fumes into the atmosphere.

The hotel had been something of a problem. Twenty-five dollars, no less, for a room. Dinner was only possible in the hotel bar which served all the locals. Here a man with demonic eyes, dangerous eyebrows and wildly frizzy hair had set about me with such ardour that I had abandoned my kebabs and rice and fled, asking reception to bring them to my room, where they were delivered cold some time later. In the morning the staff informed me that my bill would be halved as I had not shared my room. I probably otherwise would not have noticed that the table next to mine at breakfast in the coffee bar was occupied by three prostitutes, heavily made up with fake suntan and looking vaguely Brazilian.

As for visiting the ethnographic museum, the hotel had insisted on arranging for their van to take me there and bring me straight back, commenting that there was no bus and that any taxi would charge an extortionate amount as soon as they saw I was foreign. They expressed some surprise that my only reason for being in Razgrad was an interest in embroidered cushions.

Razgrad itself was a dreary conglomeration of blocks of flats — shabby, jerry-built, cheek by jowl — rusting swings and slides and cowpats in the thin weedy grass around them. I saw no church and the abandoned mosques had their windows smashed or boarded up and the БНРП of the Bulgarian National Radical Party daubed on them in green spray paint. Small groups of people hung around waiting for buses. It was profoundly depressing, a modern desert, and my quest seemed to be fizzling out in a void. I thought despairingly of Carl Schuster.

It was a group of anthropologists in Vienna who had come up with the idea early this century that if the repertoire of patterns in the folk art of an isolated region of the world is studied, symbols will be discovered that date from ancient, even prehistoric, times. If the same is done in another isolated region similar symbols will be found and the early migrations of peoples can be tracked. It had been thrown out of the window as a theory long ago, but Schuster had continued to believe in it. In the decorative device of depicting human joints marked with circles or with patterns of eyes he had found contacts between America and Oceania. He had considered the similarity of patterns based on linked human forms carved on house posts and totem poles and had compared them through Europe, Asia and the Americas with menhirs, painting on skin robes and tattooing. From this he had concluded the Tehuleche Indians of Patagonia to be 'a remnant of an ancient Asiatic racial stock which migrated to the New World before the time when the parent stock separated into Proto-Australoid and Proto-Europoid branches in the Old World.'

He had found these same patterns on shards of Chalcolithic sites near Persepolis and in the decorative arts of the fourth millennium BC in Spain. He had faith in the theory that such observations showed that it was in the general region of Western Asia that 'higher forms of civilisation seem to have developed first, and whence it seems that their influence gradually spread, through obscure prehistoric channels, to remote parts of the world'. He concentrated in the 1930s on the provinces of Western China and had collected and studied the blue and white peasant embroideries there. The patterns he had found – the swastika, the solar rosette, the pomegranate, the tulip – were the ones I had come across so often, the universal symbols of the sun and of fertility.

But the concept of linking patterns to migrations of peoples was flawed; I had known that before I started out. None the less the embroidered pattern of the amulet, or the amulet itself, had surfaced here and there on my journeys. Maybe rather than pinpointing migration as a link between Central Asia and Eastern Europe it symbolized a common human response to calamities not understood: to those women who died in childbirth, replaced by milk mothers; to the vagaries of rivers like the Indus that suddenly rose, swamping civilizations; to the power of fire, the cycle of trees, the course of the sun. What people had lived in Razgrad and had put their faith in the amulet?

The cowpats had not at first – though rather curious in such a location – seemed particularly significant. But wandering around I soon became aware that on the balconies of the flats not only was urban-style washing hung out to dry, but also rural chillis and corncobs. Vines had even been grown up the façades from the ground below, reaching the balconies of the third floor, their side-shoots trained across the railings of those below. Though the blocks of flats and the mechanical diggers were relentlessly encroaching, it was obvious that Razgrad was at heart a village.

Its core was a colony of little peasant smallholdings: cottages surrounded by garden plots where old women in headscarves scattered seed to chickens and old men sharpened knives. On washing lines pigs' entrails dried in the sun; on verandahs pumpkins were laid out in rows; on wooden gates black bows, ill-focused photographs of the deceased and words of mourning etiquette were fixed with rusting pins. It was the domain of the old.

The first woman I accosted was walking down the wide cracked street, bent, the hem of her coat curving up at the back, her slippers shuffling. '*Da*' she knew the amulet, she nodded, shutting the gate of her garden behind her. I continued along the street, horses and carts were the only traffic. The horses flaunted red pompoms on their foreheads that bobbed up and down as they trotted along, and had strings of blue beads round their necks, but no amulet. I came next upon a small group of women knitting and crocheting. Yes, they knew the amulet: '*Muska*' they said. Did they embroider it? Did they use it on cushions? I was unable to ask in Bulgarian and wandered on.

The next woman was sitting on a bench in the sun, on the pavement outside her gate. Yes, she had woven her blue and red striped apron herself and had embroidered it. Did she know this muska? She nodded, got up and went indoors. I could already see the cushion, typical of Razgrad, embroidered with the amulet pattern, that she was going to bring me, but she came out instead with a ghastly black satin apron embroidered with roses in acrylic threads. I tried not to look crestfallen and drew its pattern in my notebook to please her.

The three women on the next bench, fat-thighed, legs akimbo, looked completely blank as I showed them the amulet and tried to engage them in conversation about embroidery. A man walked down the middle of the road and they called him over – maybe he was educated and could help. But no, he spoke only Bulgarian. We all nodded thanks and I strolled on. An old woman was sitting on the pavement painting a cart in vivid blue – the wheels, the spokes, the sides, the shafts, everything. Another group of women were sitting in a garage peeling huge piles of parsnips. None of them seemed to know anything about amulets or even embroidery. My despair was deepening.

A few streets on a car pulled up beside me. It was the man who had walked down the road and tried to help. He had a young boy with him. 'Son. English' said the lad. I explained my problem, asked him to thank his father for thinking of going to fetch him and enquired whether he could interpret for me. Sadly he was only at the 'what's-your-name-where-are-you-from' stage. I engaged him in conversation on the subject of what his name was and where he was from so that his father could listen with pride. It was soon evident that more was needed and we drove off to find his English teacher.

The teacher was bustling around the school gates, briefcase in one hand and plastic shopping bag in the other. She immediately apologized for her English and explained that it was philosophy that she had read at university. For six years. But it was of teachers of English that there was a terrible shortage so she had been pushed through a crash course. She never stopped talking. 'People who draw, that's what we need, people who draw. They understand these things. It's probably from Macedonia, your pattern. There's a man from Macedonia at the glass factory. He may not speak to us – his grandmother died last week. But he knows about drawing.'

We shot off in the man's car to the glass factory. The Macedonian was quite happy to speak to us and was sure the pattern came from the Rhodope Mountains. We were back to the idea that it was over the next hill, Kalash, Gilgit, Swat. The teacher continued 'Rhodope or Macedonia, that'll be it.' She was very dogmatic. I tried to explain that I knew both these areas and had never found the amulet there, but it was impossible to interrupt the flow. 'The history museum. That's it. The history museum – all about when Razgrad was Roman. They'll know.' We shot off to the museum. Closed. 'The art gallery. That's it. The director will know.' We shot off to the art gallery. The director wasn't there. 'The antibiotics plant. Someone there will know.' No one did.

I continually tried to interrupt to say 'Could you come with me to the old women, could you just ask do they know this pattern, what does it mean to them and tell me what they say.' It was impossible.

'A bookshop, that's it. They will know.' We shot off to the shops but there was no serious bookshop. She still went on talking: she was married with two daughters, worked full time but mother helped; she had been an ardent member of the Communist Party, had taken everything they said for the truth, had not understood. Now she could see how wrong she had been and firmly believed in the Socialist Party.

Finally it dawned on her we were getting nowhere. 'My English teacher, that's it. She'll be able to help.' We said goodbye, with profuse thanks, to her pupil and his father and walked to where she thought her teacher lived. The door of the flat was opened gingerly by an old couple, revealing a dim wood-panelled hallway. Yes, their daughter still lived there with them – what else could one do in Bulgaria? – but she was teaching. We found her. A lively young woman wearing white glasses, who understood what I wanted right away. 'I have a friend who's an ethnographer at the museum here. He's just the person you need.'

'Museum? Ethnography museum?'

'Yes, but it's not opening till next year so most people don't know about it.'

The End of the Trail

At first glance Dr Madzharov cut a boyish dash: jeans, pale blue sweater, black hair curled in a cap around his head, like a young Greek god. But a closer look revealed the deep bags under his eyes that betrayed a life of juggling an underpaid job, cramped accommodation, a small child, and a wife on twelve-hour night shifts. He was an academic to the tips of his fingers, precise, cautious, loath to come to conclusions when there was the slightest hint of anything he termed 'problematic'.

I began by showing him the photograph of the amulet embroidered on the Kohistani shawl. 'I'm not sure I agree with my colleague in Sofia that this is a cushion from Razgrad. There's something just not quite right about it.' He shook his head gently. I enlightened him immediately and told him I had been following this pattern between Central Asia and Eastern Europe and the photograph was of the Kohistani end of the trail. He became very excited. 'Just look at those rhombs' he exclaimed. 'Now those three rhombs above the triangles, the left one is exactly Razgrad. And the one on the right too, but the middle one is problematic.' He leapt to his feet and rushed around his small office taking books and files of photographs from the shelves. 'Rhombs, just look, here this one, just the same.'

The rhombs that excited him so much were patterns of the Kàpantsi, ancient Bulgarians, Proto-Bulgarians, who had come to the Razgrad region in the sixth or seventh century. The pattern on the right they called 'frog's step'. 'That's not what it is, of course. It's solar. All embroidery patterns are symbols, even if the women have forgotten what they mean.' The name the women gave to the pattern on the left escaped him but they also used it as a sign on the walls of their houses.

'For protection against the evil eye?'

'Problematic. Archaeologists know what it means. They say that is what it is for.' The middle rhomb with chequered patterning was also problematic and Dr Madzharov leapt to his feet once again to fetch out more books and photos.

As for the amulet, this was a pattern of the Kusulbash or Alians, so-called because they follow Ali.

'Shi'ite then, like the Iranians?' He nodded.

'Are they anything to do with the Ali-Ilahis of Luristan who were supposed to be able to eat, or at least sit in fire?'

'Problematic.'

They were regarded as non-Muslims, I added.

'The Alians too are not true Muslims, they still keep vestiges of Zoroastrian belief. Here, take this little book, keep it. The introduction is good. But from page nine problematic, then from page thirty-five trustworthy.' It was in Bulgarian, in Cyrillic script, but the photographs, though in blurry black and white, I could understand. They were of people in distinctly Turkish clothing. The sashes at their waists – men's and women's – were embroidered with a floral motif thrice repeated, in the typical style of Ottoman Turkey. They were the flowers of the court tiles and textiles of Topkapi, and of the ceramics of Iznik. But there were pictures too of rags hanging from trees, of phallic wooden grave markers, of revered stones, of solar patterns around water sources. 'The Alians use the symbol of the sun in everything. They worship the sun and fire, but most of all they worship water. And they hang on their churches – that they call teke and not mosques – straw amulets with dangling appendages tied with rags.' Just as in Harran.

'They came from Pakistan or Afghanistan, through Asia Minor. Maybe in the fifteenth century or in the sixteenth after the Turks conquered the Balkans or maybe a bit before.' Too late, but it sounded very promising.

'Would they have gone south at all, say to Baluchistan, Iran?' I asked. A slight frown brushed Dr Madzharov's forehead, almost imperceptibly, vanishing as rapidly as the thought that had inspired it. He raised his eyebrows gently and shook his head.

'The amulet is one of their patterns' he continued 'but with five pendants not three. They call it the hand of Fatima but it is much older than Islam. It symbolizes the various meanings of the hand: the sincerity of man, the creatures nearest to God – that is, goddesses – and the votive function of protection. In churches here it is made of wax and silver and placed near the altar.'

'But isn't a hand as a protective symbol raised?' I asked.

Dr Madzharov nodded. 'Of course your amulet may not have come here with the Alians. It may have been here long before.'

'Could it have anything to do with the people of the necropolis in Varna? Did the same people live here in Razgrad?'

Dr Madzharov looked approvingly at me. 'We are researching.'

'Your amulet is most likely to have come here with the Proto-Bulgars, though they later joined together with the Alians. The Alians were unorthodox Muslims and when they reached this region they found these earlier settlers, unorthodox Christian and still with old pagan beliefs, the Kàpantsi we were talking about. They had settled here in the Razgrad district and in Targovishte, a few kilometres to the south.'

Darkness fell and Dr Madzharov didn't notice. 'The name Kàpantsi may come from kàpishte, denoting an ancient Proto-Bulgarian pagan shrine. Or they were called Kàpantsi because kàpanka was the name of the women's shirts. That was because of the unique embroidery on the sleeves: all dots, *kapky* in Bulgarian.'

'Romanian blouse sleeves are also embroidered with dots.'

Dr Madzharov nodded. 'There are relations between these people, the Dracian – the oldest culture of the Balkans – the Proto-Bulgarians, the Slavs and the Hungarians – they were nomads too.'

He jumped up again and fetched more photographs and books, finally switching on the light. 'Here, have this little book on the cushions. You'll see Professor Koev says they are not cushions but pillows for the first night of the marriage bed. Two rhombs together to bring the couple together. This is the same as your rhomb on the right you see. But not the middle one' said Dr Madzharov, peering at my photo again. It seemed churlish to say I wasn't interested in the rhombs but in the triangles, and Dr Madzharov fetched out more books.

'Then there are the Chuvash, one of the ancient Turkic-speaking peoples whose language belongs to the Bulgar linguistic family. They live in the mid Volga region. Historians are sure there's a connection between the Chuvash and the Kàpantsi – the dialect here has a lot of Turkish words not used in other parts of Bulgaria. Ethnographers are sure too. There's an embroidery pattern on the neck of Chuvash shifts that we also have here in Razgrad, but nowhere else. Their legends seem to prove they came from even further east than the Volga, around the Urals.'

Dr Madzharov placed a large book on the costume of the Chuvash in front of me and dashed off to fetch his child from the crêche.

Red is the most powerful, the most vibrant of colours: it is the blood of life and of sacrifice, it is fire and the power of the sun. In embroidery almost everywhere red threads and fabrics are associated with youth and marriage, with spirit worship, demons and talismanic charms. Even the Varna tombs had been heavily daubed with red. In the Chuvash costume, though the shape of the dress was totally different, red was everywhere – as in Kohistan. The old patterns – the swastika, the tree of life, the tulip, the eight-pointed star – were all there; the cowries, the coin-hung headdresses, the fringes with tiny white beads like the Turkmen's. And of course the amulet. In red cloth and with hanging tassels, sometimes seven, sometimes five, sometimes three. My head was spinning.

Dr Madzharov returned with a pale quiet little boy. 'If the Chuvash and the Kàpantsi or Proto-Bulgars both came from Asia through the mid Volga region' I asked hesitantly 'as that's way north of the Caspian I suppose they must have come north of the Black Sea and not from the south?'

'Of course' said Dr Madzharov. 'Our people came from the north. They came from the Golden Horde, north of the Caspian and the Black Sea.' He appeared to be wrestling again with the idea he had dismissed from his mind earlier on, unable this time to let it go. The bags under his eyes sunk deeper. He frowned. 'Yes, from the north, from the Golden Horde' he said. 'Our people came from the Golden Horde.' He shifted uneasily and finally looked straight at me.

'You went the wrong way' he said.

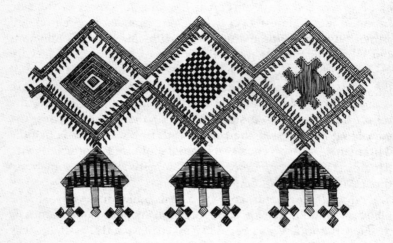

Glossary

Kohistan

burqa shroud covering woman entirely from head to foot, with small mesh visor over eyes
charpoy simple wood-framed bed strung with rope
djinn evil spirits of Muslim mythology
Mehtar chieftain of Chitral
mujahed Afghan freedom fighter
naan flat, slightly leavened bread
paratha flat cake of flour, water and ghee (clarified butter)
paseo [Sp] quattro passi [It] ritual evening stroll
shalwar kameez loose trouser and long tunic outfit worn by both men and women in Pakistan

Indus

betel leaf of Piper betle, chewed and spat out, leaving red stain
chapatti flat unleavened bread
chowkidar caretaker
ikat weaving technique where the design is dyed into the threads before weaving, giving a blurred effect
memsahib Indian term for married European lady
Nawab Muslim noble
NOC No Objection Certificate – permit issued by Pakistan Government
shisha mirrorglass used in embroidery

Makran

dhow Arab ship of the Indian Ocean with triangular sail
Gichkis from the early eighteenth century the most powerful tribe of Makran
halwa Turkish sweetmeat made of sesame seeds and honey
joghi snake charmer caste
keraz underground water channel (also *qanat*)
lac a resin used to colour woods
Mir aristocrat, especially of dominant races
mullah Muslim teacher or priest
pish *Nannorhops ritchieana*, a stemless dwarf palm common on rocky ground

271

putto   cherub of Renaissance and Baroque art
qanat   underground water channel (also *keraz*)

Iran

chador   woman's shroud, covering head and body but leaving face free
dupatta   woman's shawl worn with shalwar kameez
faisanjan   dish of chicken cooked with walnuts and pomegranate juice
feranghi   foreigner
ghee   clarified butter, especially from buffalo
kebab   small pieces of meat cooked on skewer
saroz   Indo-Iranian lute
Seljuk   Turkic peoples from Central Asia who ruled in Iran from the
   mid-eleventh century and later in Anatolia
yashmak   woman's veil leaving only eyes uncovered

Afghanistan

angur   grapes
gul dozi   embroidery, generally floral
purdah   seclusion of women

Kurdistan

keffiyeh   check headcloth, especially as worn by Palestinian Arabs
kepenek   Turkish sleeveless felt cloak
oya   Turkish needlelace or crochet edging for scarves
salaam aleikum   Arabic greeting 'peace be on you'

Anatolia

madrasha   theological college

Bulgaria

barquentine   three-masted vessel, with the fore-mast square-rigged, and
   the main-mast and mizzen-mast fore-and-aft-rigged
joual   the French language of Quebec, so called from the pronunciation
   of 'cheval'
muska   amulet

Sources

Kohistan

pp 45–6, 257: G.W. Leitner, *The Hunza & Nagyr Handbook*, London 1889

p 40: Sir Aurel Stein, *On Alexander's Track to the Indus*, London 1929

Makran

p 90: Denys Bray, *The Life History of a Brahui*, London 1913

pp 78, 83, 86, 92–3: *Gazeteer of Makran*, Quetta 1905

p 72: Col. Sir Thomas Holdich, *The Indian Borderland 1880–1900*, London 1901

p 73: Lieut. Henry Pottinger, *Travels in Beloochistan and Sinde*, London 1816

Iran

pp 119, 120, 121–2: C.E. Biddulph, *Four Months in Persia*, London 1892

pp 152–3: Thomas Bois, *Connaissance des Kurdes*, Beyrouth 1965

p 127: Edward Fitzgerald, *Rubáiyát of Omar-Khayyàm*, London 1859

p 123: The Bible, Luke 20:25

p 152: Major Frederick Millingen, *Wild Life Among the Koords*, London 1870

p 119: A.R. Neligan, *Hints for Residents and Travellers in Persia*, London 1914

pp 120, 139: E.O. Walker, 'Telegraphic Communication between England and India: its present condition and future development'. *Journal of the Society of Arts*, No 2152 Vol XLII, February 16 1894

Afghanistan

p 182: Sir Alexander Burnes, *Cabool*, London 1842

p 176: W. Crooke, *The Native Races of Northern India*, London 1906

p 197: Lowell Thomas, *Beyond Khyber Pass*, London n.d.

Anatolia

p 242: Isabella Bird, *Journeys in Persia & Kurdistan*, London 1891, 1989

pp 239–40: The Bible, Genesis 11:31, 12:4–5

Bulgaria

pp 257–8: John Biddulph, *Tribes of the Hindoo Koosh*, Calcutta 1880

pp 261–2: Carl Schuster, *Genealogical Patterns in the Old and New Worlds*, Sao Paulo 1954

— *Kapkaps with Human Figures from the Solomon Islands*, Budapest 1964

Letters of advice received before leaving home were from:

Professor Dr Karl Jettmar of Heidelberg University

Dr Peter Andrews of the Ethnographic Institute of Cologne University

Mr Jerry Anderson of Karachi

Opinions on the origin of the Kohistani costume were also given by:

Dr Benko Puntev of the Ethnographic Institute of the National Museum of Bulgaria, Sofia

Dr Dzheny Madzharov of the Historical Museum, Razgrad

Dr Jürgen Frembgen of the State Ethnographic Museum of Munich

Dr Nabholz-Kartaschoff of the Ethnographic Museum of Basel

All are acknowledged with great appreciation.

Index